THE WORLD IS RVLED & GOVERNED by OPINION.

B.M. 272

Heading to verses by Henry Peacham, 1641. Hollar

pp. 25–26

# ENGLISH POLITICAL CARICATURE

## TO 1792

A STUDY OF OPINION AND
PROPAGANDA

BY

M. DOROTHY GEORGE
LITT.D.
*Hon. Fellow of Girton College*

OXFORD
AT THE CLARENDON PRESS
1959

*Oxford University Press, Amen House, London E.C.4*

GLASGOW  NEW YORK  TORONTO  MELBOURNE  WELLINGTON
BOMBAY  CALCUTTA  MADRAS  KARACHI  KUALA LUMPUR
CAPE TOWN  IBADAN  NAIROBI  ACCRA

PRINTED IN GREAT BRITAIN
AT THE UNIVERSITY PRESS, OXFORD
BY VIVIAN RIDLER
PRINTER TO THE UNIVERSITY

# PREFACE

IN the vast literature of the subject it might be misleading to select especially relevant works for mention. Some authorities are given in footnotes and in the Index of Artists. Others will be found in the British Museum *Catalogue of Political and Personal Satires* to which the numbers in square brackets in the text refer—volumes i–iv, 1870–83, by F. G. Stephens (art critic and minor Pre-Raphaelite) cover the period to 1770; volumes v–vi, 1935–8, by myself, deal with the years from 1771 to 1792.

I am very grateful to Dr. E. H. Gombrich and Mr. Charles Mitchell for their help and encouragement, and to Mrs. William Martin and Mr. Lawrence Towner for valuable information. I am also much indebted to the Print Room staff of the British Museum, especially to Mr. A. Aspital.

*February 1959*

# CONTENTS

# LIST OF ILLUSTRATIONS

Acknowledgements are made to the British Museum for all plates except 12 and 17, which are from the Bodleian Library, Oxford.

Frontispiece. *The World is Ruled and Governed by Opinion*, heading to verses by Henry Peacham, 1641, engraved by Hollar

# INTRODUCTION

THE subject of this book is pictorial propaganda in England—the political or controversial print, which, especially in its earlier phases, is distinct from its older relation, comic art. To be politically effective the picture must be capable of rapid production and distribution; the political songs of the Middle Ages had these qualities—only the inventions of paper, printing, and engraving made graphic propaganda possible. There is no need to stress the interest of the outstanding cartoon[1]—to use the modern term—as a vivid occasional illustration of politics. One can scarcely think of Bismarck's dismissal without remembering Tenniel's *Dropping the Pilot*. And of all forms of propaganda the picture can be the most deadly. But, in general, historians—apt to neglect iconography—disregard the wonderful material buried—the word is hardly an exaggeration—in the great mass of English satirical engravings. They reflect the rhythm and tempo of the national life, showing the immediate reactions to events and illuminating opinion and propaganda, with their myths and fantasies, catchwords and slogans. And though many prints were propagandist in the sense that they were intended to influence opinion, deliberate propaganda, paid or organized, is seemingly rare, but sometimes important. The prints were commercial ventures which had to be popular; their great interest is that in the main they reflect opinion. And since they illustrate, not the past, but a sequence of presents in a series of dissolving views, a chronological treatment is imposed.[2]

The object of the book is to find the pattern in the shifting kaleidoscope, not to take the thread of history, as we now see it, and find appropriate illustrations. All political caricature tends to be radical, oppositionist, disruptive. In the eighteenth century and after, the bias against authority was more extreme. Ministerial journalists were inevitably denounced as venal

[1] The word was used ironically in this sense by Leech (*Punch*, No. 105) during the 1843 exhibition of cartoons for mural decorations in the new Houses of Parliament. After some time it established itself as the word for a large political drawing in the illustrated papers. M. H. Spielmann, *Encycl. Brit.*, Cambridge, 1911, *s.v.* Cartoon. Leech was anticipated in a plate to the *Westminster Magazine*, 'The Political Cartoon for the Year 1775' [5288].

[2] The prints to be discussed here are chiefly those in the collections of the British Museum. These, of course, are not complete—almost any collection of satirical prints will have some that are not in the Museum. But they contain most of the more important, and the prints are sufficiently representative to be a guide to trends of opinion. Many must have disappeared, especially cheap flimsy woodcuts and the seditious ones that were handed about or posted up surreptitiously. The grosser ones too would tend to be eliminated from collections.

hirelings—a judgement somehow not applicable to the paid hacks of opposition—and any such person as a public relations officer would have been thought an outrage. Johnson's *Dictionary* derivation of Gazetteer speaks for itself: 'It was lately a term of the utmost infamy, being usually applied to Wretches who were hired to vindicate the Court.' Horace Walpole in 1770, deploring the licence of the press, saw no remedy: 'Ministers are and ought to be lawful game, yet the law could not except them as proper to be abused.'[1] Autocracy in France in the *ancien régime* was said to be tempered by epigram, and in Russia by assassination. In England oligarchy was tempered by caricatures as well as by the press.[2]

The prints can be libellous to an extreme degree, and (after the Revolution) with impunity. This was misleading to foreign observers. In 1802 (when English visitors were flocking to France) prints by Gillray disparaging to the Ministry were posted up in Calais to confront travellers going through the passport bureau. 'I felt not a little indignant', wrote Raimbach the engraver, 'at perceiving, in addition to the tone of official arrogance, the wall of an anteroom in which we waited was decorated with the masterly caricatures of Gillray, ridiculing the chief personages of the English administration . . .'[3] In the prints we see how very far *lèse-majesté* could go. It is usual to think of Gillray as the most savagely uninhibited of English caricaturists. He is challenged (though not in wit or ability) by the anonymous engravers of the 1760's and in 1777–80, and again by the caricaturists of 1819–20.

But the prints reflect also a basic patriotism and loyalty, often in conflict with the voice of faction—though faction finds violent expression in these many-sided cartoons which range from naïveté to sophistication. In the mid-nineteenth century Taine found that 'whereas we *suffer* our Government, the English *support* theirs',[4] and the same could probably be said much earlier—the support being consistent with recurrent indignation and contempt, violently expressed, so that at first sight the prints might seem to demonstrate the opposite of this: they belong to 'the history that is present politics', and that, to quote Professor Brogan, 'is mainly composed of envy, malice and all uncharitableness'.[5] As Boyer-Brun said in

---

[1] *Memoirs of the Reign of George III*, 1845, iv. 168.

[2] Cf. 'L'Angleterre est une monarchie composée, mitigée par des caricatures': Charles Nodier quoted Grand-Carteret, *Les Mœurs et la caricature en France*, 1888.

[3] *Memoirs*, 1843, pp. 104 f.

[4] *Notes on England*, trans. E. Hyams, 1957, p. 179. The contrasted use of the extinguisher symbol in France and in England seems significant: see M. D. George, *English Political Caricature 1793–1832: a Study of Opinion and Propaganda*, Oxford, 1959 (hereafter referred to as *E.P.C. 1793–1832*), p. 19, Pl. 8.                    [5] *The Study of Politics*, 1946.

1792, 'Les caricatures sont le thermomètre qui indique le degré de l'opinion publique'.[1]

The caricatures are documents in an endless discussion on politics and persons, war and diplomacy. They soon acquired a virtual immunity from prosecution, and a variety and vitality untrammelled by authority, indeed, usually in opposition to it. They were a recognized weapon of controversy, national and sometimes international, to a degree that gives them an importance outside the scope of the modern cartoon. Crises and scandals and vendettas evoked prints and counter-prints, sometimes commissioned by those concerned. Some prints have inscriptions that turn them into graphic pamphlets. They were important also as virtually the only pictorial rendering of passing events. They are history, concrete, personal, and tendentious, seen through contemporary eyes. Like all history they are a seamless web in which the pattern is always changing.

Inseparable from the pictorial pattern of national life found in a sequence of prints is their imagery, the framework of allegory and metaphor which both reflects and colours opinion, which is deeply traditional and yet responds to the fashion of the moment. When English graphic satire established itself it inherited a symbolical language that was international. Allegory was the spirit of the age and all illustration tended to be symbolical. The normal progression for many of these symbols was from the images—pious or ribald—of the Middle Ages, through their Reformation or Renaissance transformations. Though there are earlier examples of the political print in Italy and France, it was Luther who first used pictorial propaganda on a massive scale and in the service of a revolutionary movement. With him it sprang to life, fully armed. He was a pamphleteer of genius, with a great school of wood-engravers, the Cranachs and others, at his disposal, and he had mastered the essentials: he attacked power and pomp in a way dear to the populace. 'The Devil', he wrote, 'knows well that when the foolish people hear high sounding words of abuse, they are taken in and blindly believe them without any further ground or reason.' In a letter of 2 June 1525 he wrote of the efficacy of prints, songs, words, and jests: 'on all the walls, on every sort of paper or playing cards, priests and monks are to be so portrayed that the people are disgusted when they see or hear of the clergy. . . . The clergy have departed from the hearts of the people.' When he ridiculed monks and nuns he was in succession to a traditional art expressed in wood and stone in churches and in illuminated manuscripts, including the margins of Missals and Books of Hours. A worsted

---

[1] *Histoire des caricatures de la révolte des français*, Paris, 1792.

adversary is apt to over-rate the share of propaganda in his defeat (no need to look farther than to German tributes to British propaganda after World War I): A Catholic historian of Leo X attributes the success of the Reformation to this propaganda in its cruder aspects, and he has a chapter 'Du rire, employé par la Réforme comme instrument de propagande'.[1] It would indeed be hard to find in the later history of graphic satire anything to outstrip Luther's achievement.

Luther's prints ranged from crude images on flysheets appealing to the illiterate to Bible illustrations. Pictorial flysheets circulated in Germany up to the Thirty Years War, but with the revolt of the Netherlands Holland became the chief source of pictorial propaganda. Dutch prints and medals went all over Europe, and since these early satires were largely directed against Spain and the Jesuits they were peculiarly acceptable in England. Reformation images, deriving mainly from Germany and Holland, are found in a long line of anti-clerical prints on the Continent and No-Popery ones in England. Their first appearance in an English guise seems to have been in the illustrations to the Elizabethan editions of Fox's *Book of Martyrs* and in the cuts in Stephen Bateman's *The Doome* in 1581, a chronicle of marvels and portents, related with complete credulity. Some of these militantly Protestant symbols have a special interest and a very long history.

An outstanding example of the medieval image transformed by the Reformation and passing into the language of political allegory is the balance in which the souls of the dead—naked infants—are weighed between good and evil, Heaven and Hell. There were many Reformation versions of the familiar theme. A classic example is a Dutch print copied by Carel Allard: two monks try to drag down a scale containing the papal keys and a book, presumed to be the Summa of Aquinas. But it is hopelessly outweighed by the Bible; on one side stand the Pope and his hierarchy, on the other Huss, Calvin, Melancthon, and Luther. In a variant published in Geneva a demon drags at the Popish scale.[2] There is a similar but simpler English design in the 1576 edition of *Fox's Martyrs* [Pl. 1]: 'A lively picture describyng the weight and substaunce of God's most blessed word, agaynst the doctrines and vanities of mens traditions.' Justice holds the scales in which *Verbum Dei* outweighs 'all the Decreta of the Pope and his Wrath', despite the efforts of a demon. The symbolical and propagandist potency of the contrasted symbols of the Bible and of

[1] J. M. V. Audin, *Histoire de Léo X*, Paris, 1844.
[2] Doumergue, *Iconographie calvinienne*, Lausanne, 1909, pp. 183-5.

Popish 'trinkets' or 'trumpery' is manifest in prints of the Great Rebellion. In a long succession of English political prints, countries or persons, documents or symbols are weighed in a balance; the theme is applied to the balance of power and the balance of parties.

Other medieval images appropriated by Reformation artists derived from the *Book of Revelation* which had taken strong hold of the people's imagination. It had been illustrated in block books and their manuscript sources. Dürer had immortalized it on traditional lines. In the first issue (September 1522) of Luther's New Testament with cuts by Cranach, traditional in character, the Pope is Antichrist: the Scarlet Woman or Whore wears the Papal tiara, and so does the Beast with seven heads whose number was 666. Fallen Babylon is clearly Rome with the Castle of Sant'Angelo and other well-known landmarks.[1] A monster with seven heads or more, verging sometimes towards a medieval dragon, sometimes a hydra, sometimes a blend of Beast and hydra, became part of the stock-in-trade of the satirical artist. It may represent a person or persons, or sometimes a grievance, such as Excise or 'Corruption'. Sometimes the monster is explicitly related to Rome and the Beast, as 'Whore' always is. The seven heads and ten crowns were supposed to be Rome's seven hills and ten provinces. Any outstanding *bête noire* is liable to be identified with the Beast.[2] In a very interesting Puritan example (by a Dutch engraver) the seven heads of 'Rome's Monster on his monstrous Beast' [378] are the seven deadly sins as in the Middle Ages.[3] On a memorial medal of Charles I struck in Saxony in 1649, a seven-headed monster rampages above the dead King with the motto *Heu Quaenam Haec Insania Vulgi*! ('Alas what a madness is this of the rabble').[4]

One of the earliest and most noteworthy products of Luther's campaign was the *Passional Christi und Antichristi* with contrasted cuts by Hans Cranach illustrating the life of Christ and the activities of the Pope: Christ washes a poor man's feet; princes kiss the Pope's toe. In English satires, from a cut in *Fox's Martyrs* in 1576 to a poster against Gladstone in 1885,[5] kissing the papal toe recurs as a symbol of abject subservience to Rome. The papal slipper or toe figures repeatedly in the grossly disrespectful cartoons of Italian anti-clerical newspapers in the early years of this century.

[1] In a later edition, at the instance of Frederick the Wise, the tiaras were reduced to harmless crowns, but other details remained, and in the 1534 issue the tiaras were restored.

[2] In English prints one finds Laud, the Stuarts, Cromwell, Bute, the Coalition of Fox and North, and Napoleon.

[3] As in the misericord at New College, Oxford: A. D. Anderson, *Misericords*, 1954, fig. 20.

[4] Hawkins and Grueber, *Medallic Illustrations of the History of Great Britain . . .*, 1885, i. 350-1.          [5] *England's Pope* [B.M. 1850. e. 5/43*].

The famous German Reformation medal or token[1] has had a prolonged influence on graphic satire, if we regard it as the fountain-head of innumerable versions of the reversible head or *phisionomie à double visage*. On the obverse is a profile of the Pope which when inverted becomes the Devil; the reverse is a cardinal-fool, similarly conjoined. It is attributed to the decade from 1537, a counter-token to a Catholic one of Pope and Emperor current during the Diet of Augsburg and the Council of Trent. The motto is *Ecclesia perversa tenet faciem Diaboli*, which suggests Luther as its inspirer, and it has in fact been attributed to his friend, Nicholas van Amsdorf. The little tokens, of which there are many variants, were well known in France, Holland, and England. The design was adapted to pottery, draughtsmen, gems, and seals. It was copied in a cut to Bateman's *The Doome* [Pl. 2]. The double head, so drawn that the nose of one face becomes the chin of the other, was a popular conceit in England and France in the later eighteenth century, sometimes applied to politics, sometimes to such notions as before and after marriage. In political satires the original design was often closely adhered to. In 1761 Henry Fox (a fox) and the Duke of Newcastle are Devil and fool [Pl. 28], and in 1770 Fox, now Lord Holland, is again the Devil with Bute as fool [4416]. In a French print the duc d'Aguillon is conjoined with a fishwife; he was reputed to have joined the Versailles mob on 5 October 1789, disguised as a *poissarde*. In a large bold design of 1871 Napoleon III, violently caricatured, is conjoined with an ass, the two profiles being 'Badinguet allant à la Guerre!!!' and 'Badinguet revenant de la Guerre'.[2] Another favourite device for the double personality which had a long life and many variations, was the body or head vertically divided into contrasted halves, and this was used also to make one person out of two, usually in sinister co-operation—as in the Coalition of Fox and North.

Related to the double-headed image is a profile head of the Pope constructed of emblematical objects disparaging (in Protestant eyes) to the Papacy. This begins with Tobie Stimmer's *Gorgoneum Caput* in 1571; there is a Dutch adaptation (two states); like the Pope-Devil token it was copied in *The Doome* [Pl. 2], and it too has had a prolonged influence on satirical art. On the Catholic side, Arcimboldo produced for Maximilian II a derisory portrait of Calvin; the nose is a frog, the face bits of plucked chicken, the mouth a gaping fish's head, the beard a fish's tail.[3] The genre

[1] F. P. Barnard, *Satirical and Controversial Medals of the Reformation*, Oxford, 1927. He found no engravings of the medals; there are, however, several.     [2] In the London Library.
[3] Now in Stockholm. Doumergue, op. cit., pp. 152–3, pl. xxiii. There is an engraving of a Pope's head constructed of a bell, cups, and plates: *Collection Hennin*, Paris, x. 55.

was used by the German artist Voltz for his famous 'corpse head' of Napoleon which had so many copies and adaptations. The Napoleon print of 1814 (the 'Hieroglyphic Portrait')[1] was imitated in 1871 for an even more venomous head of Napoleon III by Belloguet in a French series, *Pilorie-Phrénologie*, in which there is also an emblematical head of Pius IX. Thus the line of composite emblematical heads reaches from Pope to Pope across three centuries. These heads have analogies with the type of facetious or satirical print, common to folk-prints and satires, and popular both in England and France, in which persons are constructed of appropriate inanimate objects. There are outstanding examples by Hollar [Pl. 4] and Hogarth [Pl. 21].

One medieval image was so familiar that it is unnecessary to seek a specific origin for its adaptation to politics. This is 'Hell Mouth', the fanged and flaming 'jaws of Hell' into which victims are dragged or pushed by demons. In the later Middle Ages the conception was popularized by the Mystery play, where the elaborate movable machinery, the flames and flying demons, made it a favourite scene. The mouth might be round and cavernous, as in the Guthlac Roll at the end of the twelfth century, or long and angular like a crocodile's jaws. It was used repeatedly in English polemical prints for the public enemy of the day; Napoleon and Wellington (in 1832) are both so disposed of. There are other images common—like the balance—to medieval, renaissance, and modern imagery, for instance, the wheel of Fortune or of Time. Death with his javelin persists—the Death of the *Danse Macabre*, the grinning posturing skeleton, not the earlier and more austere figure of *Les trois rois morts et les trois vifs*.

Besides Reformation imagery, chiefly Germanic in origin, there is the renaissance symbolism of the Emblem, Italian in spirit, popularized by the often-translated *Emblemata* of Alciati, first published in 1531. English satirical art was profoundly affected by the popularity of Emblem Books:[2] in form and phraseology seventeenth-century prints are permeated with the art of the Emblem. These books were one of the most typical expressions of allegory. At the end of the sixteenth century illustrations in English books were still rare, but after Geoffrey Whitney's *Choice of Emblems* (printed by Plantin in 1585) Emblem Books became increasingly popular, with Quarles, whose emblems were engraved by William Marshall, as the outstanding emblematist. A typical Emblem Book was a series of little engravings which might range from illustrated metaphors to more elaborate

---

[1] See *E.P.C. 1793–1832*, Pl. 58.
[2] See Rosemary Freeman, *English Emblem Books*, 1948.

scenes, each with a motto and a moral exposition, usually in verse. The form of the Emblem Book was used by William Blake and adapted to politics by William Hone, so that its influence long survived its seventeenth-century vogue. Typical emblems (often rooted in the past) were the Eye of Providence with its beam of light, the arm or hand extending from clouds, the lighted candle, the tree (flourishing, decayed, or cut down), Time, the globe, suns and moons (with inset faces), signs of the Zodiac, the Phoenix, the wreath of laurel or oak, or more elaborate illustrations such as the Æsopian fox and grapes, or the fall of Phaeton or of Icarus.

The obligation of political satire to the Emblem Book is expressed in the term 'Emblematical' or 'Hieroglyphical' print, which survived till late in the eighteenth century. But the influence of the emblem was naturally at its height during the first enthusiasm for these books. Many, perhaps most, of the early political prints are emblematical in the strict sense of the term. For instance, *A Rot Among the Bishops*[1] is 'An Ægyptian Dish drest after the English Fashion with a Tribute for Mr. Quarles of never dying memory, set forth in four silent Parables'. By a natural process the word emblem was soon used for any picture with a moral or political significance.

Many emblems were heraldic, and burlesque heraldry is one of the oldest and most long-lived forms of graphic satire: the supporters, the quarterings, the crest, and the motto were great opportunities for insult or ridicule. An early Reformation woodcut from the Cranach studio is a travesty of the papal arms: the Keys are broken, and a hand clutches a money-bag.

The rebus or pictorial writing, a seventeenth-century word for an ancient device, is a variant of the emblem. In England it took shape chiefly in the 'Hieroglyphical Letter', a puzzle print which was sometimes political, sometimes facetious. The most striking examples seem to belong to the later half of the eighteenth century [Pl. 49]; the earliest ones in the British Museum are attributed to 1710 and are non-political. The device is much older. The calligrapher and engraver Palatino published in 1540 an often reprinted guide to scripts and alphabets which included a 'Sonetto Figurato' on four plates, exactly on the principle of the later puzzle-print, verses in which little pictures are interspersed with letters and words. Much earlier again was the rebus in heraldry.

The symbolical frontispiece or title-page, so popular in the seventeenth century, was an extension of the emblem. It is often in an architectural setting; sometimes it is a number of small pictures within a framework

[1] See p. 19.

to symbolize the contents of a book. Emblem-wise, this was usually explained in verse headed 'The Meaning of the Emblem', or 'The Mind of the Frontispiece', or some such phrase. When a political tract had a frontispiece this was almost always a satirical or at least a symbolical design, and such prints were sometimes also issued separately.[1] The frontispiece has great importance in graphic satire. In the first place it was a superb instrument for conveying the bite of a polemical or scurrilous work, a safer and often more effective medium than words for the expression of dangerous notions. Secondly, it was a source of political imagery. From its architectural and monumental setting derives a long sequence of satirical monuments in polemical prints.[2] Britannia does not I think, appear in English graphic satire till after her personification on medals. But, before the medals, she sits enthroned on her rock in the title-page to Camden's *Britannia* (1609), and again, framed in an arch, on the title-page of Drayton's *Poly-Olbion* (1613). And though she was established by the Restoration medals of 1660, there is no better representation of the stereotyped Britannia of the cartoon than the title-page of Clarendon's *History* (1702).

The folk-print, rare in England in comparison with France and Germany, made its contribution to political imagery. There is the simple illustration of the proverb or proverbial phrase, such as 'labour in vain' in which old women with mops and brushes try to 'wash a blackamoor white'. This was repeatedly used as a political parable from the late eighteenth century at least. The illustrated metaphor of the nose at the grindstone was used in English prints for Laud, Charles II, the Pope, Louis XIV, Britannia, George III and Napoleon. There is also 'Nobody' a bodiless man whose legs are joined to his shoulders, a folk-print conceit of the early seventeenth century repeatedly applied to politics [Pl. 58].

Three outstanding folk-print subjects have the special interest that they were common to England and France and with one possible exception to Germany, and that they survived with only minor modifications from the sixteenth or seventeenth to the nineteenth century. The most interesting, from the political philosophy that underlies it, is that known in England as 'The Four [or Five—or more] Alls', and in France as *Les Quatre Vérités*. In the most usual form the four are the King who says 'I rule all', the parson or bishop ('I pray for all'), the soldier ('I fight for all'), the farmer or peasant, or—later—John Bull ('I pay for all'). Often there is a final figure, the Devil or Death, 'I take you all'. In 1803–4 the theme was

[1] Conversely, the already published print was sometimes used as a frontispiece.
[2] Cf. Pls. 19, 24; *E.P.C. 1793–1832*, pl. 49.

twice used in a Napoleon satire, *The Three Plagues of Europe*. In 1832 and later variants in crude woodcut were adapted to condemnations of the whole social and political system. The 'Alls' have survived as a device on inn signboards.

The *World Turned Upside Down*—in old French *Le Monde bestorné*—has ancient origins in the marginal drolleries of manuscripts; the tables are turned by, for instance, the hare hunting the hounds or the huntsman, mice pursuing the cat, geese hanging a fox. As a folk-print its standard form is a collection of little oblong scenes, usually sixteen arranged in four rows. As a chapbook the little scenes survived into the nineteenth century. Taylor, the Water Poet, a Royalist, combines a selection of the usual scenes to illustrate two pamphlets,[1] whose political lesson is the reverse of the folk-print spirit—delight in the humiliation of the mighty. Another image for the topsy-turvy world is an inverted terrestrial globe, used both politically and on inn-signs.

It goes without saying that these main streams of influence on pictorial satire were not canalized, that there was much infiltration and cross-fertilization. They were, of course, profoundly affected by the pressure of events and the trend of politics. It is a characteristic of these early English prints that the comic is rare—and that caricature in the strict sense of the word has no place, or almost none. It is important to remember that in the earlier prints it was the idea that was important, not the execution, and that the idea was supplied to the engraver, not by him, though doubtless he often contributed conventional imagery.

Another characteristic of the earlier prints is their association with verse. Elaborate engravings have the form of broadsides with an engraved or printed text. Verses or songs often have headings which range from small woodcuts often from an old block to large engravings. Tradition, and the model of the Emblem Book and the frontispiece, made a verse explanation the natural appendage to a print. What was once general (though not universal) long survived as an occasional practice. Many Napoleon satires are illustrated broadsides, and there are survivals or revivals of the form in the 1820's and 1830's, while for street-papers there was no break in continuity, and woodcuts with a verse commentary only gradually succumbed to a changing world after a long process of degeneration.

Progressively the cartoonists' framework expands as originality gains on convention. Historical parallels and allusions are persistent and revealing.

[1] See p. 26.

Literary settings begin with Shakespeare and Milton (in that order) and they keep their supremacy. The next favourites perhaps are *Gulliver* and *Don Quixote*. There are a few popular plays, headed by the *Beggar's Opera*. John Bull joins Britannia, but with a considerable time lag from Arbuthnot's fable of 1712. Repeatedly, the mountain delivers its mouse, the cat pulls chestnuts from the fire. Card-playing, chess, and cock-fighting begin early and are successively followed by ninepins, the race-course, cricket, and pugilism. The Temple of the Constitution is a recurrent symbol, a little outmoded but not displaced by the greater realism of the late eighteenth century.

Not till the fifties of the eighteenth century was the exaggeration of form or feature on which portrait caricature depends used in English political satires. This seems strange, since 'caricatura' or overloading, the French *charge*, began in Italy about 1600 (Leonardo's heads being regarded as grotesques). Annibale Carracci invented both the art and the word and defined the caricaturist's task: 'to grasp the perfect deformity and thus reveal the very essence of a personality. The caricature, like every other work of art, is more true to life than life itself.'[1] From the 1730's, personal caricature, good-humoured and intimate, became fashionable among English dilettanti in Italy and was much influenced by the cari-catures of Ghezzi. In the fifties George Townshend began to exercise what Horace Walpole called his 'talent for buffoonery' on political subjects and the word caricatura or caricature established itself as the name for a satirical print. By this time Hogarth had profoundly influenced graphic satire by the scenic story-telling of his print-sequences and had greatly raised the prestige of the engraving. Consequently, the old-fashioned 'hieroglyphical' print, usually dependent on a verbal explanation, with a mass of detail, sometimes intentionally cryptic, gave way gradually to the 'caricature' with an immediate appeal to the eye, sold plain or coloured, but generally coloured. Despite this transformation, much of the old symbolism remained and was adapted to the new look. It is one of Gillray's great merits to combine allegory and fantasy with excellent personal cari-cature and to subordinate both to his design.

More remains to be said about the transition, which culminated in the classic age of English caricature. In the meantime, how can the long neglect of personal caricature in England be explained? Even Titus Oates, with a chin that would have been a caricaturist's godsend, is favourably, indeed flat-teringly, depicted, even when he is 'an incarnate Imp of Hell'. Cartoonists

[1] E. H. Gombrich and F. Kris, *Caricature*, 1940, pp. 10-12.

were as insulting as they knew how to be to a succession of victims from Sir Giles Mompesson to Sir Robert Walpole, but though these might be given the attributes of a fiend there was no uglification of feature: their characteristics are expressed symbolically, or they are put in some discreditable situation—taking a bribe or conferring with the Devil. This was a convention that long survived. To represent men as animals—a form of satire common to most ages and countries—is, it may be said, caricature. 'When men's features are drawn with some resemblance to some other animals the Italians call it to be drawn in caricature', wrote Sir Thomas Browne in 1690. In Prince Rupert as a wolf [Pl. 11] dressed up as a cavalier there is something of caricature, but not in the stricter sense— facial similarity is not attempted. Nor is it when Roger L'Estrange is dog 'Touzer' [Pl. 15], though here there is more of the spirit of mockery.

Was the political climate unfavourable to caricature? Perhaps, and even after 1660 the prints have more of the spirit of 'the good old cause' of 1641 than of *Hudibras*. Were those who engraved political satire incapable of (deliberate) personal caricature or were they too deeply wedded to the emblematical to attempt it? Most of these prints were anonymous and the work of craftsmen rather than of artists, though a few are by the best engravers of the day, Hollar, Faithorne, Gaywood, William Marshall. A gifted amateur, known to history as 'the Protestant Joiner', and ignored by writers on caricature, has some claim to have made one of the earliest approaches to the spirit of political caricature in England.[1]

Up to about the middle of the eighteenth century, then, personal caricature remained essentially an Italian art. 'Young man you come from Italy', the Duchess of Marlborough said to Bubb Dodington in 1710; 'they tell me of a new invention there called caricatura drawing. Can you find someone that will make me a caricature of Lady Masham describing her covered with running sores and ulcers that I may send the Queen to give her a slight idea of her favourite?'[2] It would seem that the caricature she envisaged was emblematical in character.[3] In 1742 Gray, writing to Chute in Florence, remarked on the vogue for graphic satire in England, and suggested that he should find and dispatch an Italian artist who should

---

[1] See p. 53.

[2] Quoted without reference by Bohun Lynch, *A History of Caricature*, 1926.

[3] By an odd coincidence there is in the British Museum a print (1710) of an ugly old beggar woman in a London street, sold in 1881 as a caricature of Lady Masham. The print, however, is one by Laroon the younger of a notorious beggar known as 'Blind Granny' (the caption of one state of the print). It is just possible that Lady Masham was so travestied, or that the portrait of a beggar was maliciously handed about as a caricature of the lady. But evidence is lacking.

visit Holland on the way to learn taste.[1] By the 1780's political caricature was regarded as peculiarly an English art and an English weapon. 'Il faut compter au nombre des privilèges de cette nation', wrote Archenholtz, 'la liberté de faire des gravures satiriques, qui tournent au ridicule les ennemis du jour. Le François les chansonne, le Hollandois plus pesant frappe des medailles; l'Anglois a choisi la gravure, comme le plus propre à donner de la publicité à la satire.'[2]

Though the earliest English prints are scarcely caricatures, seldom intentionally comic, and only by exception works of art, they have a peculiar fascination and they are historic documents. Through their inherited imagery and the pressure of events they treat politics as a struggle between right and wrong, truth and falsehood, and especially between Protestants and Catholics.

[1] Letters, ed. D. C. Tovey, 1900, i. 108.
[2] Tableau de l'Angleterre, Bruxelles, 1788, i. 149–50. He writes as an eye-witness of events in London between 1771 and 1784.

# I

## THE GREAT REBELLION: 'THE WORLD IS RULED AND GOVERNED BY OPINION'

THE beginnings of the English polemical print were conditioned by the dissensions between King and ¡Parliament that led to the Great Rebellion, though its ancestral strains were largely continental. There is no special category to be isolated, but a great variety of forms, from the crude woodcut on pamphlet or ballad to the extremely elaborate engraving; 'picture', 'sculpture', 'figure', 'emblem' are the words used. Nor is there any clear distinction between the polemical print and 'straight' illustration. The vogue of Emblem Book and frontispiece established the picture as the natural way to epitomize and stress the content of a book or pamphlet. In the more elaborate prints the aim is to convey symbolically, or in a blend of symbolism and realism, the complexities of a political situation. 'The picture is the Emblem of the Times' is a phrase that recurs. These prints, like the frontispiece and title-page, were usually expounded in verse, sometimes in prose, or a mixture of both. The 'straight' portrait might have an inscription turning it into a satire, and this again was often in verse. All this made the picture a potent form of propaganda, and the output of prints was clearly influenced by the rise and fall of political passions. What light do they throw on the period? They reflect, not of course underlying motives (hidden from contemporaries) but the more emotional and irrational aspects of the conflict. They illuminate its assumptions, prejudices, and illusions—opinions passionately held. When they were deliberate propaganda, they were on occasion directed at the London mob and the apprentices, forces to be reckoned with, and exploited by rumours of plots and Papists.

These civil war satires are interesting also for their imagery. If the symbolism of the Middle Ages and the Reformation was the seed-bed of the English cartoon, its nursery was the graphic satire of the Great Rebellion, when many of the perennial devices of the political caricaturist made a seemingly first appearance.

As a prelude to the English political print we may consider an important

Dutch print by Peter van der Heyden,[1] which belongs to Anglo-Dutch history. It is based on Titian's picture of Diana discovering the unchastity of her nymph Callisto. Queen Elizabeth is Diana (she is also the naked Truth brought to light by Time). Callisto is the Papacy, that is, the lewd nymph who here stands for the Whore of Babylon; she has laid an assortment of baneful eggs; from one crawls a dragon, Gregory XIII; among the other hatchings are a second dragon (the Inquisition), the 'Mort van Paris' (the St. Bartholomew massacre), and Balthasar, the murderer of William the Silent. The date is thus between the murder in July 1584 and (presumably) the death of Gregory XIII in the following April. The four nymphs grouped round Diana in Titian's picture have become the Netherlands provinces in revolt from Spain. Such a tribute to Elizabeth in a Dutch print, at this time, was surely aimed at overcoming her resistance to a Dutch alliance: the pact with the Netherlands followed in August 1585. Was it intended to stress the plea of the Dutch envoys that she should accept the sovereignty of the four provinces? And is it one of those rare prints intended to influence opinion at the highest levels? It is at all events an early print in the long series, Dutch and English, on Anglo-Dutch relations, a recurrent manifestation of a hate-love relationship, as well as a typical contribution to anti-Rome propaganda.

This and other Dutch prints must have circulated in England. When did English graphic satire begin? Coke in his *Reports* (1600–10) mentions the various forms of libel as writings, emblems, and pictures.[2] The year 1621 saw the publication of two outstanding prints, illustrating the two chief grievances of James I's third parliament—Monopolies and the negotiations of the Spanish marriage. Both are English, though one was engraved in Holland; the latter has importance and significance as a classic, repeatedly adapted to meet new alarms of 'Popery' or invasion. This is the *Double Deliveraunce* [Pl. 3] from the two great perils for which Parliament gave thanks in its daily prayers. It is an elaborate engraving 'Invented by Samuell Ward preacher at Ipswich' and 'Imprinted at Amsterdam anno 1621'. Between the dates '1588' and '1605' is an inscription in Latin and English: 'To God. In memorye of the double deliveraunce from yᵉ invincible Navie and yᵉ unmatcheable powder Treason.' On one side of the plate Spanish galleons sail in a horned crescent, assailed by winds and by a single fireship. On the other is the 'Parliament House' towards which 'Faux' advances, dark-lantern in hand.

[1] See Frances Yates, 'Queen Elizabeth as Astræa', *Journal of the Warburg Institute*, 1947, x. 76.
[2] Report of the case *de famosis libellis*: Stephen, *History of the Criminal Law*, 1883, ii. 305.

The sun of Jehovah dominates both designs and directs a slanting beam of light upon the lantern. In the centre the Pope, the King of Spain, and others sit in conclave, the Devil presiding: they plot the Powder Treason. Inset is a tiny view of 'Tylburie Camp', where ranks of pikemen are visited by the Queen. Here is a graphic rendering of the Englishman's belief in the intervention of Providence in behalf of his country on the most famous of all occasions. It was also deliberate propaganda against the Spanish marriage, as well as an insult to the King of Spain, and as such it evoked a protest from the Spanish Ambassador which led to Ward's arrest and his examination before the Privy Council. Thomas Scott, a Puritan who, like Ward, could well be termed factious, used the incident in his pamphlet against the proposed marriage of Prince Charles, *Vox Populi, Part II*; this purports to be authentic news from Spain, 'faithfully translated out of the Spanish copy by a well wisher to England and Holland', and the fabrication was widely accepted as fact. Gondomar, 'in the likeness of Matchiavell', reveals to 'the Spanish Parliament . . . His treacherous and subtile Practices to the ruin as well of England as of the Netherlands'. Gondomar remarks, 'and I thinke Ward of Ipswich escaped not safely for his lewd and profane picture of 88 and their Powder Treason . . .'. He advises 'Be sure to have going in the North and West . . . a small rowling Presse for little pictures of Saints. . . . Have a care whensoever any Booke or Picture come out to our prejudice, set some friend to buy them all up, though you burne them forthwith, which fail not to send us of every sort three at the least, for they will be unto us of great use.' This (and other remarks in the long tract) is early testimony to the propaganda value of the picture (already established on the Continent). Scott illustrated his own pamphlet with three plates to authenticate his fabrication and curdle Protestant blood: Gondomar making his report; an 'infernal conclave' in Spain; a conference of English 'Jesuits and Priests' (names in full) plotting to deliver England to Spain. These and other prints reflect both the extent to which England was bedevilled by alarms of Popery and plots (potent from their element of fact) and the propaganda value of such scares. In the public mind recent history was largely a succession of plots. Plots are the subject of an elaborate print, *c.* 1627, *Popish Plots and Treasons, from the Beginning of the Reign of Queen Elizabeth* [13]. There are sixteen little scenes, arranged chronologically, most of them assassination plots. Number 12 is the Armada, number 16 the Powder Plot. In a final scene the Prince of Wales returns after the failure of the marriage overtures, and the whole is summed up in an elaborate tailpiece of the True Church trampling on the malignant

Church of Rome and Spain. Here, with the fires of Smithfield, is the background of Civil War emotions as well as of the achievements of Oates and Bedloe.

Contemporary copies and adaptations of the *Double Deliveraunce* show its immediate impact. The most remarkable is in needlework, a close copy of the original by Dame Dorothy Selby, 'a Dorcas'.[1] On her tomb, carved by Edward Marshall, is an incised slab with the same scene and verses.[2] Surely this must be the only popular print to survive both in silk and in stone. Recurring adaptations, in whole or in part, until the early nineteenth century, symbolizing threats of invasion, 'hellish conclaves' or 'consults' (in Popish Plot language), or encroachments of Popery, are vivid examples of historical memory, as well as illustrations of the extent to which engravers drew upon a repertory of old prints. The Powder Plot detail was revived when fears of Popery became acute; probably every Fifth of November Guy derives remotely from Ward's 'Faux' of 1621.

The other print of that year, *The Description of Giles Mompesson, late Knight* . . . [91], is less spectacular but foreshadows the long series of pictorial attacks on the scapegoat and *bête noire*. It depicts the fate of Sir Giles Mompesson who was probably the original of Sir Giles Overreach in Massinger's play, *A New Way to Pay Old Debts*. He was impeached and sentenced for the most hated of the monopolies, that for the licensing of inns. Monopolies, theoretically suppressed, survived the Act of 1624 by virtue of an enormous loophole to become a source of revenue in the eleven years personal rule. The wrath they engendered is fully documented in prints of 1641. In the interval there are very few; indeed, for the first hundred years of the English polemical print—say from 1620 to 1720— prints were more or less sporadic, chiefly a product of civil strife, war, or near-rebellion.

With the opening of the Long Parliament the polemical print comes into its own, a product of the ferment of ideas. In the pamphlet war that preceded the fighting war prints pick out the highlights as seen by the man in the street, or so it would seem. Speaking very roughly, some 150 extant prints belong to 1641 or the last weeks of 1640, as compared with about 50 for 1642,[3] with fluctuating but smaller totals thereafter, dwindling away

[1] Photograph in V. and A., No. 71047. See J. L. Nevinson, 'English Domestic Embroidery Pictures', *Walpole Society*, xxviii. 1 ff.

[2] Sir E. Harrison, *History of Ightham Church*, 1932, p. 16.

[3] This reverses the relative proportion, as between 1641 and 1642, of the tracts collected by Thomason. The outbreak of war seems to have impeded the craft of the engraver, but not of the printer.

after 1653. In the complicated variety of Great Rebellion prints it is
dangerous to generalize, but some things stand out. First, and especially
at the beginning, Parliament and the Puritans have the best of it; Royalist
prints are rare and generally cautious: prints voiced the then dominant
opinion in London; they did not lend themselves like ballads (which are
predominantly Royalist) to clandestine production and sale. And one must
presume the disappearance of many cheap woodcuts on flimsy paper.[1]
As the Royalist reaction gained ground, prints became scarcer. Secondly,
though anti-Royalist, the prints are not anti-monarchical (with some
exceptions to be considered later), and Charles is treated with respect.
Thirdly, the prevailing approach is religious, or at least sectarian or ecclesiastical, with fear of Popery as the overriding theme.

In the simplified panorama of the prints the main preoccupations at the
opening of the Long Parliament appear as hatred of Prelacy and the Court
of High Commission (with the glorification of the Protestant Martyrs,
Bastwick, Burton, and Prynne), the grievance of Monopolies, the fate of
Strafford. It was Laud's misfortune to be involved in all these things, and
he is the chief target of pictorial insult. The mighty explosion of hatred
is graphically expressed in prints well designed to fan the flame. The attack
is part of the attack on bishops in general, especially after these had made
their protest and were imprisoned in the Tower at the end of 1641. The
pervading theory is that Prelacy was not merely half-way to Popery, as
many believed, but a cloak for Popery in its most dangerous form, a standing conspiracy to deliver England to Rome, with Laud as conspirator in
chief. More rationally, Laud is the cruel but defeated enemy of Bastwick
and the others; he is responsible for all grievances, the cause of the trouble
with the Scots—'the little wheele that turns all' in fact. He is in the long
succession of 'evil counsellors' and 'over great subjects' who are resented
as upstarts, a line of attack to which all Ministers of the Crown were liable,
and which is repeatedly expressed by a comparison of the bugbear of the
moment with Wolsey. This was particularly applicable to Laud, reputed
to aim at a Cardinal's hat. *Canterburies Dreame* . . . [198] is illustrated by a
cut of Wolsey's ghost lamenting the fate of those who, like himself, had
tried 'to set the mitre on a level with the Crown'. From the first, Laud is
threatened with execution, and at the end of his long imprisonment there
is exultation at his death. To study the prints is to see him as a sacrifice to
popular resentment and a frenzied fear of Rome, but it must be remem-

[1] The woodcuts that survive are on pamphlets or broadsides; cuts bound with copies of
*Eikon Basilike* are an exception; see p. 35.

bered that those who were anxious to preserve the hierarchy found it
prudent to make a scapegoat of the Archbishop.

Many, if not most, of the forms of pictorial insult used in the seventeenth century were directed against Laud. In 1641 the illustrated squib
in the form of a play was new (it was used against George IV in 1820).
The topics of *A New Play called Canterburie—his Change of Diot* [174]
are Laud's treatment of Burton and the others, his supposed intrigues
with Rome, and his punishment by direct action. Each act is headed by a
woodcut. In the first he dines off the ears of the three Protestant Martyrs,
having himself cut them off. In the second, attempting to sharpen his
knife at a carpenter's grindstone, he is seized by its owner, who holds his
nose to the stone; 'A Jesuit, a Confessor' (Father Philips) staunches his
face with holy water. In the third (repeated on the title) priest and Archbishop have been seized and popped into a cage by the carpenter and his
wife, while Archie Armstrong, the King's jester, laughs at them—he had
been dismissed from Court for disrespect to Laud. These last two cuts
anticipate a number of punitive cages and grindstones. An engraving by
Marshall of Laud tied to a post by a rope round his neck was copied several
times on inflammatory tracts and broadsides: to quote one [161] where he
is threatened with the gallows:

> By wicked counsels faine he would have set
> The Scots and us together by the eares;
> A Patriarks place, the Levite long'd to get
> to sit bith Pope, in one of *Peters* chairse.
>> And haveing dranke so deepe of Babels cup,
>> Was it not time d'ee thinke to chaine him up?

Such things were rabble raising, and Laud complained, not only of
libels and ballads 'sung up and down the streets . . . as full of falsehood
as of gall', but of 'base pictures . . . putting me in a cage and fastning me
to a post by a chaine at my shoulder. And divers of these libels made men
sport in taverns and ale-houses, where too many were as drunck with
malice as with the liquor they sucked in.'[1]

The adaptation of the Emblem Book to politics is exceptional; a striking
example, typical of opinion in 1641, is Thomas Stirry's *A Rot amongst the
Bishops, Or, a Terrible Tempest in the Sea of Canterbury, Set forth in lively
Emblems to please the judicious Reader* [190]. The four 'Emblems' are expounded in verse. First, the ship 'High Commission' sails towards the

[1] H. Trevor Roper, *Archbishop Laud*, 1940, p. 412.

mouth of Hell; on board are Laud, Bishop Wren, and those hated officials Doctors Duck and Lamb (often depicted); Laud's notorious 'etcetera oath' has been thrown into the sea, which is 'The Church and Commonwealth of England'. Next, the ship is blasted by lightning from the hand of Justice. The last two are realistic: Laud going to the Tower; Laud looking from the Tower towards a gallows. It was natural that among the exultations at his death in 1645 there should be, as in 1641, a print [420] in which he enters Hell Mouth in the medieval manner, this time in company with a Pope, a cardinal, a monk, and a bishop (it is interesting to note that this is described as 'Charons ferry-boat').

Laud is explicitly connected with Rome and Antichrist in a venomous pamphlet published to coincide with his attainder and anticipating the verdict, *A Prophecie Of the Life, Reigne and Death of William Laud . . . by an Exposition on part of the 13 and 15 Chapters of the Revelation . . .* [408], one of the many expositions of the 'Number of the Beast' in relation to public enemies—applied, needless to say, with special virtuosity to Napoleon. Laud sits in a chair of state; on his antlered forehead is the number 666; the Devil offers him a cardinal's hat: one servant attends with Popish 'trinkets', another with a roll of tobacco signifying the tobacco patent. In the eighteenth and early nineteenth centuries the disgorging of spoils was often depicted in the most literal manner: examples are Napoleon, Suvórof (in 1799), Lord Melville (in 1805). Laud suffers the indignity in a print of *c.* 1641 [412]; superintended by Henry Burton he is forced to throw up the tobacco patent, his 'canons and constitutions', and is threatened with the hangman. The theme is elaborated in *The Bishops Potion* [177], one of the tracts illustrated by the cut of Laud tied to a post.

Laudian prints (there are many more) have been considered at some length because, to judge from the prints, no other topic or person during the Great Rebellion was such a public obsession for so long. The attitude towards him is something of an opinion-gauge. When, in 1651, his *Sermons* were published, it is clear that there had been a change of mental climate. And when, in 1653, he is actually enshrined in a frontispiece as a pendant to Charles I, one might guess (apart from other evidence) that the change had gathered momentum.

Prints on Strafford can hardly be separated from those on Laud; their association was familiar to all. One of the relatively few without Laud is a woodcut in which he is rowed across the Styx to be welcomed in Hades by Noy, the Attorney-General who had escaped retribution by dying in

1632. This is on a pamphlet, *A Description of the passage of Thomas late Earle of Strafford over the River of Styx* . . . [197]. The small cut anticipates some notable prints in which Charon ferries the defeated or the departed —a convenient device for depicting *bêtes noires* in Hell: Gillray used it for a ribald satire on the defeat of the Whigs in 1807; Napoleon and many Bonapartists are received by Robespierre and others in an elaborate French travesty (in 1815) of part of Michelangelo's *Last Judgment*.

The prints suggest that in 1640–1 resentment at monopolies was a mass-emotion second only to fear of Rome and hatred of Laud. And Laud was traduced as a monopolist. He was accused in Parliament by Harbottle Grimston of 'sharking and taking in the tobacco shops' (through a licensing system). 'The Projector and the Patentee' were partners in infamy: they stood for shady devices secured by intrigue and Court favour to exploit the public under various pretexts of regulating trade and securing quality. For the Crown there was unparliamentary revenue (not very much), with a huge rake-off for the lucky few. The citizen suffered in his purse and his liberties by high prices, shortages, inferior quality, and vexatious regulations. Such was the case against patents of monopoly, experienced in countless individual grievances. (A case has been made for them and some were not without a quota of good intentions.) An engraving by Hollar [Pl. 4], copied and adapted in other prints, symbolizes the Patentee (the description was applied also to the Projector—'Mr. Tenterhooke'). It is a striking example of the application to politics of the folk-print in which persons are constructed of objects connected with their calling. A man with a wolf's head has fish-hook fingers which pull strings attached to money bags; his legs are screws. The rest of the body is made up of things that had been the subjects of monopoly: wine, playing-cards, coals, soap, pins, &c. He is a 'Wolfe like devourer of the Common wealth / That robs by Patent, worse than any stealth / . . . Strong scrues support him that hath scru'd us all / And now we live, to see this strong man fall.'

Though this and some other prints are comprehensive indictments, the most hated of the Monopolies was that of wine, and the public rage was directed against the cousins Kilvert and Abel, Projector and Patentee of the grant. More particularly at Abel: 'every man limnes his picture, and scarce any stationer in Towne, but has some Pamphlet, Sonnet or Ballet in his praise'. Thus a broadside of 1641 associating the 'downfall of wines' with the death of Strafford and the imprisonment of Laud. Abel and Kilvert were imprisoned by order of Parliament in 1640. A portrait of

Alderman Abel with a wine-barrel under his arm (copied from a plate by Hollar) is one of three which decorate a well-known verse pamphlet by Thomas Heywood: '*Reader, Here you'le plainly see Judgment perverted by these three: A Priest, A Judge, A Patentee.*' The priest of course is Laud, the judge is Sir Robert Berkley who justified ship money and was impeached in February 1641.

All the prints on Monopolies record the downfall of the Patentee: in 1641 Monopolies officially ceased, to be replaced (from 1643) by the parliamentary levy of excise duties—which were to acquire a deep and lasting hatred. Portraits by Hollar of Abel, and of Prynne, Bastwick, and Burton, have inscriptions recording the crimes of the first, the virtues and sufferings of the others; these and many other prints illustrate the extent to which the first actions of the Long Parliament appeared as punishment of evil-doers and succour of the righteous—a turning of tables which in the case of bishops was also a rescue from Popery. An interesting representation of the deliverance from Rome is Hollar's print of Time carrying the Pope 'backe to *Rome*' [Pl. 5]: 'This trunke of trash & Romish Trumperies.' These include a bishop's mitre and cap.

For 1641 then the prints reflect the news of the day to a greater extent than after the outbreak of war. Besides the main preoccupations with Laud, Strafford, and Monopolies, there was the flight abroad, first of Windebank to France and then of Lord Finch to The Hague, and both men were often associated with Laud. A portrait of Finch with wings did duty several times. Another favourite subject, in its own right as well as in relation to Laud, was the end of the Court of High Commission and the disappearance of the Ecclesiastical Courts; prints and pamphlets exult at the cessation of interference with religious exercises and with matters of every-day life. In a tract of 1641 there is an illuminating summary of the chief news: *Old Newes newly revived: or, The Discovery of all occurrences Happened since the beginning of the Parliament: As the confusion of Patents, the Deputies death, Canterburies imprisonment, Secretary Windebank, L. Finch, Doctor Roane, Sir John Sucklin and his associates flight, the fall of Wines, the desolation of Doctors Commons, the misery of the Papists, Judge Barckleyes imprisonment, and the ruine of Alderman Abels Monopoly. Most exactly compiled in a short discourse between Mr. Inquisitive a Countrey Gentleman, and Master Intelligencer, a Newesmonger.* The woodcut on the title attempts to summarize this summary. The tenor of the tract is exultation at the unmixed blessings bestowed by Parliament, notably immediate relief from the vexations suffered in the Ecclesiastical Courts. The speakers adjourn to a tavern to drink the health of Parliament in wine at a reduced price.

This was a spirit that could not survive the impact of war and heavy taxes. The near-unanimity of the prints of 1641 was broken, not by open defence of what in the prevailing mood was scarcely defensible, but in attacks on the sudden 'Swarme of Sectaries', and the preaching of illiterate tradesmen and mechanics. The proliferation of sects and congregations, suddenly freed from restrictions, and preaching that was eccentric and fanatical, lent themselves to ridicule; most of the early pamphlets are anonymous, but John Taylor the Water Poet signed several and wrote others, and engaged in violent controversy with Henry Walker, the leather-seller (or ironmonger) with a London congregation who was to become a chaplain to Cromwell, and a leading London journalist, but who has no place in the *D.N.B.*[1] Most of the tracts are unillustrated, but some cuts stand out, because each did duty several times and they convey the spirit of this pamphlet campaign. There is the tub-preacher holding forth to a congregation originally at the Nag's Head in Coleman street, but adapted also to other localities. This illustrates Taylor's doggerel tract: *A Swarm of Sectaries and Schismatiques: Wherein is discovered their strange preach- (or prating) of such as are by their trades Coblers, Tinkers, Pedlars, Weavers, Sowgelders and Chymney-Sweepers* (an interesting list of the callings at the bottom of the social ladder). It served also for *Lucifers Lacky* . . . [210] on the 'dissembling Brownist'[2] with the added motto, 'When Women Preach and Coblers Pray, / The Fiends in Hell make holiday.' The tub-preacher was to become (in word and picture) a symbol of the ranting nonconformist. *Religions Enemies, with a Brief and Ingenious Relation, as by Anabaptists, Brownists, Papists, Familists, Atheists, and Foolists, sawcily presuming to tosse Religion in a Blanquet* [245] is another of Taylor's tracts. The tossers, who toss the Bible, are the first four of the title. This is interesting as an early attempt to associate Popery, not with Anglicanism but with the sects, and also for the appropriation of the Bible as an Anglican emblem. The Puritans had made their own this embodiment of Truth versus Error—often symbolized by Prayer Book or Mass Book. Parliamentary troops sometimes went into action with banners on which a Bible was depicted. On a broadside of 1641, *Good Newes for all*

---

[1] See J. B. Williams, 'Henry Walker, Journalist of the Commonwealth', *Nineteenth Century*, Mar. 1908.

[2] The name Independent had not yet established itself, and the usual term was Brownist from Robert Browne, died *c.* 1633, the separatist regarded as the founder of Independency (or Congregationalism).

*True-Hearted Subjects* [226], is the device of the Arms of the City combined
with an open Bible. When the Bible became an attribute of the dead King
it was one of the indications of the massive shift of opinion in 1649. At first,
the attack on the sectaries was Anglican-Royalist and chiefly voiced by
such a light-weight as John Taylor. But from 1644, when toleration became a great national issue as between Presbyterians and Independents,
pamphleteering against the sects was taken up by Presbyterians and became altogether more important.

As against the preaching cobblers the retort was denunciation of the fat
idle priest, pluralist, and non-resident. This traditional theme (never
less appropriate) was expressed in a simple symbolism [Pl. 6], used and
elaborated by the political anti-clericals of the eighteenth and nineteenth
centuries [Pl. 23].

If the Royalist stereotype of a Puritan was a ranting preacher, that of the
Puritan for his adversaries was a 'Popish Cavalier', raffish and dissipated.
The debauched and roistering Cavalier is admirably portrayed in a broadside dated 1641, *The Sucklington Faction: or (Sucklings) Roaring Boyes*
[Pl. 7]: 'Here sits the prodigall Children; the younger brethren
(Luk. 15. 2) acting yᵉ parts of hotspur Cavaliers and disguised ding-
thriftes, habiting themselves after the fashions of the world, as one that is
to travaile into a farre Countrey.' They are prodigal sons, proud, profligate,
indolent, and drunken. The engraving (with a satirical verse on tobacco)
has an expressive realism, Hogarthian in spirit and competence, unlike the
allegorical designs of the period. Here are the younger sons who haunted
the Court, flouted their elders, and formed Sir John Suckling's much derided troop of gorgeously dressed and ineffective soldiers who accompanied
Charles to Scotland in 1639. The use of the word Cavalier is noteworthy.
With 'Round-Head' it was a new term in the winter of 1641–2. Lilly the
astrologer, speaking of what he saw that Christmas, writes: 'The Courtiers
againe, wearing long Haire and lockes, and always sworded, at last were
called by these men [Puritans] Cavaliers, and so after this broken language
all that adhered unto the Parliament were termed Round-heads; all that
took part . . . for his Majestie, cavaliers, few of the vulgar knowing the
sense of the word Cavalier.'[1] 'Round-Head' (as it was first written) was
much resented, and a counter-term 'Rattle-Head' was produced but failed
to establish itself. A little pamphlet war developed in 1642, well illustrated
in a broadside [Pl. 8] in which the Roundhead (a Puritan minister) is
'Sound-Head', the 'Priestly-Prelate' is 'Rattle-Head', and the true

[1] *Monarchy and No Monarchy*, 1652, p. 107.

Roundhead is a 'Balld-pate Fryar'. The Rattle-Head, half-Bishop, half-Jesuit, rejects Truth (the Bible) and accepts a crucifix from the friar:

> See heer, Malignants Foolerie
> Retorted on them properly,
> The Sound-Head, Round-Head, Rattle-Head
> Well plac'd, where best is merited.

The bisected body, sometimes Janus-headed, was then and long remained a favourite device to indicate a double personality, a secret enemy, a hypocrite, a Mr. Facing-both-ways. In Great Rebellion prints it is chiefly used, as here, and as in *The Kingdomes Monster* [Pl. 9] for the crypto-Papist. Archbishop Williams (in 1642)[1] dressed as soldier *cum* bishop-Jesuit is one of a succession of bisected soldier-clerics.

At the end of 1642 'The unheard of invention of the Round-heads' was attributed in *Magna Britannia Divisa* [143] to 'the dissolute Scollers of Oxford and Cambridge' who were 'Authors of the Round-Heads and of 27 other Masques and Disguisements, heads, cheefs, extravagant opinions or Religions in England . . .'. John Taylor (no scholar) describes the round-head in *Heads of all Fashions . . . allegorically showing the diversities of Religion in these distempered times*:

> But as this head is understood of late
> Some hold it acarce a friend to th'King and State,
> And some suppose it whereso'er it lurch
> To be a great disturber of the Church.

The Rattle-Heads do not seem to have made a corresponding protest against the term Malignant. Whatever may have been the material and moral strength of the two sides on the outbreak of war, Henry Peacham, a Royalist, admitted that opinion, as voiced in pamphlet and broadside, was hostile: the retort was to represent it as fickle and confused. This is the tenor of a very interesting plate by Hollar on the pamphlet war, *The World is Ruled & Governed by Opinion* [Frontispiece], which illustrates lines by Peacham. Opinion, with the world on her lap, sits in her tree, which is watered by Folly; its fruits, 'shaken off with everie little wind', are 'idle books and libells' (pamphlets and broadsides with titles belonging to 1641) which 'in everie street in everie stall you find'. On her arm is a chameleon, her emblem because it 'can assume all Cullors saving white' —that is, except truth. She is blinded by her hat in which is a turret

---

[1] In Hollar's portrait [340 and 341].

representing the Tower of Babel. Below the design is a dialogue: Opinion answers Viator's questions. Asked if she cannot remedy the confusion, she answers,

> Ah no then should I perish in the throng
> O' th giddie Vulgar, without feare or shame
> Who censure all thinges bee they right or wrong. . . .
> Because that Follie giveth life to these
> I but retaile the fruites of idle Aire
> Sith now all Humors utter what they please
> To th' loathing loading of each Mart and Faire:

Some of John Taylor's tracts are among the papers in the tree, as well as counter-tracts by Henry Walker. Peacham carried the argument farther in *Square-Caps turned into Round-Heads: or, the Bishops Vindication and the Brownists Conviction. Being a Dialogue between Time, and Opinion, shewing the folly of the one and the worthiness of the other* [338]. This, Peacham's last work, is remarkable (in 1642) for its open defence of bishops, especially the Archbishop. Opinion, with her chameleon, turns a wheel so that five heads of Roundheads are uppermost, and five bishop's caps below:

> Time doth Opinion call into accompt,
> Who turnes the Bishops downe and Round-Heads mount:
> Upon Her lofty Wheele their Noddels are;
> But her Camelian feedeth upon aire.

The chameleon was an emblem of duplicity and inconstancy from its changing colour, nimble tongue, and supposed capacity to live on air.[1] Here Opinion replaces the traditional Fortune or Time. John Taylor, in the same year, expresses a similar notion—an inverted world—in the ancient imagery that illustrates *Mad Fashions, Od Fashions, All out of Fashions, or the Emblems of these Distracted times* [Pl. 6].

In 1642 the pamphlet war was slipping into the fighting war and in August the King set up his standard at Nottingham. By the end of the year it was apparent that neither side would get an easy victory. This is the background for a Civil War print of a type much rarer than the broadside and pamphlet illustrations that multiplied after 1640—the large, elaborate engraving intended to depict the complexities of a political situation. Among the relatively few extant the most ambitious is *Magna*

---

[1] In *Magna Britannia Divisa* (see below) Archbishop Williams and Bishops Duppa and Towers are 'the Prelatical Camelions'.

[2] Taylor uses the same cut for a tract of 1647 *A Plea for Prerogative: or, Give Caesar his Due* . . . [E. 154/24].

*Britannia Divisa* [143], dated 31 December 1642, with an Amsterdam imprint. To discuss it at length would be to plunge into the intricacies of home and foreign affairs, but the general purport is clear. It is an attempt —violently partisan—to depict the causes, events, and personalities of the war—'this Popish War'. The design is on two large sheets (probably intended to be pasted side by side on a wall) with lengthy marginal explanations printed in French and English. The genre is continental and there are analogies with that remarkable production the *Mappemonde Nouvelle Papistique* of 1566 (printed at Geneva and dedicated to Queen Elizabeth).[1] This is on sixteen sheets intended to form a large wall-map. Figures and buildings seen from above are grouped in a symbolical map which is framed in the gaping jaws of Hell—an interesting application of the ancient device. So too the Civil War print, also *contre-Rome*, is an extremely complicated view of places and people in a vaguely geographical setting. But this print, though linked with the past, foreshadows the future; in its mass of political allusions it outdoes the intricacies of English eighteenth-century cartoons. The viewpoint is ultra-Presbyterian: a die-hard aversion to the peace-talks of 1642–3, combined with seeming respect for the King who is the victim of evil counsellors and foreign intrigue. There are many allusions to foreign affairs, notably Richelieu's attitude to Spain, his death, and even the conspiracy of Cinq-mars. On one sheet is the *Professio Christiana, or the King and the Parliament;* on the other the *Processio Romana, or King without his Parliament.* On the first are the achievements of the parliamentary side from events in Scotland in 1637–9, beginning with a view of Edinburgh Castle. The King's unsuccessful attack on Hull in April 1642 is depicted: on the banner of the town is an angel with an open book, *Biblia Sacra.* In another group Charles receives gifts of money and plate for the war (against himself), and an army, 'raised by the King and Parliament',[2] is put under the Earl of Essex 'for the defence of the Protestant Religion, the securitie of his Majesties person and Parlement, the preservation of the laws, liberties and peace of the Kingdom . . . against the aggression violence and oppression of this Procession'. The war is thus between Christianity and Rome. The details are explained in notes numbered from A to V.

On the other sheet, and in even greater profusion of detail, is a long pro-

---

[1] Reproduced in part, Grand-Carteret, *L'Histoire, la Vie* . . ., Paris, 1927, ii. 122, and attributed to Pierre Eskrich. There is said to be an impression in the British Museum, but I have traced only the explanatory text (190 pp.).

[2] Cf. *The Whigs Idol* . . ., a Tory ballad on Presbyterians, *c.* 1709, who (in 1642) 'Yet drew for *King* and Parliament!! / As if the Wind could stand *North South*'; see p. 72.

cession or masque containing groups and single figures numbered from 1 to 90. Since this is a 'Popish War' and the Procession 'a Bloudy Plot', it is headed by monks with a processional cross: 'The Episcopal War' (in Scotland) is identified with 'the Roman religion': the Irish rebellion is prominent. Friars, Jesuits, Father Philips (the Queen's confessor), Papal emissaries, the Pope, and cardinals are depicted. The Pope is treated with crudity: he is laden with the 'Masse-God'; the usual 'trinkets' or 'trumpery' are excreted by his mule, with the unusual addition of 'Gregorian Almanacks', that is, the reformed calendar accepted only in Catholic countries. The mule excretes also dispensations directing princes 'to keep no faith with heretiques'—a phrase that echoes through No-Popery propaganda for another two centuries. His conclave is voiced by cardinals, who blow through trumpets 'To Kings and Princes Let your Government be arbitrary, abuse the goodnesse of your People, hold them in ignorance, use them like Beasts, and (this Procession finisht) we shall make you carry the sadle and they the Pack-sadle.' With these 'Perfidious Counsels and tyrannical advices' is associated the invention and use of the term Round-Head already noted. The procession ends at the Tower, where Laud and Bishop Wren and other Malignant prisoners are 'the timpanists of this confusion': unable to take part they ring the bells. The climax is a view of the Church on a pinnacle, reformed by 'a good Synod' (then sitting at Westminster): bishops who 'daunce on the Sabath day' are falling 'to their Episcopall down-fall within the abisses', while two (Presbyterian) ministers climb the hill to replace them. Here is Milton's 'New Presbyter' displacing the 'Old Priest'. This ecclesiastical extremism is combined with a quasi-loyalist attitude consistent with the conventions of the Parliamentarians, and prophetic of the combination of Presbyterians and Royalists that led to the Restoration. It may be significant that the King's attempted arrest of the five members is absent. Hollar's pictorial map of the three kingdoms [144] is another political survey, less complicated, and devoted half to British, half to Imperial and Bohemian history—one of the English episodes is the attempt to arrest Pym and the others, as a pendant to the defenestration of Prague.

Prints illustrating incidents of the war are few, the concern is with persons, with plots (there is a very elaborate one on Waller's Plot), and with the dangers of Popery which meant especially soldiers from Ireland. A notable example is *The Kingdomes Monster uncloaked from Heaven: The Popish Conspirators, Malignant Plotters, and cruell Irish . . .* [Pl. 9], a nightmare vision of fear and hate. Two hands reach down to draw aside a cloak and reveal the Monster: on three stalk-like necks are three clusters of heads representing 'Papist Conspiritors', 'Bloudy Irish', and 'Mallignant-Plotters'; the body is half-Papist, half-Cavalier, and the Monster is about to destroy—with fire and sword—the Church, the Parliament, the Kingdom, and the City.

At this time (September 1643) Newcastle's 'Papist Army' had defeated the Fairfaxes in Yorkshire and negotiations were afoot for Irish troops (they were sent to Cheshire in November). Reinforcements from Ireland were a continual source of hope for one side and dread for the other. As the Irish scene shifted, these might be either from the King's troops in Ireland or be recruited from Irish rebels—'the bloudy Irish'. A broadside of 1642 ridicules the first: *The English-Irish Souldier With his new Discipline* . . . [Pl. 10]. There is an interesting analogy with a print of a Hessian in America laden with food in 1778, *A Hessian Grenadeir* [5483]; both express contemptuous dislike of the forces of the Crown, and it is noteworthy that on both occasions the thieving soldier was an enormity. With the formation of the New Model Army (April 1645) the contrast between the forces of King and Parliament became more glaring; as the Royalists admitted, 'In our Army we have the sins of men (drinking and wenching) but in yours you have those of devils, spiritual pride and rebellion.' Two broadsides illustrate the contrast: *The Mercenary Souldier* and *The Zealous Souldier*.[1] One is a Cavalier, cloaked and sworded, the other a man in improbable armour, brandishing a huge sword. One says, 'I came not forth to do my countrey good / I came to rob and take my fill of pleasure. . . .' The other asks, 'can one happier Die / Then for to fall in Battaile, to maintaine / Gods worship, Truth, extirpate Popery. . . .'

Prince Rupert was the Cavalier's hero, the Roundhead's bugbear, and, despite his Protestant antecedents and former popularity, it is only the bugbear that figures here, usually with his famous white poodle, Boy, who was credited with supercanine powers. A minor bugbear was Colonel Lunsford, and legendary atrocities were attributed to both. To quote Cleveland's *Rupertismus* on these pamphlet tales of horror:

> They fear the giblets of his train, they fear
> Even his dog, that four-legged Cavalier
> He that devours the scraps that Lunsford makes
> Whose picture feeds upon the child in steaks, . . . .

The shooting of Boy at Marston Moor by a soldier 'who had skill in

[1] B.M., 669, f. 10/49, 50.

Necromancy' is the subject of *A Dogs Elegy, Or Ruperts Tears* . . ., [395], with 'Witch, Pope and Devill' as chief mourners. The most virulent attack on Rupert is *Englands Wolfe with Eagles Claws* [Pl. 11], illustrating a broadside published after his departure from England, and interesting as an approach to caricature.

With the end of the first Civil War in 1646 the prints reflect growing disillusionment, a sharpening of the issues as between the two parties, and new and growing animosities between Parliament and Army, Presbyterian and Independent. In the prints this last is the dominant subject of 1646-7. The Army was mainly Independent, though with many other sects, and the Independents stood for freedom of conscience and complete toleration for the sects (Popery and Prelacy always excepted); the Presbyterians, with their majority in Parliament, were for a State Church, rigidly organized and utterly intolerant, and were anxious to disband the Army and so leave themselves supreme. The split, or rather chasm, was manifest with Parliament's rejection of the Army's plea for 'tender consciences', and the Army was further embittered by the Parliament's attitude towards their arrears of pay. Despite the constitutional issues involved, the religious and sectarian aspects of the controversy dominate the prints, and, as always, each side associates the other with Popery, and assumes for itself the part of champion against Rome. The situation is strikingly displayed in a pic-torial broadside of September 1646, *The Watchmans Warning-Peece, or Parliament Souldiers Predilection, shewing*[1]

> That if our Armies lay down Arms
> Before the Work is at an End
> We may expect
> Yet worser Harms
> More pretious Lives and States to spend.

Reason walks in a rocky landscape menaced by enemies—Papists, a dragon (the Pope), a spotted leopard (Prelacy), and by a still more crafty adversary explained in the last verse:

> The crooked serpent creeps upon the Earth,
> An Antichristian Presbyter by birth
> His head from Rome, his taile and body so
> With them to Aye-Perdition he shall go.

Watchman's plea is for London to be guarded by an army. The 'Antichristian Presbyter' had already been attacked in April in a pictorial broad-

---

[1] B.M., E. 354/10.

side, *Dictated Thoughts* [647], a protest against intolerance and an emblematical plea for 'tender consciences'. Pope, Priest, and Presbyter, linked by a chain, stab 'Tender Conscience' to the heart. A Presbyterian retort followed, but not till November: *A Reply to Dictated Thoughtes by a More Proper Emblem* [653]; an Independent takes the place of Presbyter, and is styled 'Profane Libertin or advocate for a general Toleration', he has a double face and tramples on the Bible. He and two others, the Pope and a bishop with the 'Liturgie', stab a burning heart representing the 'honest hearts' which they unite to wound.

The same engraving was used for another Presbyterian thrust, *Proper Persecution . . .* [657] directed especially against Richard Overton, a Leveller who had attacked the Westminster Assembly of Presbyterian divines (the Synod) in pamphlets signed Martin Marpriest (professing to be the son of Martin Marprelate (John Penry), enemy of the Elizabethan bishops). Overton was attacked in yet another anti-toleration print, *The Picture of an English Persecutor, or A foole ridden Ante Presbeterian Sectary* [670]; he crawls on hands and knees with a fool riding on his back. It must be remembered that Presbyterian intolerance was extreme indeed. To quote one of their divines, 'To let men serve God according to their own persuasion is to cast out one devil that seven more might enter.'[1] The Presbyterians had taken up the Anglican theme of 1641–2 against sectaries and schismatics; the most comprehensive attack was in Thomas Edwards's *Gangræna*. The conflict evoked Milton's sonnet 'On the new forcers of conscience under the Long PARLIAMENT', with the famous last line, '*New Presbyter* is but *Old Priest* writ large'. Presbyterian attacks include a broadside (January 1647), *A Catalogue of the severall Sects and Opinions in England and other Nations* [666] with portraits of twelve sectaries; the first is a Jesuit (with Guy Faux's lantern); six, the Independent, is 'Libertin' wearing a sword and breaking the Tables of the Law; the last is 'Divorcer' (surely intended for Milton), who is thrashing his wife.

Royalists naturally cashed in on the dissensions of their enemies. In December 1646 Samuel Sheppard produced a verse tract, *The Times displayed in Six Sestyads* [656] with a print of 'Three Grand Enimies of Church and State'. These are 'Profane Liberty' (an Independent), 'Envious Hypocresie' (a Presbyterian with six masks) and 'Jesuiticall Pollicie'. Daniel Featley's Anglican contribution (in 1645) had been *Dippers Dipt* with a striking title-page.

A pictorial plea for unity followed in March, *A Pious And Seasonable*

[1] Quoted, C. H. Firth, *Cromwell*, 1934, p. 152.

*Perswasive to the Sonnes of Zion Soveraignely useful for Composing their Un-brotherly Devisions* [675]. An Independent, 'a Godly dissenting Brother', takes the hand of 'a Godly Brother of the Presbyterian way', to the dismay of a 'Romish Prelate' (Anglican) and an 'English Jesuite', who watch together, saying, 'Ah lass wee are utterly undone, our designe is spoyled, they are agreed.'

However, the rift between the Godly Brothers and between Parliament and Army deepened, while both sides manœuvred for possession of the King, who was trying to play off one against the other. Charles, who was handed over by the Scottish army to a Parliamentary Commissioner at the end of January, was brought to Holmby House. There, forestalling the secret intentions of the Presbyterians, he was seized by Cornet Joyce (2 June) and taken to Newmarket. The Army marched towards London, and Parliament was forced to temporize and then to yield. But this was deeply resented by the citizens, apprentices, and mob. The Presbyterians prepared to fight, putting their weak forces under Major-General Massey. The futile attempt to resist Fairfax's veterans is the subject of a cocksure pamphlet [686] decorated by a cut of two fighting cocks (one of many political cockfights): 'Presbyterian John revived' against 'Independent Craven a dying.' In the language of pamphlets and squibs the Presbyterian was now 'Sir John Presbyter', or 'Presbyterian Jack', or 'Mr Persecutor' and was a target for both Independents and Royalists. An early example of burlesque heraldry (1647 or later) is *Atchievement of Sir John Presbyter* [702], a Royalist satire, bitterly hostile to sectaries and Presbyterians, and using, as became customary, the jargon of heraldry for the elaboration of insults.

Besides these envenomed exchanges between the Godly Brothers, there is a more subtle exposition of the Independent *versus* Presbyterian theme in an emblematical design of October 1647, *Truth flatters not: Plaine dealing the best* [697]. Four figures are dominated by the eye and sword of Jehovah: they are 'Heresie' (the Pope on his seven-headed Beast), 'Prelate', 'Priste' holding a crown upon a sword, who is clearly though not quite explicitly a Presbyterian minister, in fact, 'Old Priest writ large'; a weathercock in his hat indicates his recent veering towards royalism. Last is 'Veritie', a woman holding a Bible and saying, 'Learne of mee to be meeke and lowlie.' It is made plain that she is an Independent or a sectarian preacher by the fact that 'Scorner', a Cavalier, points at her saying, 'A silly tubb preacher.' Each speaks, under compulsion to speak truth. The 'Priste'-Presbyterian:

I hate the Pope, his poysoned cup,
        and trinkets all.
The Bishops deeds, and Romish weeds
        to me are gall.
Yet well I know, what Layicks owe
        unto our Coat,
Reverence all way, good livings pay,
        is our just lot.
Sects and unlearned, up-start Jackes
        doth us defraud,
Who to our shame, our power and name,
        have over-aw'd.

This line of attack is exceptional among the imputations of Popery and Prelacy.

There is a note of triumph in John Spittlehouse's *Rome Ruin'd by White-hall . . . a Confutation of the three Degrees of Popery, viz. Papacy, Prelacy, and Presbitery . . .* In a plate headed 'An Emblem of Antichrist in his threefould Hierarchies . . .' a triple-headed Pope—Cerberus—stands between 'Presbiter' and 'Prellat'. All three deplore their ruin. This is an Army viewpoint, with a dedication to Fairfax. Published at the end of 1650, it represents the achievements of Independents over Presbyterians by the King's death and Cromwell's victories.

To return to 1647. Alongside the bitter controversies between the Godly Brothers, we can trace in the prints the growth of Royalism and, perhaps, the counter-trend towards republicanism. In January the common interest of Parliament, Synod, and Army is expressed (optimistically) in what may have been a plea for unity. In *Englands Miraculous Preservation Emblematically Described, Erected for a perpetual Monument to Posterity* [660], Royalists, dying and dead, submerge in the water surrounding an ark which contains the Houses of Parliament and the Westminster Assembly; the Queen floats siren-like next Charles. There are six medallion portraits of generals, including Fairfax and Cromwell. A very different view is that of a print dedicated to the Earl of Northumberland, undated, but probably belonging to 1646: *Syons Calamitye or Englands Miserye Hieroglyphically delineated* [373]. Disillusionment, war-weariness, Anglicanism, and moderate Royalism are expressed in a complicated symbolism expounded in verse beginning 'Alas Poore England!'. Two buckets in a well indicate the alternations of opinion.

Similar disillusionment is the note of a broadside (February 1647) by a Somerset country gentleman with a grievance—Humphrey Willis. His

Royalism is sharpened by resentment at the jack-in-office and the new rich, and he uses imagery for a topsy-turvy world to illustrate verses: *Times Whirligig, or, The Blew-new-made-Gentleman mounted* [668]. A Committee-man tramples on an inverted globe saying, 'Take him Marshal'; at the North–South Pole is an orb without the crown. The verses are a plea for peace: 'arbitrary power' was the only thing to fight against and that fight has succeeded 'Beyond what we could hope or wish . . . / If we sometimes had from our Prince / A lash or two, what have we since? . . . O what an ague hath this land / Look how it shakes, how tottering stands; / How pants for some Physitian . . .'. *The Committee Man* [228] is a spectacled owl in a frankly Royalist print of about the same date which deplores revolutionary change: 'O Tempora, O Mores . . .'.

On the King's imprisonment little more remains than a crude cut that served for several loyal pamphlets; Charles looks from a barred window in Carisbrooke Castle, saying, 'Behold your King'. The execution evoked a flood of loyal papers, not only in English, but in Dutch, German, French, and Latin, some with conventional illustrations. Here, it is the plate to *Eikon Basilike* [Pl. 12] that demands attention as supreme among poli-tical-allegorical frontispieces—not aesthetically, but as an historical docu-ment, and as probably the most effective piece of pictorial propaganda of the Great Rebellion. First, for its association with the famous book and as part of its message. Then, for its multiplied variants and adaptations, and finally as a design with a life of its own. In a minor degree it shares the prolonged controversy that has raged round the authorship of 'The King's Book';[1] was Marshall's plate designed by Charles or by Dr. Gauden? By the Doctor, if we are to believe his own letter to Clarendon: 'this book and figure were wholly and only of my invention making and designe . . .'. But Royston, who printed the earliest editions, said that the design was sent him by the King: 'his Majestie sent another figure to bee engraven on copper and annexed to the Booke . . .'. And according to Dr. Edward Hooker[2] the King 'drew' the frontispiece and 'pencilled' the mottoes on the right side, he and Marshall supplying those for the rock and the palm-tree. Drawing was one of the King's accomplishments, and there is the

---

[1] This account is based on Dr. F. F. Madan's *New Bibliography of the Eikon Basilike . . .*, Oxford, 1950. His conclusion is that loose papers written by the King reached Gauden, who on his own initiative used them as the basis for a book, and sent the completed manuscript to Charles at Newport. After some hesitation the King accepted this as what he intended to write, and 'corrected and heightened' it for the Press. This has not been univerally accepted so that the controversy is even yet not ended.

[2] Corrector of the Press to William Dugard and author of the *Apothegmata Carolina* 1649, extracts from the *Eikon*.

perhaps suggestive fact that the text chosen for his coronation service had been 'Be thou faithful unto death and I will give thee a crown of Life'. It seems possible that the design, or part of it, was his.[1] It replaced an earlier one sent to Royston: three crowns indented on a crown of thorns. Three crowns remained the core of the symbolism of the famous plate, which from the first was an essential part of the book. Kneeling before an open Bible,[2] Charles spurns the world, rejects a crown of gold, accepts a crown of martyrdom, awaits a crown of glory. The other half of the design is a characteristic example of the emblem. The palm, weighted but erect, and the storm-beaten rock symbolize the King's faith and steadfastness. The palm was believed to have the power of straightening itself against a weight, and Dryden, alluding to Marshall's plate, transferred the imagery to Cromwell:

> His palms, though under weights they did not stand,
> Still thrived; no winter could his laurels fade.[3]

The rapid printing of edition after edition by different printers involved repeated re-engravings and copies of the plate: thirty-five pre-Restoration variants have been traced. Seven were engraved by Marshall; the boldness of his signature is an early indication of the immunity of the artist as compared with author and printer. Three of the others, one a crude woodcut, cannot be connected with any edition and were probably made for the printsellers; each has survived only from having been inserted in a single copy of the *Eikon*, and more variants of these perishable separate prints may have existed. Adaptations of the design were made for editions printed outside England—some of great interest. There were post-Restoration adaptations and in 1703 the original version illustrated a broadside of the King's sayings. An enlarged copy was made for a mid-eighteenth-century printseller, a cartoon, cheaply produced as if for a wide circulation; two versions exist, with different inscriptions. The one in the British Museum Print Room is *The Emblem of the Royal Martyr King*

---

[1] The profile of the first version has a more amateurish look than the three-quarter face which Marshall introduced when he re-engraved the plate.

[2] To stress that he was a good Protestant. The point is made in two of the verse 'Explanations' of the frontispiece:

> That hee's no Papist neither, look before him,
> Gods word, no Missal there, doth so declare him.

And:

> [Charles speaks] . . . my book upon my bord,
> Explains my heart, my hope is in thy Word.

[3] *Heroick Stanzas upon Oliver Cromwell*, 1659.

*Charles y^e first in his sufferings*; there is no reference to the *Eikon*. The famous design survived also in more remarkable forms. With the Restoration it apparently blossomed into stained-glass windows and paintings in churches. Two embroidery pictures still survive; one is in the V. & A. In this the design is enriched by the standing figure of a youthful Charles II, armed and erect, hand on his sword, as a pendant to the kneeling King; two angels hold a crown above his head. This oriflamme must have been kept carefully hidden before the Restoration.

The *Eikon* frontispiece figures in its own right in a pamphlet published early in 1649: *Frontispiece of the Kings Book opened. With a Poem annexed: the In-Security of Princes*. This contains also two of the sets of explanatory verses that were an important adjunct of the plate, as of most 'emblems'. For the *Eikon* no less than six were printed or engraved, five being connected with specific editions, one known only from the pamphlet. A seventh exists in manuscript in Thomason's hand.[1] Such verses were a perfect medium for loyal sentiments, and surely there must be others in the commonplace books so often found among seventeenth-century manuscripts in country houses.

In 1649 two other frontispieces played leading parts in the controversy that sprang up over the *Eikon*. But this was not the controversy based on conflict of evidence: that began only in 1690, when Dr. Gauden's claim to have written the book and the acceptance of his authorship by Charles II and his brother were first made known. The problem was different in 1649—the urgent need to discredit a book so damaging to the régime, so daunting to the regicides. Milton declared in *Eikonoklastes* that its influence was such that all except some few were 'ready to fall flatt and give adoration to the Kings image and memory'. The publication, immediately after the execution, written in the first person, but unsigned, astonished the country, indeed Europe. Only one line of attack was really practicable: to declare the book spurious and father it upon some ambitious cleric. Hence the first (anonymous) attack; the title parodies that of the *Eikon*: ΕΙΚѠΝ Α'Α ΛΗΘΙΝΗ, *The Portraiture of Truths most sacred Majesty . . . Wherin the false coulours are wash'd off, wherewith the Painter-stainer had Bedawbed Truth, the late King, and the Parliament in his counterfeit Piece.* There could be no better testimony to the effect of the *Eikon*: in 'many before well affected persons . . . I found an Idol-worship crept in among you and found you adoring the counterfeit Pourtraicture of one you sometimes knew no Saint . . .'. The author is alleged to be a 'court parasite

---

[1] 'Explayning the frontispiece of the Kings Book.' [B.M., E. 550/4.]

preaching up prerogative . . .'. The gist of the argument is in the frontispiece and its accompanying doggerel: a hand from the upper margin draws
aside a curtain to reveal the author, a cleric in a doctor's cap:

> The curtain's drawne: all may perceive the plot,
> And him who truely the blacke babe[1] begot. . . .
> Presumptuous Preist, to skip into the throne,
> And make the *King*, his bastard issue owne
>> The Authour therefore hath conceiv'd it meet
>> The Doctor should doe penaunce in this sheet.

The retort was rapid,[2] considering that a plate had to be engraved, ΕΙΚΩΝ
Η ΠΙΣΤΗ, *Or, the faithfull Pourtraicture of a loyal Subject, in vindication of
Eikon Basilike . . . In answer to an insolent book. . . .* Charles sits, hand on
an open book, an elbow resting on a skull. A man in a fool's cap is about
to snatch off the crown and replace it by a doctor's cap, but is restrained
by a Cavalier. The verses begin as before and end:

> Though as a King in's actions he did shine
> Yet in his writings he may be divine
>> Do not then say one skips into the throne
>> The Doctor and the King may both be one.[3]

This seems to point prophetically to the double authorship theory, but
the Cavalier of course makes a complimentary play upon words.

Many more examples of the political frontispiece could be cited. Its
introduction into a non-political book is noteworthy. Marshall's plate to
the second edition of Quarles' *The Shepheards Oracles* (a posthumous work
of 1646) is frankly Royalist. The Tree of Religion is defended by Charles
with sword and sceptre and watered by a bishop, while it is attacked by a
Jesuit and by Protestant dissenters. One of these, standing in a tub, fires
at the tree; he has already transfixed on his spear a bishop's cap, the
Liturgy, and 'Cannons'. Others try to root it up. The branches are Faith,
Hope, Charity, and Good Works, and the last two are being cut off.
A protecting hand descends from Heaven. The usual verse explanation is
absent and the only allusion in the text is to

> . . . these base sycophants that lye
> Close gnawing at the root, as well as those
> That with the Romish Axe, strike downright blows
> On the main body of Religions Tree. . . .

[1] The *Eikon* in its dark binding was sometimes stigmatized as 'the black babe'.

[2] Thomason acquired the tracts on 26 Aug. and 11 Sept. This seems to disqualify Endymion
Porter (buried 20 Aug.) as author of the second.

[3] The verses seem to be the model for those on print and counter-print on the Sacheverell
controversy, see p. 69.

After the King's death the situation called for official propaganda on the grand scale to counteract the shock to the country. On the highest level this was supplied by Milton, who as Secretary for Foreign Tongues was the chief literary supporter of the new Commonwealth. There were also severe measures of press control. A wave of pictorial propaganda from 1649 and especially in 1651–2 has signs of official inspiration, its purpose being to discredit the Stuarts and build up Cromwell. There are reasons to connect this with Henry Walker, John Taylor's adversary, now a leading journalist and one of Cromwell's chaplains; he was to show himself a shameless time-server in 1660 when he produced a sanctimonious eulogy of Charles II. Out of a set of four pictorial broadsides two have been attributed to Walker, on grounds of style and imprint.[1] On the same grounds the fourth should also be his. Besides these, Walker's printer published two portrait-broadsides listing Cromwell's achievements, the portrait engraved from the painting by Robert Walker of Cromwell as a victorious general, one version of which is now in the National Portrait Gallery. In this anti-monarchical propaganda three interlaced lines of approach are conspicuous. One was the use of astrology and of 'prophecies', allegedly ancient, to show that monarcy was doomed to end with Charles I. Another was to discredit the Stuarts by attacks on James I and his Court, sometimes also on Charles I (as in Milton's *Tenure of Kings and Magistrates*), and by accounts of the violent deaths of Stuart sovereigns. The third, pictorially the most striking, is found on broadsides on Charles II's relations with the Scots. Resentment at the prospect of an invasion of Scots, perhaps also of the still more dreaded Irish, produced an excellent climate for anti-monarchical propaganda.

The first, February 1651, is *The True Manner of the Crowning of Charles the Second King of Scotland . . . Together with a declaration of his life . . . and a close view of his Court and Counsell*. On this is an engraved equestrian portrait of Charles II in armour with a battle raging in the background. The text, besides imputations on the young man's character and conduct, is propaganda on the usual lines: 'What are the great fruitlesse boastings of *English* Malignants, the vaine hopes of *Irish* Papists...'. The second, July 1651, livelier than the vituperative manifestoes attributed to Walker, has a print, often reproduced, but without attention to its context. The design is effectively simple, with a certain humour unusual in Civil

---

[1] J. B. Williams (Muddiman) in *Camb. Hist. Engl. Lit.* vii. 355–6. He thinks that Robert Ibbitson rarely published any other author's writings, but he published official papers. In 1653 he was put forward for the office of printer to the Council of State, but did not get it: H. R. Plomer, *Dictionary of Booksellers and Printers . . .*, 1641–67, 1907.

War prints. Picture and text are an excellent rendering of the situation and a clever appeal to anti-Scottish sentiment. And it has a second string in its use of prophecy: *Old Sayings and Predictions verified and fulfilled, touching the young King of Scotland and his Gued Subjects* [812] is illustrated by 'The Scots holding their young Kings nose to ye grinstone'. The verses begin:

> This Embleme needs no learned Exposition,
> The World knows well the sad condition
> Of regall Power, and Prerogative
> Dead, and dethron'd in *England*, now alive
> In *Scotland*, where they seeme to love the Lad,
> If hee'l be more obsequious than his Dad,
> And Act according to Kirk Principles,
> More subtile then were Delphick Oracles, . . .

There is a final appeal to 'true *English* hearts' to make a speedy end of 'these wars', that 'the *Scots* (though late) may see / What 'tis attends the STEWARDS family'. Then follows an 'old Prophesie of a Jesuite [*sic*] in Hen. VII time, of all the Kings and Queens that should succeed in *England* thus, Mars, Puer, Alecto, Virgo, Vulpes, Leo, Nullus'—no King will succeed Charles I. This 'prophecy' was worked hard in 1651–2.[1] It was inscribed on a portrait of Charles I which is the frontispiece to a scurrilous production, *The None-such Charles, his Character*[2]—a title appropriated from Fabian Philipps's royalist tract. And it appeared again on the portraits of James I prefixed to two libellous publications by Sir Anthony Weldon, one being *A Cat may look at a King*: a woodcut of a cat looks across at the portrait. Robert Vaughan in 1651 (unaware of the rout of Worcester) engraved a counter-print to Republican manifestoes, a 'picture' with a 'traiterous inscription' for which he was indicted at the Middlesex Sessions:[3] 'Charles Sonne of Charles the Martyr . . . Nowe in the head of a gallant and numerous army of the valliant and faithfull Scottes marching by the favour and mightines of his maker, towards the possession of the rest of his fathers Crownes . . .'.

The chief astrologer of the day, William Lilly, came into action in

[1] Another 'prophecy' in 1651 is *The Black Dutch Almanack or Predictions and Astronomicall Observations foreshewing what will further happen to the King of Scots and other Kings and Commonwealths . . .*' This professed to include an old prophecy found in Dutch; in a rhyming jingle it foretold the flight of Charles from Britain, never to return.

[2] Probably by John Hall, appointed official writer at a salary of £100 a year: J. B. Williams, *History of English Journalism*, 1908, p. 103.

[3] On 14 Oct. 1651: a jury acquitted him on 28 Apr. 1652: Jeaffreson, *Middlesex County Records*, 1888, iii. 206, 287.

August 1651 with *Monarchy or no Monarchy in England. Grebner, his Prophecy.* This contains emphatic approval of Charles's execution and a prophecy that England should no more be governed by a king. He professes to embody his predictions in sixteen 'Enigmaticall' plates, which he would have explained, he says, 'had the courtesie of the present times deserved it at my hands'. The end of monarchy (a mole sniffing at a crown) and the overthrow of pulpits and preachers—presumably Presbyterians—are depicted. Though after 1660 Lilly declared himself a crypto-Royalist who had given secret aid to Charles I, his *Monarchy* was Republican propaganda. Was it commissioned? It seems not unlikely; in 1648 he had been officially called upon to attend the siege of Colchester to encourage the soldiers with prophecies of speedy victory. He also contributed in 1651 to the disparagement of Stuart kings in his *True History of King James and King Charles I.*

To return to the Charles II broadsides. The title of the third, *A Mad Designe* [814], November 1651, has had some publicity through its adoption by David Low as a generic name for cartoon.[1] But in the political language of the day 'design' connotes plan (bad or good), scheme, conspiracy, and here it clearly refers to the subject of the print: Charles intends to appeal for foreign and papal aid. The broadside, attributed to Walker, is a complicated emblematical representation of Charles's fate after Worcester, combined with an attack on Scots and Presbyterians. It is a processional design, with analogies to *Magna Britannia Divisa*, filled with personal allusions and allegations of Popish intrigue.

The fourth broadside, October 1652, exulting over 'the rout of Worcester', symbolizes the destruction of monarchy. In *The Woefull Mirrour of Monarchy* [813] Death triumphs. There is a 'List of the Family from which Charles the second king of Scotland descended, that sat in the fatall Throne of *Scotland* and came to untimely ends'. Starting with Charles I, this goes backwards to the legendary kings (fourth century B.C.) imagined by the Scottish historians Boece and Buchanan. The number of the Beast, 666, is applied comprehensively to Charles II and his ancestors; James I and his elder son are said, as often at this time, to have been poisoned. (This was a crime attributed to Charles I and Buckingham.) Hatred of the Scots had a propaganda value that is exploited in the frontispiece to *The*

---

[1] Low follows M. H. Spielmann (*Encycl. Brit.* 11th ed. *s.v.* Cartoon) who writes 'The Mad Designe' of the reign of Charles I [*sic*] became the 'cartoon' of the reign of Queen Victoria. Low adds, 'the unappreciative monarch [Charles I] was moved to anger against "these Madde Designes"': *British Cartoonists*, 1942, p. 8. Titles of tracts illustrate contemporary usage: *The Pretended Design of Levelling . . .* 1647; *Designes Unmasqued . . .* 1669.

*Dissembling Scot Set forth in his true Coulours* ... [852], 1 February 1653, an early example of the *bête noire* whose body is inscribed with all manner of vices and crimes; Charles Fox and Napoleon, among others, were thus indicted. The Scot is 'Persecutor', that is, Presbyterian.

From 1653 polemical prints are scarce. Cromwell's expulsion of the Long Parliament is applauded in an illustrated broadside, *The Parliament Routed: or, Here's a House to be let* [856], with an introductory quatrain which ends 'O Lord protect the Generall, that He / May be the Agent of our Unitie'.[1] English attacks on Cromwell hardly begin before 1660. But there are many Dutch pictorial insults, and in these the whole anti-Cromwell legend may be found: he is tyrant, hypocrite, self-seeker, man of blood; he is vain and arrogant. The King's execution figures often in these prints; it is usually Fairfax who is executioner-in-chief—he is, for instance, Cromwell's hound, 'the bloodhound Fairfax'. In 1656 Cromwell is Antichrist, on the seven-headed Beast [897], and the extent to which he remained an obsession with the Dutch is seen in his reappearance in prints of 1780 as the embodiment of English arrogance and violence. In England, too, Cromwell is one of those few who survive in folk-memory and graphic satire as cautionary embodiments of political crimes. In the long-drawn-out chorus of pictorial dispraise there are a few exceptions—marking crises of resentment at military or diplomatic failure.

In the war of 1651–4, as in other wars, the Dutch used the satirical print and the medal as national weapons. The war-engendered hate was reinforced, not only by commercial jealousies, but by Stuart associations due to Princess Mary's marriage to William of Orange and to the Cavalier colony in Holland, with Charles II's headquarters there. Royalist propaganda flowed from Dutch presses. In their use of graphic satire the Dutch were far in advance of their adversaries, and English counter-prints were few. Only three survive in the national collection, notably a complicated allegory in the Dutch manner which heads a broadside of 1652, *Dr. Dorislaws Ghost, Presented by Time to unmask the Vizards of the Hollanders* [837]; one item in this represents the long resented 'Massacre at Amboyna' in 1623, adapted from the frontispiece to *A True Relation . . . of the Massacre* [839], published in November 1651; another incident in the plate (taken from the *Double Deliveraunce*) is 'the treacherous assault of Van Tromp upon the English ships'. The tenor of the print is Dutch craft and cruelty. Dorislaus, Commonwealth emissary to Holland, had been

---

[1] See the remarkable emblematic tribute to Cromwell by Faithorne, 1658, *The Embleme of Englands Distractions*, reproduced *History Today*, viii. 603. In B.M.

murdered by Royalists at The Hague. It seems strange that a Dutch version was published at Amsterdam in the same year. Finally, in January
1654 there was *The Great Butter Box* [854], a coarse and clumsy pictorial
broadside which is a grosser rendering of the gibes that had appeared in
Marvell's *The Character of Holland* written, as official poet,[1] in 1653, in
which the country is 'This undisgested vomit of the sea', its governors
(Hogan Mogan) 'the hogs, as all their subjects boors', and the Dutch
skipper 'butter Coloss, Tunned up with several towns of beer'.

Occasional English prints before 1660 suggest the approach, desired or
dreaded, of the Restoration. Resentment at Puritan rule speaks for itself in
the title of a tract published at Christmas 1652, *The Vindication of Christmas. Or his Twelve Yeares Observations upon the Times, concerning the
lamentable Game called Sweepstake: acted by General Plunder, and Major
General Tax: . . . a Description of that oppressing Ringworm called Excize;
and the manner how our high and mighty Christmas-Ale that formerly
would knock down Hercules, & trip up the heels of a Giant, strook into
a deep Consumption with a blow from Westminster.* This has a woodcut of
Christmas (in a long robe and bearded) repulsed by a soldier and welcomed by a countryman [848]. By an Act of 1644 the day was to be kept as
a fast on the ground that it was a heathen festival. Another sign of the times
is open defence of the Anglican Church—when Dr. Gauden (a time-server
who had taken the Covenant and kept his benefices) came into the open
in 1653 with *Hieraspistes, a Defence of the Ministry and Ministers of the
Church of England*, it was clear that the weather was changing: in the frontispiece Charles I and Laud (with a Bible) are martyrs defending the faith.
Edward Chisenhale was a Royalist who had been fined for delinquency;
his *Catholick History* in the same year is a glorification of the Church of
England; in the frontispiece the Church is *Veritas*, the Romish Church
(with Pope and Devil) is *Vanitas*.

The often-used device of ghosts in colloquy served for a sequence of
tracts. In March 1658 there was an anti-monarchical dialogue between
Henry VIII and Charles I in Windsor Chapel [910]: both confess to many
crimes. (Here one is reminded of the macabre scene in the chapel in 1813
when the two coffins were opened in the presence of the Regent.) But in
June 1659 the ghosts of Charles and Cromwell [924] meet: 'Oliver the late
usurping Pretender' entreats the King for pardon. And, in March 1661,
the ghosts of Cromwell and Bradshaw meet at Tyburn [947], with those of
other regicides, exhumed or executed.

[1] Legouis, *André Marvell, Poète, Puritain, Patriote*, 1928, p. 176.

With the Restoration there was an outburst of squibs and lampoons and violent diatribes against the regicides, and it was inevitable that Cromwell should be Antichrist. In a satirical portrait he is 'the true Emblem of Antichrist', and this is also the theme of a tract by Abraham Nelson, professedly written in 1654, published in 1660, *A Perfect description of Antichrist . . . wherein is plainely shewed that Oliver Cromwell was Antichrist.*

These Great Rebellion prints, miscellaneous as they are, fall into successive phases. First, an outburst of pictorial pamphleteering—violent opinions, suddenly freed from restrictions and violently expressed. The spirit is Puritan-Presbyterian with a few relatively cautious Royalist-Anglican prints. Hollar's allegory, *The World is Ruled & Governed by Opinion* [Frontispiece] stands out as significant though far from typical. Secondly, the bitter strife between Presbyterian and Independent dominates the scene, and is fought out in print and counter-print, with an occasional plea for unity in face of the enemy, while an occasional Royalist print tries to turn the discord to advantage. With the crisis of the King's death the enormous effect of *Eikon Basilike*, despite press restrictions, is reflected in the many variants of the frontispiece. To counteract the sense of outrage in the country there is evidence of deliberate propaganda in a sequence of illustrated broadsides which are anti-monarchical, anti-Stuart, in some degree anti-Presbyterian, and there is reason to believe that these were officially or semi-officially inspired. On the constitutional crises that followed there is almost nothing, apart from approval of Cromwell's expulsion of the Rump in April 1653. Until 1660 attacks on Cromwell are almost wholly Dutch; the many Dutch prints insulting to the Commonwealth and the Protector, before and during the naval war, evoked a very limited pictorial retort.

Throughout, the constitutional and legal aspects of the struggle are barely touched on. There is one little *Plea for Prerogative*,[1] one or two incidental allusions to 'Arbitrary Government'; but the Star Chamber is not mentioned. There are protests against a topsy-turvy world, resentment at the upstart, especially the 'Committee Man', and at the attempt to make, Christmas a fast day. The approach to such topics is almost wholly Royalist, although a majority of the prints are Puritan in spirit. Controversies are seen in terms of religion: the changes are rung on Popery, Prelacy, Presbyterian, Independent, sectaries. Doubtless the prevailing imagery, with its personification of qualities—Hypocrisy, Vanity, Verity,

[1] By John Taylor; see p. 26, n. 2.

Discord, and the like—was peculiarly suited to religious themes, but then
the imagery reflected the mental and moral climate. Not till the 1660
edition of Clement Walker's *History of Independency Part II* (for which he
was imprisoned in 1649) have I found any of those symbols of the Constitution which belong to the graphic imagery of the eighteenth century: in
the frontispiece Cromwell, poised insecurely on a globe which rests on
Hell Mouth, directs the cutting down and rooting up of the 'Royall Oake
of Brittayne'; the fruits of the tree, besides *Eikon Basilike* and the Bible,
are 'Magna Charta',[1] 'Statutes', and 'Reportes'—emblems of liberty and
law. Liberty indeed, destined to a dominant role in English political imagery,
appears only in the guise of 'Profane Liberty' or 'Libertin' (otherwise
Congregationalist). Yet the Great Seal of the Commonwealth had the
legend 'In the first Year of Freedom'. It is noteworthy that Liberty had
long been an important Dutch symbol. On a medal of 1575 the Hat of
Liberty (afterwards to acquire the form of cap—the *pileus* that French
Revolutionary symbolism transformed into a Phrygian cap) has the motto
*Libertas aurea cujus Habenas ratio*, 'Golden Liberty whose reins are held
by Reason'.

In the matter of imagery, though devices of the later cartoonists have
been noted, there are striking absences. No Britannia, despite her appearance on title-pages; no British Lion with one partial exception. In fact
these symbols were ready to hand. The Dutch Lion was well established,
but the corresponding Dutch emblem for England was a dog, and long
remained so (in happier days it had been a rose).[2] In Dutch prints Anglo-
Dutch wars are fights between the Dutch Lion and English Dog. The
partial exception is a plate by Hollar illustrating complimentary verses by
Henry Peacham on the marriage of Princess Mary in 1641, *En Surculis
Arbor*.[3] The two lions rampant face each other, their paws supporting an
orange tree (another political emblem making an appearance):

> Two Lions sterne, one red the other gold
>     The Holland and our English heere you see,
> The Orange Tree do equallie uphold,
>     In perfect League and endless Amitie. . . .

But here the English Lion is still partly at least heraldic.

Britannia reached the political print by way of the medal. First, a Dutch

[1] 'Magna Charta' appears in the tribute to Cromwell by Faithorne, 1658, see p. 41 n.
[2] On a Dutch medal of 1587 is a plough drawn by a pair of oxen; on one is the Belgic Lion,
on the other a rose for England: Van Loon, *Hist. métallique des pays bas*, La Haye, 1732–7, i. 371.
[3] B.M., C. 20. f. 2/288.

satirical medal of 1655 (obverse, the head of Cromwell); the Protector kneels with his head in Britannia's lap, presenting his bared back to the French and Spanish Ambassadors, who obsequiously compete for an alliance with England. The medal has another interest. It was copied for an English satirical print of 1739, an attack on Walpole, *The Naked Truth* [2417]: '. . . so submissive were those great powers in those days and so much aw'd that they dreaded a frown from the Protector'.[1]

On English medals Britannia first appeared on those struck in 1660 for the Restoration: always seated by the sea, sometimes on a globe; usually with shield and spear (as on the famous naval medal for which Frances Stuart sat in 1667 and which became the form stereotyped on the penny). That is to say, she derived from coins of the Roman occupation;[2] first, from Hadrian's *as* of A.D. 119—a Graeco-Roman personification of the country—and also on coins (A.D. 140–3) of Antonius Pius when she was seated either on a rock or a floating globe.[3] We shall find her (seemingly) first appearance in an English political print in a copy of a Dutch satire.

And although Irish, Welsh, and Scots are attacked in the prints on political grounds, only the Scot has a distinctive appearance or dress, and that is limited to his cap. The Scots were 'blue caps' as Falstaff calls them, and in the prints described every (conspicuous) Scot wears a flat round cap coloured blue, as yet the only use of colour. The Scot is not 'Sawney',[4] but 'Jockey'[5]—otherwise ne'erdoweel or beggar. Both Scots and Welsh speak dialect, very slight in the case of the Scot, but the Welshman uses a burlesqued Anglo-Welsh according to the literary and theatrical conventions of the day.

[1] Inscription on the second state [894], title, *The Difference of Times between those Times and these Times*. Cf. pp. 98, 108.

[2] J. M. C. Toynbee, *The Hadrianic School, a Chapter in the History of Graeco-Roman Art*, 1934, pp. 55 ff.

[3] The coin of A.D. 155, on which she is *Britannia capta*, seated dejectedly on a rock, spear and shield beside her, and with dishevelled hair, has a resemblance (probably fortuitous) to some of the Britannias of the cartoonist. This was the form known to Henry Peacham:

> With hair dishevelled and in mournful case
>   Who spurnes a shippe with scepter in her hand,
> Thus Britain's drawne, in old Antiquities
>   What time the Romanes, overran her land
> Who first devis'd her sitting in this plight,
>   As then their Captive, and abandon'd quite.
>                     *Minerva Britannia*, 1612, p. 108.

[4] The earliest instance of Sawney in the *O.E.D.* is 1700, but cf. Lacy's play, *Sawney the Scot* (1667): J. O. Bartley, *Teague, Shenkin and Sawney*, Cork, 1954, p. 89.

[5] The Scots are 'the Bretheren Blue' and 'the Jockies' in verses (attributed to Cleveland) in the first number of *Mercurius Pragmaticus for King Charles II*, 10–17 Sept. 1649: J. B. Williams, *History of English Journalism*, 1908, p. 85.

# II

## CHARLES II. THE PLOT

AFTER the Restoration pictorial propaganda has three main preoccupations. First, invective against the regicides, ridicule of the
Rump. Pictorially, all is loyalty; but the seditious press was caus-
ing uneasiness. Secondly, attacks on the Dutch, more especially during the
two wars, retaliation for a Dutch caricature campaign against England,
during one of the more violent phases of the hate-love relationship.
Thirdly, the grand crisis, exploding in the Popish Plot and culminating
in the Exclusion Bills. The reign, beginning as it did with the Declaration
of Breda, was a prolonged struggle between the King and a changing, but
(till 1681) formidable, opposition for the support of public opinion, an
opposition always latent and becoming apparent as early as 1667. Finance,
ecclesiastical divisions and legacies of the Civil War were the foundation,
but the conflict was inflamed by the intrigues of Louis XIV and the skill
of his ambassadors, acting on the constant principle that Charles and his
Parliament must never be on good terms.[1] The press was of supreme importance: prints had only a small part among the mass of publications in
which pamphlets, verse satires, lampoons, ballads, squibs, 'prophecies',
and 'dying speeches' had the major share, together with sermons and the
many libels circulated in manuscript. But prints illuminate key points, and
those on the Popish Plot have a notable place in the history of English
graphic satire.

The anti-regicide phase of 1660–1 provokes comparisons with the anti-
Laudian phase of 1640–1 and after—speaking always in terms of prints.
Though the mood and the issues differed, there are some striking analogies,
with Hugh Peters corresponding to Laud as arch-villain and chief target.
Peters had been the outstanding Cromwellian cleric, a leader of the Independents and an army chaplain whose preaching was unrestrained even by
the standards of the day—a 'Pulpit Incendiary' who had inflamed minds
during the King's trial. He was regarded as the embodiment of the

---

[1] Barillon to Louis XIV, on 2 Feb. 1682, N.S.: 'The greatest security your Majesty can have
is based on the difficulty, not to say impossibility, of a reconciliation with parliament. This
reconciliation can never be to the interest of your Majesty, it must ever be traversed with care
and secrecy by those who serve your Majesty.' P.R.O. Paris (Baschet) Transcripts.

violence and fanaticism of the Interregnum. Like Laud he was the subject of macabre jests and crude ferocity. In one print [967–8] he stands upon the Book of Common Prayer, the Articles, Canons, Homilies, a crown and mitre; he draws towards himself huge money-bags covered with inscriptions denoting the contributions and sequestrations of the war. A devil whispers in his ear; behind is a church, standing for St. Paul's; Peters says: 'Make it a Stable let it out to yᵉ Jews.' In one of several satirical portraits [971]—and here the comparison is with Archbishop Williams—he is dressed half in armour, half in a minister's gown (he had been colonel of a regiment of foot in Cromwell's army in Ireland).[1] In the background are allusions to his horrible execution; he hangs from a gibbet with the legend *Inde Pendens*, a pun much admired and often repeated. If Peters corresponds to Laud, Cromwell evokes comparisons with Strafford—the Protector with the Deputy.

All this connotes that turning of the wheel of Fortune or of Time so longed for by the Royalists. And this is the theme of a large crude woodcut [965], used for two verse broadsides; it expresses the mood of 1660 and has something of a folk-print character. As in 1641, here is the turning of tables, but in reverse. The grandees of the Interregnum, whose punishment was pending, are now shut up in the pound, travestied as animals: *The Tryall of Traytors, or, The Rump in the Pound, Wherein is presented the Lively Shapes and Bloody Actings of the Chief of those Grand Traytors who subscribed to the horrid Murder of that Blessed Martyr Charles. . . .* They are dominated by a wheel, containing a map of the world, between 'Hasilrig the Fox' (who turns it) and Speaker Lenthall as an ass. The animals are flanked by the Devil—'The Rumps Scout'—and by Harrison, a squirrel, who looks from a prison window. With the characteristic inconsequence of folk symbolism[2] the delighted spectator is dressed as a fool: he is 'Jack Spy-Knave' who 'laughs to see / These Traytors pounded and himself so free. / Thus is poor *England* freed from future harms. . . .' There is much praise for Monck. The verses begin: 'Behold and view, Times wheel is turned round / *Subjects* are free, whilst *Traytors* in the *Pound* / Do ly, for bloody Murder. . . .' As Peacham had prophesied in 1642, Time has called Opinion to account.

When Puritan rule was followed by the two most frivolous decades of English national life, we should expect changes in the political print. And

---

[1] J. B. Williams, *History of English Journalism*, 1908, p. 127 and n.

[2] There is also characteristic carelessness as to the roles of the characters, all classed as regicides: Haselrig (fox), Lenthall (ass), Scobell (cat), Desborough (boar), Hewson (bear), Vane (wolf), John Cook (ram), Peters (buck), Thomas Scott (goat).

so there are, though old preoccupations persist, especially fanatic fear of Popery. A new form of political satire—new in England—was the adaptation of the pictorial playing-card to politics—when printed in sheets they became wall-decorations. The seemingly first example is a set on the Rump Parliament, which is apparently pre-Restoration (*c.* 1659) and was probably made in Holland for the Cavalier colony. This treats serious subjects with a levity that was new. On the ten of clubs Cromwell kneels: 'Oliver seeking his God while the King is murthered by his order'; in the background is the execution. That there were grosser prints than any that have survived is clear from the attack on the Rump 'hung up' in the Exchange, and described by Pepys (on 7 February) as an example of the 'great and general contempt' for it among both 'good and bad'.

But the Dutch had gone farther in the use of levity and ridicule. On 28 November 1663 Pepys recorded: 'I have been told two or three times, but to day for certain I am told how in Holland publickly they have pictured our King with reproach. One way is with his pockets turned the wrong side outward, hanging out empty; another with two courtiers picking of his pockets; and a third leading of two ladies, while others abuse him; which amounts to great contempt.' This was part of a campaign of disparagement. Relations with the Dutch were dominated by naval and commercial rivalry with interests clashing in most parts of the world, each with bitter grievances against the other. Mutual antipathies were tempered (or sharpened) by the old idea of a Protestant league against the Catholic powers, sanctioned and sanctified by the memory of Elizabeth's pact with the Netherlands. English prints express detestation of the Hollanders as ungrateful, treacherous, and altogether contemptible. The Dutch use of prints in foreign countries to discredit the English is the subject of a diatribe by Dr. Samuel Collins provoked by his experiences in Moscow, where from 1660 to 1669 he was physician to the Tsar.

The Dutch [he writes] like locusts swarm in Moscow and eat the bread out of the Englishmens mouths, they are more in number, and richer, and spare no gift to attain their ends.

He goes on:

The Hollanders have another advantage by rendering the English cheap and ridiculous by their lying pictures and libelling pamphlets,'this makes the Russians think us a ruined Nation. They represent us by a Lyon painted with three crowns reversed and without a tail, and by many Mastive Dogs, whose ears are cropped and tails cut, with many such scandalous prints, being more ingenious in the use of their Pencils than Pens. These stories take much with a barbarous people. . . .[1]

Henry Stubbe maintained that Dutch pictorial insults were a justification for the war of 1672. He cites Dr. Collins and reproduces the humiliated British Lion—three crowns were an emblem on Restoration medals.

For these insolent Hollanders have advanced themselves to their present grandeur and height as well as vastness of trade [so he writes in 1672 when the Dutch saved themselves from invasion by cutting the dykes] by affronting the high merchants . . . defaming and abusing their Prince and by exposing them to scorn and derision by ridiculous pictures and odious medals. . . . It is no justification for the States General to say that these are for the most part the actions of individuals. . . . It is enough . . . that the States themselves published some and that no solicitations and complaints could make them recall, or suppress the others.[2]

Stubbe continues in his second pamphlet, *A Further Justification of the present War* . . .:

The Provocations of the Dutch by their Pictures, Medals and Monuments (all publick and authorized by the States, or commonly tolerated) were such as would have justified a more early War. . . . There was not a Port in Europe wherein the drunken Dutch sea-men and their officers did not revile and abuse our English merchants and others of our Countrymen . . . trayling the English Colours defiled with Excrements through their streets and at the stern of their Boats. . . . Whereby foreigners were perswaded that the Dutch had totally destroyed the naval strength of these Realms in general and themselves the sovereigns of the British seas. Curious prints were divulged every where of the English Phœbus [Phaeton] being overthrown, not by the Thunderbolts of Jove, but Valour of the United Provinces. Britannia, or Old England, was no longer seated on her Globe, with her Feet in the Sea, but prostrate on the dry Land, Holland being mounted on an Elephant and trampling on her. Also a Boor cutting of the Tailes of the English Mastifes whereof some ran away, others sate licking their Soares, others stood barking at a distance. Another Boor was employing his Hatchet to kill a multitude of Adders with this Inscription: The English Dogs and Vipers destroyed by the Valour of the Hollanders in such a manner that they shall give the World no further Trouble. By these Artifices not only the Merchants of England have been discouraged in their Trading, the foreign Princes alienated from her, and their Subjects induced to believe that the English were so odious, so detestable a People, that they deserved not to be considered in place of Commerce.

He concludes that all this has 'done England more Prejudice than their

[1] Collins, *Survey of Muscovy*, ch. 26.
[2] Henry Stubbe, *A Justification of the present War against the United Netherlands*, 1672.

Ships and Canons'. Stubbe illustrates his two tracts with copies of the prints he describes. One [Pl. 13] is a composite of dovetailed subjects which had probably (in Holland) been first issued separately, and comparison with the Dutch original shows that the copy, though inferior and slightly reduced, is accurate. Here are Phaeton (overthrown by the seven arrows of the United Provinces), Britannia, the mutilated English curs, the adders, and a peering Jesuit. There is also a menacing or inquisitive bear, then standing for any northern country—usually Sweden. A fox wearing a ribbon (looking up at the Jesuit) is supposed to be Charles II. This is the earliest example known to me of Britannia in a satirical print: she holds a peacock, emblem of pride; she has slipped from her globe and is trampled on by the Dutch Maid, who holds a victor's palm branch and leans against 'her Elephant'.

As in Oliver's time, English retorts to Dutch graphic satire made a poor showing. Marvell's *Character of Holland* was reprinted as a broadside for both wars—in 1665 and 1672—probably without the author's consent. The strain of coarse invective begun in *Butter Box* continued. Insults to the country and its inhabitants were piled up in two pictorial verse broadsides, *The Dutch Boare Dissected, or a Description of Hogg-Land* . . . [1028] and *The Egg of Dutch Rebellion* [1045] (partly an attack on the De Witts). The Dutch are fat clumsy fellows, addicted to cheese, brandy, and herrings. They return England's former aid with 'base Pranks'. They are frogs or 'froglanders', or live in a land cumbered with frogs (anticipating many later caricatures on frog-Dutchmen). Both broadsides exude jealousy of Dutch commercial achievements. In *The Low Estate of the Low-Countrey Countess of Holland on her Death-Bed* . . . [1040] the country is personified by an old woman, aged a hundred, dropsical—that is swamped by the cutting of the dykes—and *in extremis*. Addiction to satirical prints and medals is implied:

> She that on Pictures doted so, may here
> Herself the Picture see of a *dear year*

but even now there is hope—'a Doctor from the Hague;' . . .

> Who knows what vertues in an *Orange* dwell
> An Orange only tis can make her well. . . .[1]

Meanwhile the opposition to Charles was swelling, aided by a campaign of disparagement for which the material was all too abundant. The anti-

[1] By the revolution of July 1672 William of Orange became Stadtholder, Captain General, and Admiral.

thesis between the Court and the Country parties had been established, with the dissenting interest as the backbone of the Country Party, and associated with the doctrine of the wholesale corruption of members of Parliament by the Government—pensioners were 'state vermin',[1] and the Court Party, like the Anglican clergy, were 'Popishly affected'. The term 'Patriot', assumed by the Opposition, already had the significance of the days of Wilkes and Dr. Johnson. The Anglican viewpoint was expressed by South in a sermon: 'What can be expected if a company of bold, crafty, designing villains shall be incessantly buzzing into the rabble's ears tyranny and arbitrary power, pensioners and evil counsellors on the one hand, and pointing out themselves for the only patrons of liberty and property and the redressers of grievances on the other?'[2]

Even before the Press Act (for the licensing of presses and publications) expired in 1679 propaganda was carried to heights—or depths—seldom equalled. This was a revolutionary agitation, directed at the populace. Oates's bombshell almost coincided with the revelations (contrived by Barillon and the Opposition) which showed that Danby had taken part in Charles's intrigues with Louis XIV, involving demands for French gold in return for the dissolution of Parliament. Both revelations came as a climax to the long campaign by the Opposition to show the country that the Court party designed 'to change religion and government'—to introduce Popery and Slavery. Of course there was some foundation for this, but the Whigs (as they were now to be called) relied largely on misrepresentation. The most damaging of all the stories was that James and the Jesuits had started the fire of 1666 and others since then—unfortunately there had been many in London. This was propagated in a series of 'Fire Libels' from 1667 onwards, at first secretly; after the Plot new and enlarged versions came out openly. Bedloe's *Narrative*, one of the Plot classics, was largely compiled from these libels. The frontispiece to *Pyrotechnica Loyalana* . . . [1030], published in 1667, gives some idea of this propaganda, though James does not appear. It is a medley of Jesuits setting fire to the globe with fireballs, with the Pope plying bellows, Jesuits storing combustibles in a cellar, and 'G.Faux' with his lantern entering another cellar; Hubert[3] is there with his fireball. Thus the Plot was prepared for.

[1] Vermin as a term of abuse dates from 1562: *O.E.D.* Cf. Rolle, *Abridgement*, 1656: 'He is a corrupt man, he is a Vermine in the Commonwealth'. 'Vermin'—human rats or insects—recur in these prints, notably in 1831.

[2] *Sermons*, vi. 56–57 (preached *temp.* James II).

[3] Hubert, a Frenchman, 'a mopish besotted fellow', was hanged on his own confession that he had started the fire with a fireball, having been hired to do it: Pepys, *Diary*, 24 Feb. 1667. Analogies with Van der Lubbe and the burning of the Reichstag are striking.

Nevertheless, it nearly miscarried at the beginning, through its own absurdities and the scepticism of the chief victim, the King. But Godfrey's murder had a shattering effect; he was the London magistrate to whom Oates had made his depositions and it was everywhere accepted as an attempt by Jesuits to 'stifle the Plot'. The agitation against Papists rose to panic heights, Protestants were taught to expect a general massacre, and Londoners expected to be burnt in their beds, maidservants being allegedly bribed to introduce fireballs. All this was taken as proof of a design to introduce Popery and Slavery and was aimed mainly at the Duke of York as a 'Popish Successor'.

The propaganda is spotlighted by the prints. 'Among other ways [of expressing horror of Popery] this of exposing their Hellish Contrivances by Picture was not thought the most contemptible'; thus the 'Explanation' of a large Plot broadside in twelve scenes [1088]. There are Popish Plot playing-cards, fifty-two little designs, sold either as cards or on sheets 'fit to adorn studies and houses'. Some of the designs were used also on an almanack 'which may not unfitly be called the Christian Almanack fit for Shops Houses and Studies . . . the price Sixpence'.[1] There are many Popish Plot prints, often in a sequence of little designs on the various episodes; these usually include a 'consult' in Rome (Pope, Devil, and an eavesdropping Oates); Godfrey's murder is a central theme, treated with much imaginative detail. There are of course emblematic portraits of Oates as the saviour of the nation. An adaptation of the Emblem Book to the Plot is *The Protestants Vade Mecum or Popery display'd in its proper Colours in thirty Emblems . . .*[2] beginning with Jesuits in counsel in the reign of Henry VIII, number viii is 'King Charles the First murder'd' (Oates had made the Jesuits responsible for this). The burning of London is number ix; all the rest are on the Plot, with four on Godfrey, whose murder remains a great unsolved mystery.

The spirit of the campaign as carried on from the Whig headquarters at the Green Ribbon Club (at the King's Head tavern at the Fleet Street end of Chancery Lane) is well conveyed in the elaborate prints on the Pope burnings on Queen Elizabeth's accession day, 17 November, which took place at Temple Bar in 1679, 1680, and 1681, after torchlight processions from Aldgate, *The Solemn Mock Procession of the Pope, Cardinalls, Jesuits, Fryers, &c. . . .* [1072, 1084, 1085]. A leading feature in the procession of pageants was Godfrey's dead body supported on a horse by one of the

---

[1] Advertisement, *True Domestic Intelligence*, 26 Dec. 1679, quoted, Willshire, *Catalogue of Playing and other Cards in the British Museum*, 1876, p. 244.     [2] B.M., G. 18365.

'murderers', a Jesuit: 'the manner he was carried from Somerset House to Primrose Hill'. Another pageant was 'the Popes Chief Physitian with *Jesuites Powder* in one hand . . .' exclaiming 'This for 15 thousand Pound', to show that he was Wakeman, the Queen's physician whose acquittal on a charge of conspiring with the Queen to poison the King had been the first—and bitterly resented—check to the Plot. In 1680 there were additional pageants, the Meal Tub plotters, Roger L'Estrange and four 'Protestants in Masquerade', a retort to his cartoon and his pamphlets. There was seemingly no print in 1681.

With Roger L'Estrange and his enemy, Stephen Colledge, we come to what from our viewpoint is the core of the Plot, a group of prints, one by L'Estrange, six by Colledge, unique in the history of English graphic satire as weapons in a campaign for and against revolution by men taking leading parts in the struggle. At first almost alone L'Estrange resisted the tide of propaganda that had seemed irresistible. This old Cavalier and high Tory was a brilliant pamphleteer and journalist whose pen had made many enemies.[1] Colledge, 'the Protestant Joiner' and maker of the 'Protestant flail', was a very active agent of Shaftesbury and the Green Ribbon Club: his trial for treason and his 'Dying Speech' made him a minor Protestant martyr. These seven prints have more claim than those so far produced to be considered cartoons in the modern sense. L'Estrange may or may not have done more than 'invent' the design and write the verses, but Colledge's prints were almost certainly drawn and engraved by himself.[2] How far he was the 'inventor' is another matter. Appropriately, this foretaste of the cartoon coincides with the appearance of 'Whigs' and 'Tories' and the first great struggle between parties in Parliament. And though to use the word cartoon before the mid-nineteenth century is an anachronism, the term is almost indispensable.

There were two main lines of counter-attack on the Whig campaign.

[1] He is the Sheva of Nahum Tate's sequel to *Absalom and Achitophel*:

> Wakeful as Judah's Lion for the Crown;
> Who for that Cause still combats in his Age,
> For which his youth with danger did engage.

[2] Six were mentioned at his trial and in L'Estrange's *Notes upon Stephen Colledge*; there may be others (see p. 55, n. 3). These attributions lack absolute proof: the chief witness against him was the perjured Dugdale. But his authorship was accepted as common knowledge, undisputed except by his denial at the trial and in his 'Declaration' of 24 Aug. (*Cal. S.P. Dom. 1680–1*, p. 416) which was not repeated in his 'Dying Speech'. A large bundle of prints and the drawing for *Raree Show* were found in his house. Stylistically, the prints are the work of an excellent craftsman; I believe that the Pope-burning print of 1680 [1085, original in C. 20. f. 6/26] is his. 'His Vein lay much toward *Doggerel* and Designing, as he has plentifully given the World to understand in his Learned *Drawings* . . .': L'Estrange, ibid., p. 28.

One was to throw doubt on the Plot witnesses; at first this was highly dangerous. It was to 'sham the Plot', to be a 'Papist in masquerade', and risk being denounced by Oates and thrown into one of the lethal London prisons. The other, also risky at first,[1] was to 'turn all to '41' as the phrase went. L'Estrange used both with consummate skill. A famous Whig pamphlet gave him his chance at the end of 1679 and he published anonymously (but the author was unmistakable) his *Answer . . . to the Appeal from the Country to the City for the Preservation of His Majestys Person, Liberty, Property, and the Protestant Religion*. This notorious pamphlet is significantly signed Junius Brutus and has the motto *Salus Populi suprema Lex*. It was a frank appeal to religious bigotry and pointed to armed resistance to arbitrary government and a Popish Successor. Readers were to picture the inevitable consequences of a Popish king: London burnt 'by the same Popish malice which set it on fire before', the Tower guns battering down their houses, their dearest relations burning at Smithfield, 'troops of Papists ravishing your wives and daughters and dashing your little childrens brains out . . .'. To this vision L'Estrange retorted: 'Imagine you see the whole nation in a flame, and brought to the same extremities of fire and sword by the same schismatical and republican malice which embroiled it before.' He then instanced with chapter and verse the bogus Popish scares during the Troubles. The Plot is mastered, 'there's hardly a Catholic dares shew his head', but 'the Kings authority is visibly arraigned'. He followed up this with his cartoon, *The Committee; or Popery in Masquerade* [Pl. 14] which appeared early in 1680. This is a satirical representation of 1641 and after with a pointed application to Whig tactics. The Committee are representatives of different sects with John Presbyter as chairman. A plotting cabal, the Junto in debate, look down on them from a balcony 'T'inspire and push an Enthusiast Rabble'; these join hands across the room with a seditious Lord Mayor with the Pope beside him. The deluded rabble, grouped round the Committee, have banners inscribed 'A thorough Reformation', 'Liberty Property' (a first appearance in a print for this slogan), and 'Religion'. Discarded on the ground are 'Magna Charta', 'Biblia Sacra', 'Councills', 'Laud against Fisher', and 'Hooker'—that is the Law, the Truth, and the Church. There are other incidents and allusions. The verses make some shrewd hits:

> *First*, make the *People* Sure; and That must be
> By Pleas for Conscience, Common Liberty:

---

[1] Narcissus Luttrell records in Feb. 1680 'about this time many libels were thrown about to disaffect the King and his people and turn all to 41'. (Apparently they could not be sold openly.)

By which Means, we secure a Popu'lar Voyce
For *Knights*, and *Burgesses*, in the next Choyce . . .
In the mean while, the Pulpits and the Presses
Must ring of *Popery*, *Grievances*, *Addresses*,
*Plots* of all *Sorts*, Invasions, Massacres, . . .

lines directly applicable to 1679–80 as well as to 1641. But the Whig campaign was concerted, engineered, and financed in a way hitherto unknown
—by subscriptions among the Party and by secret contributions from
Barillon the French Ambassador. When L'Estrange impugned John
Presbyter he could not know that Barillon was shortly to buy up two
Presbyterian preachers of repute in the City (to guard against their being
gained over by the Court or by the interests of the Prince of Orange). Such
people, he wrote to Louis, 'have great power, especially in this country,
and they can inspire others with their sentiments without shewing by
what motives they act or who is directing them'. Some weeks later he adds
that the money has been well spent—they will be useful because 'the City
of London is in part led by them, and the rest of England models itself on
London'.[1]

With his tireless and very clever pen L'Estrange was the chief enemy
of the Plot, the Court's chief defender, and, with the doubtful exception
of the Pope and the Duke, the Whigs' chief bugbear—burned in effigy,
assailed in pamphlets and lampoons, and the principal target of Stephen
Colledge, who portrayed him as a runaway cur—'I should be ungrateful',
he wrote, 'If I should not acknowledge the Honor he has done me, in
divers of his emblematical pictures. He has presented the World with six
Tousers, and L'Estrange with four pair of Gallows.'[2] Three of the Tousers[3]
survive. The first, *Strange's Case, Strangly Altered* [Pl. 15], was produced when he had found it necessary, in October 1680, to escape the
attentions of Oates and Parliament by retreating, first to Edinburgh and
then to Holland, returning in February. As a runaway cur, scourged by the
Devil, a broom tied to his tail (symbol for Henry Brome, his bookseller-
publisher), and with a pen and emblems of Popery on his head, he eludes
the hangman and deserts his patrons and masters, who are the Pope,
'Mack' (the Duke of York), and two ecclesiastics. The verses and the

---

[1] P.R.O., Paris Transcripts, 3 June, 1 July, 30 Sept., 1680, N.S.
[2] *Notes upon Stephen Colledge*, 1681, p. 29.
[3] A fourth Touser (used for two broadsides) is in Colledge's vein, and may be his, though it
is a woodcut: *Romes Hunting-Match for III Kingdomes* [1094–5]. Another Touser belongs to
1682 and cannot be his. L'Estrange figures in the Pope-burning print of 1680, which I believe
to be by Colledge.

inscription, in the guise of an advertisement for 'a *Strange* old *Yorkish Tike*', are facetiously abusive—the puns and jests strike a note new in prints (though not in pamphlets). Another Touser, *The Time-Servers* . . . [1112], followed the dismissal of the Oxford Parliament: effigies of 'An Irish Tory and a Popish Priest, and the Cur Towzer . . . all on the speed for Rome. . . .' Towzer barks 'forty one'. But the most important of Colledge's prints are the two he did for the meeting of the Oxford Parliament.

At this climax of the struggle between the Whigs and the Court the situation for the public at large—for what L'Estrange called 'the sober part of the nation'—had resolved itself into the question, was there a scheme for Popery and Arbitrary Government as the Whigs maintained, or was there a Whig design against the Monarchy and the Church, as the King and the Tories believed, and L'Estrange and a very few others re-iterated in print? The Whigs were confident, the Tories almost in despair. It was openly said, Barillon reported to Louis, 'that if the King leaves London he will not be able to return when he pleases'.[1] The Whigs' violence, their electioneering tactics,[2] their pamphleteering, their reliance on the monstrous fabrications of the Plot, proved their undoing: people came to believe that the King was in more danger from the fanatics than from the Papists.

Colledge's prints are central to this appeal to the public that underlay the proceedings at Oxford in March 1681. 'A most scandalous libel against the Government for which with other things Colledge was most justly executed'[3] was the verdict of the Whiggish Luttrell on *Raree Show* [Pl. 16]. The song, coarse and crude, but clever, gives an idea of the tavern gibes of the Green Ribbonites—they can be matched in meaning, though not in expression, in lines attributed to Marvell.[4] It was sung repeatedly with explanations by Colledge in a gathering of Whig City notables, at Lord Lovelace's house on the way to Oxford. With the print (the two are inseparable) it shows, L'Estrange thought, 'the designs of the Party' and 'looks like a song of triumph'. The King is Leviathan, embodiment of ab-solute rule—'Child of Heathen *Hobbs*, with a hey, with a hey'. His clothes are patterned with faces like the all-powerful giant on the title-page of Hobbes's book. But he is also a raree-show man with his pack on his back,

---

[1] P.R.O. Paris Transcripts, 30 Jan. 1681, N.S.

[2] M. D. George, 'Elections and Electioneering 1679–81', *Eng. Hist. Rev.* 1930.

[3] Written on his copy of the print. Dryden, *Works*, ed. Scott and Saintsbury, 1882–92, vii. 2 (where the words of *Raree Show* are printed).

[4] *Advice to a Painter to draw the Duke by*, probably by Henry Savile. Margoliouth, *The Poems and Letters of Andrew Marvell*, Oxford, 1927, i. 321.

a peep-show containing the Parliament which he is carrying off to Oxford. And he is doublefaced, half Papist, half Protestant. The song is put into the mouths of Leviathan and Topham, the Sergeant at Arms whom the Commons had been dispatching all over the country to make arrests. The King walks confidently, bent on Popery and Arbitrary Government. Topham:

> That monstrous Foul *Beast*, with a hey, with a hey,
> Has *Houses Twain* in's Chest, with a ho,

If they want to get out, says the King, they must vote 'To yield up all they have, and *Tower Lords* to save . . .', that is, the Catholic peers, of whom only Stafford was tried and executed for the Plot (in December 1680). The bubbles he blows through a long pipe symbolize the self-deluding emptiness of his words (a symbolism much used in the eighteenth century and later). Across the bridge, in Oxford, all is changed. 'Methinks he seems to Stagger . . . Who but now did so Swagger . . .'. The pack is too heavy: 'May the mighty weight at's back / Make's lecherous loyns to crack. . . .' He is stuck in the mire and Topham calls upon '*Cooper, Hughs*, and *Snow*' (officers of the Commons who have followed *Raree Show*), to pull him down so that the nation is freed and the Church can now be disposed of. The last verse begins, 'Ha-loo the *Hunts* begun, with a hey, with a hey, / Like Father, Like Son, with a ho'—a song of triumph very like a battle-cry. In the background are the buildings of Oxford with a little alehouse inscribed 'Louse Hall' (name given to a disreputable resort kept by one 'Mother Louse'[1] frequented by members of the University). Colledge explained that this stood for Whitehall 'because of its poverty'. (The Whigs counted on the King's lack of funds, not suspecting the promised subsidy from Louis.) To identify Charles with Leviathan was a stroke of wit reflecting the intense interest taken in Hobbes's book.

Like *Raree Show*, the print by Colledge known as 'Mack' or 'Mackninny' (one of the 'Tousers') illustrates the confidence with which the Whigs went to Oxford. The title speaks for itself: *A Prospect of a Popish Successor: Displayed by Hell-bred Cruelty: Popish Villainy: strange Divinity: Intended Slavery: Old Englands Misery: &c.* [1110]. James, half devil, half Papist, blows flames through a cruciform trumpet to burn London and the 'Provost House' (Edinburgh), saying, 'Thus Ile Govern Hereticks or Godfrey um.' He holds a torch to a fire where martyrs burn at the stake. A 'Church Papist' (Bishop Mews), half bishop, half Pope, stands upon a Bible; he holds out a scroll, 'A Free Pardon (in spite of God)

---

[1] David Loggan engraved a satirical portrait of her standing in front of Louse Hall [797].

for Plotters, Traytors, Murderers, Burners, Rake-hells, Tormentors, Whatsoever.' In the other hand is a crosier with which he pushes three ministers out of a church, saying, 'Out Fanaticks, In Popery' (Colledge was a Presbyterian for whom Episcopacy meant Popery). Astride the roof of a second church are four clerics and a bishop riding post haste to Rome, led by a Jesuit and followed by a devil: 'They must goe the Devill Drives: Tantivy, Tantivy, Tantivy.'[1] The devil drops 'A Pen for Towzer' upon a dog, L'Estrange, which fawns on a second Jesuit, wears a cross and rosary, and barks 'Presbiters, the Plotters, Bow, Wow, Wow.' A broom, 'H.B.', is tied to his tail, a fiddle to his back, and he holds a scroll: 'Discoveries Masquerads [his cartoon] Dialogues Apeals strange cases.' He is 'Touzer, old Ban dogg, of the Popes; but maingie...'. Below the title is the inscription 'Though Hell, Rome, and France; Have united their Powers: We defye them all Three (Sir) The Parliament's Ours: March the 21st 1680'. [1681.]

There is little doubt that these and other prints by Colledge were part of the Whig campaign:

The faction had another Order regimented [wrote Roger North], being a Detachment from the libelling Garrison in *London*, who had in Charge the Train of Artillery (if I may so term it) the Tongue and Pen Managery. . . . Besides, there was a Magazine provided for Ammunition, Libels, Lampoons, Satyrs, Pictures and Sing-songs, for the service at *Oxford*. Some adapted to deceive Men of Fortune and Education, well penned, and, perhaps, in Heroic Verse, others for the Rabble and drunken, sottish Clubs, in Ballad Doggerel, with witty Picture affixed, in dainty Conceit and Proportion; notable Eloquence for the eye! One was the King, for a Raree Show, with his box of Parliament Motions at his Back and the Saints pulling him down into a Ditch. . . . Another was called *Mac-Ninny*. . . .[2]

As propaganda both erred, like Milton's *Eikonoklastes*, in being acceptable only to party zealots.

Two other prints by Colledge are earlier, December 1680 and February 1681. In *The Contents* (*Hats for Caps*) *Contented* [1087] bishops eagerly exchange their academic caps for cardinal's hats, and their leader, Bishop Mews (who, as in 'Mack', has a patch on the cheek), kisses the Pope's toe. The other is a Plot satire, *The Catholick Gamesters or a Double Match of Bowleing* [1077].[3] The Popish Lords (then in the Tower) aim ostensibly at ninepins, actually at Godfrey, while the King looks on.

---

[1] A word for a rapid gallop, applied to Romanizing High Churchmen and high Tories. It is thought that this print is the origin of the word so used and its derivatives. *O.E.D.*

[2] *Examen*, 1740, pp. 100-1.

[3] This has the first example known to me of a device that became very popular, though not

Colledge's prints have the distinction of being the only ones to figure in an English trial for treason, a trial in which the designs of the Whigs were an issue and in which Colledge defended himself with the most remarkable skill. *Raree Show* and 'Mack' strikingly exemplify not only the violence which engendered the strong Tory reaction, but the over-confidence of the Party. The Whigs went down to Oxford assured of their power to control events, pass the Exclusion Bill, and make the King into 'a Doge of Venice' or otherwise dispose of him: 'The Parliament's Ours', as Colledge put it. The King turned the tables by dissolving Parliament, and the leaders fled to places of safety, hanged in the rope that Charles had so lavishly allowed them. How much the promise of French gold had to do with the King's victory is not here relevant: it was unknown, and if known might have undermined the popularity which was the true basis of what Roger North called a second Restoration. Surely never was the tide of opinion more completely turned. It was something more than a recoil from the excesses of the Plot; the legal conservatism, perhaps decisive in 1640–1 and 1659–60, was potent in 1681.

In literature Dryden was as characteristic of the later period of the reign as Marvell of the earlier. How does the change show itself in the prints? An expiring flare-up of the Plot was expressed (early in April 1681) in *The Happy Instruments of England's Preservation* [Pl. 17]; a print combining a view of 'The Infernall Conclave' with an apotheosis of the four chief witnesses, protected by angels. Oates says—protesting too much—'My testimony still triumphs.' Wakeman walks off from the Consult with his bribe 'to Poyson the K—'; a woman goes off with instructions 'to turn the plot upon the Presbyterians' (she is Mrs. Cellier, 'the Popish Midwife'). A tiny execution scene on Tower Hill is inscribed 'Exit Viscount Stafford'. The Whigs' bitter resentment at the reaction—so dangerous to themselves—is illustrated in 1682 in *A New Ballad, With the Definition of the Word Tory* [1121] attacking the Tories and their two propagandists, 'Towzer' and Nat Thompson, whose woodcut effigies decorate the song. Though beginning 'See how the *Tories* drives their trade / Clokes all with Fourty One', it is ostentatiously loyal: the last verse opens 'But Heaven praise our Great Monarch / And the Partner of his Bed', recently accused of conspiring to poison her husband. Far indeed from *Raree Show*.

for many years, the satirical or facetious signature or imprint, namely 'Printed at the half-way house that stood between Bothwell Bridge and Holy-Rood', a cryptic allusion to the Duke of York.

Despite much high-Tory pamphleteering and despite the mass of verse
satires on Shaftesbury and the discredited Whigs, cartooning seems to have
temporarily died with Colledge. Then as later it was essentially the voice
of opposition to authority. There is a set of Rye House Plot playing-cards
and also an illustrated broadside on the Plot [1123] with seven little scenes,
one being 'E. Shaftesbury dictating his measures' to Oates, now discredited. The fervent loyalty of the period is reflected in an outcrop of
historical compilations on the Great Rebellion with emblematical frontispieces, probably issued also as separate plates. One is Nalson's *Impartial
Collection of the Great Affairs of State* . . ., each of the two volumes (1682–
3) with a frontispiece by Robert White expounded in verse. First, Britannia,
seated and weeping, is approached by a diabolical figure, half Puritan, half
Jesuit, with his cloven hoof on a Bible [1122]. In the second [748], there
is a gesticulating crowd in the foreground interspersed with pikemen;
behind is the House of Commons (menaced by lightning) and there is also
a ship from which men throw Charles I into a stormy sea. 'But see the
temper of this barbarous Croud / Whom nothing satisfies but spoil, and
Bloud.' By the same author in 1684 is *A True Copy of the Journal of the
High Court of Justice for the Tryal of K. Charles* [743]. Cromwell, in
armour and with the legs and claws of a wolf, sits in a triumphal car driven
by the Devil and drawn by griffins. On the point of his sword he balances
a pair of scales: 'Liberty' (a bunch of feathers) outweighs solid emblems
of the monarchy and the Church. His wheels crush the bodies of Justice
and of the decapitated king. Three weeping women, chained and crowned,
represent the three kingdoms. *Arbitrary Government display'd in the
Tyrannick Usurpation of the Rump Parliament, and Oliver Cromwell* was
published in 1683 as a counter-thrust to accusations against Charles II.
The frontispiece, 'The Common wealth ruleing with a standing Army'
[1127], is a remarkable example of graphic allegory on a tiny scale. The
Commonwealth is a dragon, 'a most horrid picture' of Arbitrary Government; its fruits (excreted) are monthly assessments, loan money, taxes,
excise, and other incidents of the Interregnum. The monster is about to
devour 'Food for a Commonwealth': symbols of Laws, Customs, Episcopacy, Monarchy, Statutes, Magna Charta, Prerogatives, Privileges,
Liberties, 'Church land & tythe, gaine [money] nobility & House of Peres.'
With a chain—'Liberties'—(its tail) it encircles a group, who exclaim
'O wonderfull Reformation'. The body encloses the Parliament and tiny
armed troops cover the neck.

    Edward Pettit's *Visions of Government* . . . 1684 represents the anti-

French attitude of high-Tories, and this is well summarized in the frontispiece [1130]. Taking a sword from an angel, Charles II tramples on a
monster marked with a fleur-de-lis and with three heads—those of a sectary, a Jesuit, and a heathen Turk. Britannia, armed and helmeted, stands
by. It would seem that she is now well established as a familiar symbol.
The book is dedicated to the Duke of York: the flood of loyalty that surrounded Charles II in his last years overflowed to the advantage of James,
who profited by the calumnies with which the Whigs had assailed him,[1]
but it was manifest that dread of Popery was still active. In *Visions of the
Reformation* . . . 1683 [1126] Pettit accepts a theory put forward in Popish
Plot days by the Whigs—that the Jesuits were wirepullers 'in every particular of that Rebellion', and were responsible for the King's death. A
double-headed Presbyter is painting out the Royal Arms and replacing
them with the Arms of the Commonwealth, while the Pope steals the
crown. The sectary-Papist was a favourite Tory emblem, a counter to the
double-faced Anglican or 'Papist in Masquerade' of the Whigs.

---

[1] These were not confined to crude publications like the 'Fire libels'; 'Mack' was much
more typical of attacks on James than *Raree Show* was *vis-à-vis* Charles. There was, for instance,
*Nostradamus' Prophecy* (Jan. 1672), frankly Republican or Haringtonian, and attributed, though
doubtfully, to Marvell:

> Fire-balls shall fly, but few shall see the train,
> As far as from Whitehall to Pudding Lane . . .

*Merlin Revived or an old Prophecy found in a Manuscript in Pontefract Castle* . . . was published
as a broadside shortly before the Oxford Parliament and pointed to the death, if not the execution, of the Duke of York:

> A Senate then shall end the Strife
> And Atropos shall cut a Life,
> Rome then from England fast shall fly . . .

Accusations of arson were made in Parliament to support the Exclusion Bills by prominent
Whigs, for example by Goodwin Wharton (11 Nov. 1680), and by Henry Booth (7 Jan. 1681):
*Grey's Debates*, vii. 448; viii. 260. The Whig *canards* were summarized in Monmouth's declaration in 1685; they included poisoning Charles II and murdering the Earl of Essex (who cut his
throat in the Tower).

# III

## THE REVOLUTION. HIGH CHURCH AND LOW CHURCH

LOYALTY marked the beginning of James II's reign and was expressed in prints attacking Oates, sentenced for perjury to the pillory, flogging, and imprisonment. In one of these [1142] he is 'an incarnate Imp of Hell', dressed half as Jesuit, half as Turk. Loyalty again is the ostensible note of a set of playing-cards on Monmouth's Rebellion, but these have signs of a very different attitude, discreetly masked by tributes to correct opinion. 'Madam Lisle executed' and 'The Godly Maids of Taunton presenting their colours upon their knees to the Duke of Monmouth' suggest covert anger at savagery in the West, while 'The late Duke of Monmouths Standard Fear Nothing but God' implies, one suspects, sympathy with the Rebellion. The hatred roused by Judge Jeffreys is illustrated in prints over a long period.

The Revolution and the flight of James, with the wars that followed, are almost wholly the subjects of Dutch prints. In the French wars, satirical prints—officially inspired—were used on both sides as weapons of offence, with William III and Louis XIV as rival champions. Caricature—a word now possibly permissible if incorrect—became international—a war of prints. In this the advantage was overwhelmingly with Holland. Besides native artists, with Romeyn de Hooghe at their head, French Protestant refugees contributed to the campaign against 'Universal Monarchy' and the Jesuits. Medals were part of the graphic warfare. This is an important stage in the history of the cartoon. Prints were numerous, large, and striking (though usually over-complicated). More conspicuously than before, ridicule was used for the deflation of pomp and majesty. The ageing *Roi Soleil* was manifestly vulnerable and his mistresses were introduced with zest and spite. This was international propaganda: the Dutch prints generally had titles and inscriptions in both Dutch and French, sometimes in Dutch and English or in all three languages. There were also some German contributions and copies. Many professed falsely to be published in France, some states were printed in London (or have London imprints). But though James, his wife, his infant (depicted as the son of a miller) with

'Father Peters' (Petre), figure repeatedly in these Dutch prints, it is remarkable that English artists had almost no share in a pictorial war which thus remains outside an account of the English cartoon.

Very few English prints on the Revolution survive. The most striking is one on the capture of Judge Jeffreys, *The Lord Chancellor taken disguisd in Wapping* [1179 A]; this has the character of a cartoon, and four copies of the original, two English and two Dutch, attest its popularity. The shouts of the angry crowd are noteworthy: 'Remember ye West', 'Remember Mr Cornish' (the Presbyterian Alderman executed for the Rye House Plot), 'Remember Maudlin Colledge' (it was remembered in 1745). A devil claws at the face of what may be a disguised and prostrate Jesuit. There is one tribute to the Prince of Orange which does associate the Revolution with the war against France: *Englands Memorial. Of its Wounderfull deliverance from French tiranny and Popish oppression, Performed through Allmighty Gods infinite goodness and Mercy. By His Highness William Henry of Nassau, the High & Mighty Prince of Orange, 1688* [1186] is an allegorical design with reminiscences of *The Double Deliveraunce* and of Civil War prints. An orange-tree centres the plate; falling oranges knock down Jeffreys and remove James's crown, while Father Peters, the Queen, and her infant flee, and Louis XIV murders his Protestant subjects. There are Jesuits, devils, demon winds; the Eye of Providence beams on the tree and on the Church of England. In *The Protestant Grind-Stone* [1255] 'King' and 'Queen' press the Pope's nose to the stone, which is turned by two bishops; 'Schomberg' and two men identified as Bishop Burnet and Halifax stand by, while the Devil, a Jesuit, a monk, friar, and cardinal look on dismayed. The presence of William's commander-in-chief in Ireland connects the print with the Irish campaign. This is also the chief aspect of almost the sole surviving English contribution to the European war of prints. *The Usurpers Habit* [1267] is a portrait of Louis XIV with his dress covered with representations of battles, towns, and fortresses: 'the thefts and conquests' of France. He is seated and has taken off his hat, representing the little town of Limerick which he has been forced to surrender; there is a list of twenty-four places in French occupation whose recapture is prophesied in a verse tribute to William, ending,

> This mighty Work for William is Design'd
> The Scourge of France, and Darling of Mankind.

It is interesting to find a German copy of the *Double Deliveraunce*, with emblematical additions and verses in German, English, and Latin. This is 'invented by Samuel Ward Preacher of Ipswich, now repeated by Trans-mariner an. 1689', the title: *The Papists Powder-Treason. Deo Trin. Uni. Britanniæ bis ultori* [43, 1223]. This version was used again in 1740.

There are two sets of Revolution playing-cards, one Orangist, the other ultra-Whig, having some subjects in common: Judge Jeffreys and the Seven Bishops, which, to judge from the prints, connote the aspects of the reign that moved the public most deeply. Both sets have some significant themes. On the ace of hearts in the first set Charles II and a confidante receive treasure chests and money-bags from a French deputation: '£500 thousand pound sent from France to keep of the sitting of the Parliament.' In the second, which gives more attention to Papists and Jesuits, one of James's crimes is the punishment of Oates—the Revolution brought him a pardon and pension. Another villainy of James, shared by Charles II (names are not given), is 'The Earle of Essex's throat cut' (imprisoned for the Rye House Plot he committed suicide, evoking the Whig *canard* that he was murdered). The Assassination Plot was the subject of an old-fashioned allegorical print, *The Triumph of Providence over Hell, France, & Rome* . . . [1296]. Its many details include Louis XIV disgorging conquests and the Eye of Providence shining down on William in his travelling coach.

With Anne's reign and the War of the Spanish Succession the prints show rather less detachment from continental battles. A set of playing-cards on the war has some interesting themes. On the ace of hearts is *The French King's Dream*: by the bed are three cats; one fat for pampered favourites, one lean for the people 'exhausted by heavy Impositions', one blind for the King's Council, 'at their witts end'. This fable was repeated in 1800 with George III (who lets his Ministers govern) as both the dreamer and the blind cat [9551]. On the Knave of diamonds is the first English print on comparative national characteristics, one of a long line; a Frenchman, 'F', and an Englishman, 'E', fight, one for Ambition the other for Liberty, while a Dutchman, 'D', stoops to pick up the coins they drop.[1] This aspersion on the Dutch represents a persistent prejudice, often repeated in the prints. Throughout the eighteenth century the Dutch are selfish neutrals and war profiteers. At this date the imputation connotes more a state of mind than a fact, but it reflects acute mutual grievances.

Except for these cards, prints on the war are copied from continental

---

[1] Stephens interprets 'D' as the Duke of Marlborough taking bribes. This is not consistent with the tenor of the cards whose main subject is Marlborough's victories. There is also a card on official corruption which Stephens interprets, I think wrongly, as the Duke's peculations.

ones. *A Bridle for the French King, or an Emblem of the present Warr* [1463] is 'Done from the Original brought from Vienna'. Queen Anne, attended by a griffin, pursues Louis with a bridle, while Holland seizes him by the throat; the Emperor, aloft on a pedestal between Justice and Hope, says, 'Tyrant in vain thou dost oppose thy Spight / England & Holland both maintain my Right'.[1] Copies of Dutch prints were interpolated in the last volume of the 1707 edition of *Poems on Affairs of State*, perhaps as a device for giving novelty to a compilation many times reissued (with variations) from 1697. They are: 'A Collection of some satyrical Prints publish'd beyond Sea relating to the Affairs of Europe, since the French King plac'd his Grandson on the Throne of Spain, with their Explanations in English.' They are chiefly on continental aspects of the war; the exception is the second print: *The Sun in an Eclipse or Lewis XIV eclips'd by Queen Anne*; in the centre of a complicated design she clips the wings of the Gallic Cock. An eclipse of the sun coincided with the battle of Ramillies and evoked a number of Dutch emblematical prints on the terror of *le Roi Soleil*, 'Louis Soleiller', at such an omen. It is worth noting that this copy from the Dutch was in its turn adapted in a German print.

The sparsity and conventionality of the English prints on the wars with France suggest an isolationist frame of mind puzzled by conflicting loyalties—as if interest in the struggle against 'Universal Monarchy' had been hampered by old animosities and new grievances. Suddenly, after eighteen or twenty years of meagre pictorial output in the face of great events, there was an outburst of activity, unequalled for many years to come. The growing antagonism between Whig and Tory—now equated with High Church and Low Church—exploded in 1709 over the impeachment of Dr. Sacheverell for two high-Tory sermons, declared by the Commons to be scurrilous and seditious. A Ministry which had at last become purely Whig after starting as mainly Tory, and which had had the upper hand in a very active pamphlet and newspaper war, suddenly found itself overwhelmed by an outburst of popular disapproval in which Sacheverell became a martyred hero. This produced a pictorial war, more in tune with popular opinion than the literary war, and giving a striking view of the passions involved and the matters at stake. For the issue, seemingly trivial, was fundamental: the doctrine of passive obedience versus the Whig principle of the right of resistance, at a time when the Tory theory, taken to a logical conclusion, would seem to point to a repudiation of the Revolution and the Hanoverian succession. But the Tories were no slaves to logic, and

---

[1] Copied in woodcut for a broadside, on paper watermarked 1707.

the Church had established itself in popular favour by its stand against the Romanizing activities of James. The Tories maintained that the Whig doctrine led to rebellion: 'The Roundhead's Steps the Whigs persue.'[1] All this was a hotbed for graphic satire.

The sudden activity evoked a Tory diatribe against pictorial defamation which rates the power of the print very high: the author of *The Picture of Malice or a true Account of Dr. Sacheverell's Enemies* . . . calls the print 'a Dutch talisman . . . with a virtue far exceeding that of the Palladium, not only of guarding their cities and provinces, but also of annoying their enemies, and preserving a true balance amongst the neighbouring powers around'. And he breaks into verse which credits the print with destroying the prestige of Louis XIV, defaming Charles II, and revolutionizing the popular (pre-Reformation) attitude to the Pope:

> Swifter than heretofore the Print effac'd
> The pomp of mightiest Monarchs, and dethron'd
> The dread idea of royal majesty;
> Dwindling the prince below the pigmy size
> Witness the once Great Louis in youthful pride,
> And Charles of happy days, who both confess'd
> The magic power of mezzotinto shade. . . .[2]

Two pictorial broadsides of 1706, Whiggish, but professing allegiance to the Church, devotion to the Queen, illustrate the growing tension and show how politics had invaded everyday life. *The Oxford Almanack Explained* [1462] attacks the Tory politics introduced into the pictorial Almanack for the year; one of many items in the complicated print is the rout of the Tories, stigmatized as '*Papists, Nonjurors,* and *Jacobites,* Enemies of the Queen, Church, and Protestant Succession, appearing in very envious and deceitful postures towards the Oak and Orange-Tree &c, yet necessitated to be packing up their Popish trinkets to be gone . . . '. The other, *The High-Church Hieroglyphick* . . . [1465], denounces an inn sign, 'the sign of the Embleme Put up at . . . Stoke by *Naland* in *Suffolk.*' On the sign (as depicted in the print) demons undermine the Church, while clerics support it:

> With Brawny Shoulders strive to underprop,
> And keep the vast declining Fabrick Up:

---

[1] *Roundheads & Whigs Compar'd* [1494].

[2] The new art of mezzotint had been little used for political prints; probably the writer had in mind the series of twenty-four mezzotint caricature portraits published in Holland, *Les Héros de la Ligue* of 1691, the first being Louis XIV, travestied as *le Roi Soleil,* and with James II as *Le Roi Jacques Délogé.*

> The *High-Tantivy-Priests*, the *Tacking Elves*
> Who would, to Ruin *England*, Damn themselves.
> See the *Non-Cons*, and *Moderate-Churchmen* Laugh
> To find themselves by High-Church Fall, more safe.

The Whiggish 'moderate churchman', latitudinarian and with a tenderness for dissent, was the Tories' bugbear, attacked as an enemy of Church and Monarchy. The High Church attitude is symbolized in an undated print, *A Trimmer* [1231], several times re-issued with alterations, and probably current from the Revolution throughout Anne's reign at least. This 'half Priest half Puritan' is a split personality: 'One Legg a Pulpitt holds, a Tubb the other.'[1] 'Trimmer' has no relation to Halifax's famous 'Character', but is used, much as L'Estrange had done after the Rye House Plot, for dissenters who had conformed to the Church from interest; it expresses Tory aversion to Whiggish Revolution bishops (Burnet the most outstanding). This divided personality is a basic device of English graphic satire, and the thesis that the Low Church 'Moderate Churchman' was at heart a Presbyterian whose symbol is the tub-preacher—'still a Rebel if he durst' [1233], was central to High Church propaganda; expressed for instance in *A British Janus, Anglicé A Timeserver* [Pl. 18].

But it is odd to find the Tory author of *The Picture of Malice* already quoted asserting that 'the chief means by which all the lower order of that sort of men call'd Whigs shall ever be found to act for the ruin of a potent adversary are these three—by the Print, the Canto or Doggrell Poem, and by the Libell [pamphlet]. . . .' And that of the three the print, 'if not the first, has yet been the chief machine which his enemies have employ'd against the Doctor.' The object of his reprobation is a print of Sacheverell composing the sermon he preached at St. Paul's, inspired by the Devil and instructed by the Pope, *The High Church Champion, and His Two Seconds* [1498], the inscription

> . . . Such pamper'd Priests plead y$^e$ Pretenders Cause
> Support his faction, and dispise the Laws,
> And cry High Church is ruin'd and undone,
> If Persecution dont through Britain run.
>   What tho' this Emblem may have little in it
>   Yet since ye bought y$^e$ Sermon, buy y$^e$ Print.

Far from prints being the Whigs' 'chief machine' they were used much more by the Tories in their campaign for the Doctor. High Church

---

[1] See C. Mitchell, *Hogarth's Peregrination*, Oxford, 1952, p. xxix.

propaganda descended to rabble raising; there were alehouse gatherings, toasts, cries of 'High Church and Sacheverell', bonfires, riots, and attacks on dissenters' chapels. In the national collection there are at least five times as many High Church prints as Low Church ones between 1700 and 1711, not counting a set of pro-Sacheverell playing-cards—fifty-two little designs. And the Whig print usually evoked one or more counter-prints.

The Low Church champion was inevitably Dr. Hoadley, a far abler controversialist than Sacheverell, but far inferior in appearance and popular appeal. Many years later he figured in prints (not High Church ones) as a time-serving prelate. Only once is he favourably portrayed: in *The Living Man's Elegie* . . . [Pl. 19] two angels hold his portrait. This exultation at the sentence on Sacheverell forbidding him to preach (for three years) is a counter-print to a Tory retort to the *High Church Champion*: in *To the unknown Author of the High Church Champion* [1501] Sacheverell's portrait had been similarly upheld. Hoadley was made the embodiment of faction, rebellion, and profane Latitudinarianism. In *Guess att my Meaning* [1503], yet another counter-thrust to *The High Church Champion*, Hoadley writes his Whiggish sermon, while Cromwell stands by with an axe; on his shelves are books embodying his principles: 'Lock of Government [*sic*]', 'Sydney of Government',[1] 'Faction display'd' (by Defoe), 'Milton' (his (republican) prose works edited by Toland), 'Harringtons Oceana', 'Hobbs Leviathan', 'Burnets Pastoral Letter' (burnt by order of Parliament for maintaining that William's right to the crown was by conquest). In a similar print, the *Apparition* . . . [1569], the ghost of Cromwell introduces another Low Church library with a few more titles: 'Observator', 'Review' (Defoe's paper had defended Sacheverell's impeachment), 'Atheism', 'Fanaticism', and 'Against ye Trinity'. Hoadley's doctrines were in fact all that the High Church abhorred as subversive of religion[2] as well as of civil obedience.

These political libraries are an innovation, favoured in later prints (especially in the form of punning titles); hitherto there had been little beyond the Bible, the Prayer Book, and *Eikon Basilike*. In the lively controversy allegories were used that were to become classic themes of English political caricature. The coach, with its horses, driver, postilion, passengers, destination, victims, and vicissitudes, was a splendid vehicle for political allusions. Its substitution for the earlier notion of the symbolical

---

[1] See below, p. 160 and n.

[2] This became more apparent with the Low Church ascendancy after Anne's death, when Hoadley's sermon (Mar. 1717) 'On the Kingdom of Christ' precipitated the Bangorian controversy, a violent pamphlet war, which evoked (apparently) no pictorial war.

car (which recurs from time to time) marks a stage towards modernity, and its first appearance seems to be *Needs must when the Devil drives; or, An Emblem of what we must expect if High Church gets uppermost* [1496]. 'Perkin', the Pretender, is the passenger; Sacheverell is postilion blowing on a posthorn 'Tantive hi Oh' to show that he rides headlong to Rome; the leaders, 'Passive Obedience' and 'Non-Resistance', trample on the prostrate body of 'Property', while the next pair, Philip Stubbs and Francis Higgins (clerics partnered with Sacheverell in another Whig print [1535], *The 3 Pillars of y^e Church*) trample on 'Liberty', while the coach and the wheelers—'Slavery' and 'Popery'—pass over 'Toleration' and 'Moderation'. Fixed to the coach are a gallows and wooden shoes, emblems of French despotism. The verses expand and expound the design (with the telling lines 'Your Lands will be to Monks and Fryers given') and were answered in the similar verses of the counter-print, *Like Coachman, Like Cause, or An Emblem Of what we must expect, if Low-Church gets uppermost* [1497]. The Devil again drives, the coach is the Commonwealth, emblazoned with its arms—with a calf's head for crest, and with gallows, axe, and 'Covenant' behind. Cromwell, the passenger, says 'No Monarchy'. Hoadly (prematurely a bishop) is postilion; the leaders, 'Moderation' and 'Occasional Conformity', trample on 'Common Prayer' and on 'Episcopacy' personified in Laud. The next pair, 'Presbytery' and 'Rebellion', trample on 'Loyalty' embodied in Strafford. The wheelers, 'Republican Tirany' and 'Slavery', tread down 'Magna Charta' and 'Liberty of the Subject', while under the coach lies Charles I, or 'Monarchy'. These allusions are stressed by the background, the buildings of Whitehall. The verses of the first print end,

> Let who will say there's nothing in this print,
> I'll swear the Doctor and the Devil's in 't.

The retort:

> Let who will say there's nothing in this print,
> I'll swear the Devil and Old Noll is in 't.[1]

The calves' heads and axes, accusations of regicide and republicanism, are symbols recurring in pro-Sacheverell prints. There is no doubt that on 30 January some ultra-Whigs or old Commonwealths' men and Independents did from time to time dine off calves' heads (representing King Charles's head) with appropriate republican toasts, as a demonstration

---

[1] These verses and similar ones on other Sacheverell prints seem to derive from the *Eikon Basilike* pamphlets of 1649, see p. 37, or there is a pattern for such doggerel, common to both.

against the official fast for the day, with its Prayer Book service for the Royal Martyr.[1]

Another new theme used in some famous later prints is the funeral procession. *The Funeral of the Low-Church or the Whig's last Will and Testament* [1531] is interesting as one of the earliest election prints. A Whig makes his will, while deathbed consolation and false hopes are provided by three journalists, Defoe, Steele, and Ridpath ('Observator'); the pall on the coffin is decorated with calves' heads and axes. The verses are spoken by the dying man whose party has been routed at the election:

> . . . Triumphant Tories now assume their Powers
> And fill those Places which we once call'd ours
> Whilst we Poor Whigs our wretched Fate bemoan
> And wish we'd left Sacheverell alone—

one of the few veracious pronouncements of the pictorial war.

The prominence given to journalists on this and other prints is a sign of a new age. The three attacked here are also 'The Three Champions' in *The British Censor* [1512] a broadside headed by their portraits:

> Three Brethren in Iniquity
> That vex *the Church* and spight the *Monarchy*.

Steele's association with the other two is deplored, 'But siding with *the Party overcome*':

> Him with the *Brittish Libellers* I join,
> Nor envy him the Company of Fellows,
> That have the *Pillory* disgrac'd and may *the Gallows*.

Ridpath, 'a scotch rogue' as Swift called him in a letter to Stella, was obnoxious as an aggressive journalist and a Presbyterian foe of Episcopalians in Scotland, but the chief enemy was Defoe. *Faction Display'd* [1508], the title taken from his poem, is an attack on Whigs as Presbyterians, Latitudinarians and Deists: a seven-headed monster attacks Sacheverell; its central head is the Pope, and 'The Whore of Babylon' sits on its tail, playing a fiddle. The others are Hoadley, Defoe, Richard Baxter, Ridpath, Tindal, and Toland. They have identifying labels, the Pope has 'Solemn League and Covenant', Toland has 'Milton'; Defoe, 'Review'.

The election of four Tories for the City of London in 1710 was an outstanding feature of the Whig *débâcle*, and is the subject of two Tory prints,

---

[1] Some rowdy young aristocrats were mobbed for such a feast in 1735. Sylas Neville records his own tavern dinners on calves' heads with regicide toasts, in the seventies and later. *Diary*, ed. B. Cozens-Hardy, Oxford, 1950, pp. 96–97, &c.

*Wonders upon Wonders . . .* [1549] and *Londons Happynes in Four Loyal-Members* [1550]. Both have verses repudiating 'Perkin' and professing devotion to the house of Hanover. (There is no overt Jacobitism in the Tory prints.)

But the advance in English graphic satire produced by High Church and Low Church excitements was not followed up for many years. There is almost nothing on the Peace (though there were many Dutch prints), on the accession of the Hanoverians and the Tory rout, or on the Fifteen. A rather crude Jacobite's coat of arms [1601] seems to belong to Anne's reign; the supporters are Louis XIV and the Pope. Another coat of arms, 'The Traytor's', was advertised and described in the *Flying Post* of 10 August 1714, the traitor being Harley.[1]

Despite innovations the Sacheverell prints mark the end of an age, not the beginning of a new one. Prints were still sporadic, called out by specific excitements. More significantly, the excitements tend to be religious—politics and religion being still interwoven, and dominated by memories of '41 and '49. From the Stuarts to the Hanoverians the shift is from prints mainly ecclesiastical or sectarian to prints mainly secular. In 1670 Dr. Samuel Parker had maintained that only religious questions were capable of stirring the populace:

People are never serious in their exception against any Publick Law, unless in matters of Religion; and in that case they study for reasons to disobey, because it gratifies their Pride and Vanity to seem more knowing that their Governours in that part of Wisdom that they think most valuable. Self conceit and Spiritual Pride are strange Temptations to Disobedience. . . . But if Princes will suffer themselves to be controuled by the Pride and Insolence of these contentious Zealots, they do but tempt them to slight both their Persons and their Government.[2]

This was a plea for enforced conformity to the Church based on 'the Violence of Godly Madness' during the Troubles. The populace that had clamoured against Laud and Prelacy in 1641 were clamouring in 1710 for High Church and Sacheverell. Throughout, Popery was the main enemy with the Jesuits as arch-villains, for reasons ranging from hysteria ('there is a kind of Spell in the word Popery, it transforms Man into a Beast'),[3] through memories of the fires of Smithfield and of Popish Plots and Treasons real and fabricated, to the belief that the doctrines of resistance and tyrannicide were shared by the Church of Rome and Commonwealthsmen.

---

[1] T. Wright, *Caricature History of the Georges*, 1868, p. 10.
[2] *A Discourse of Ecclesiastical Politie . . .*, pp. 309, 311.
[3] L'Estrange, *History of the Plot*, 1680.

From 1640 to 1710 (roughly speaking) a majority of prints attack the Anglican Church, or the Presbyterians, or the Independents, or dissent in general, each being associated with Rome. Jack Presbyter was the Anglicans' chief enemy: the Presbyterians were the most powerful of the Nonconformists, the richest; they had claims to consideration for their attitude in 1659–60; they were the most disposed to infiltrate the Church (like 'The Trimmer') and, it was alleged, disrupt it from within. Most incorrectly, they were associated with Cromwell and regicide, on grounds that are pungently expressed in *The Whigs Idol, or Geneva Ballad* [1509], a Sacheverell broadside headed by Hoadley's portrait decked out with regicide and republican emblems. The 'Idol' is Jack Presbyter:

> When Monarchy began to Bleed,
> And *Treason* had a fine New name
> And *Thames* was *balderdash'd* with *Tweed*,
> And Pulpits did like Beacons flame;
> When *Jeroboam's* Calves were rear'd,
> And Laud was neither lov'd nor fear'd,
> This *Gospel Comet* first appear'd.
>
> Soone his unhallow'd Finger strip'd
> His Sov'reign Liege of Power and Land,
> And having smote his Master slip'd
> His Sword into his Fellows hand,
> But he that wears his Eys may note,
> Ofttimes the Butcher binds a Goat,
> And leaves his Boy to cut his Throat.

The last (fourteenth) verse ends:

> Yet when all's said one thing I'll swear,
> No subject like the old Cavalier,
> No Traitor like *Jack* ———.

# IV

## WALPOLE AND AFTER

THE lack of political prints in the first six years of George I's reign is surprising: rival political clubs at Tory alehouses and Whig mughouses found outlets in mobbing and rioting, bonfires and processions; the cry of 'High Church and Ormonde' replaced 'High Church and Sacheverell'. The ecclesiastical disputes blew up again at the end of 1717 in the so-called Bangorian Controversy provoked by a Low-Church-Latitudinarian sermon by Hoadley. For two years this raged in a pamphlet war that invaded the theatre, but not, it would seem, the print-shops. It died away in a public madness made for caricature—the South Sea Bubble —the Stock Exchange boom and crash produced by the inflation and collapse of shares in the South Sea Company and of other undertakings, for the most part schemes floated for the mere purpose of speculation from which brokers and buyers expected a quick profit. The similar but vaster crisis in France connected with John Law's Mississippi scheme had already been the subject of a few French prints and a mass of Dutch ones— the speculating mania having raged in Holland. Many of these were copied or imitated for the English market, but there were also some notable English satires. These Bubble prints are a landmark in English cartoon history. They were aimed at the amusement of the general public, a few of them became part of the regular stock in trade of a famous print-shop, Thomas Bowles in St. Paul's Churchyard, and were still for sale in the nineteenth century. Secondly, Hogarth, aged 23 and still a bookseller's hack, produced two emblematical satires, which stand out among the mass of Bubble prints, though compared with his own later engravings they are undistinguished. The context of all these prints is the baneful character of stock-jobbing; this was, and long remained, axiomatic: 'the pernicious art of Stock Jobbing', as it was called in a parliamentary report on the boom and crash of 1697–8, a wave of speculation followed by the expulsion of stockbrokers from the Royal Exchange so that they were forced to frequent Exchange Alley with headquarters in Garraway's coffee house.

*The Bubblers Bubbl'd or the Devil take the Hindmost* [1625] was the first of the English prints, advertised on 21 June 1720, that is, while South Sea stock was still rising, though Law's system was collapsing. This is based

on a Dutch satire, but (as in all these adaptations) the allusions and inscriptions are English. A rather simplified woodcut version was published
by Dicey of Northampton, a famous purveyor of broadsides and chap-
books. It is typical of very many prints: an architectural setting, sometimes
topographical and, if so, usually represented the *rue Quincampoix* (scene
of French stock-jobbing), Exchange Alley, or, as here, a Dutch building;
there is a combination of allegory and realism with Fortune and Folly
taking leading roles among the infatuated public. Almost always there are
allusions to specific projects, under their own or derisive titles. *Bubblers
Bubbl'd* has a list of forty-two actual schemes, '*cum multis aliis*', headed by
'Robin's Fishery for Gudgeons', the South Sea Company—Robin being
Robert Knight the cashier. Sometimes fantasies are included as in *The
Bubblers Mirrour* [1621]: 'Air Pump for the Brain' and 'Engine to remove
S. Sea House to Moorfields'—that is, to the madhouse. Much is made of
the imagery of the air—objects are air-borne or wind-tossed or cloud-
borne or inflated—there are castles in the air, kites, flying ships, as well as
bubbles. These symbols of false hopes were to reappear in the prints on
the early balloons and aeronauts. They figure in an adaptation by Pine
from the Dutch, *The Bubblers-Kingdom in the Aireal-World* [1622], where
Icarus drops his feathered wings and his shares in the Temple Mills (an
old-established business that weathered the crash) and London Assurance
(one of the two flotations of 1720 that still survive).

Two pairs of prints stand out as completely English in design, both
published by Thomas Bowles early in 1721. One pair, in mezzotint, represents the lucky and the unlucky gambler; each print is called *The
Bubblers Mirrour or Englands Folly*; to one title is added the word *Joy*
[1620], to the other *Grief* [1621]. Each is a half length portrait of a speculator
registering emotion, one fortunate, the other ruined. Each has a symbolical
coat of arms framed in bottomless cornucopias, foretelling disaster for one
man, recording it for the other; the supporters of the first are two foxes
and the crest is a head in a fool's cap. In the other the supporters are asses
and the crest is a Janus-head. The margins are covered with inscriptions:
'A List of the Bubbles, with the prices they were subscribed at and what
each sold at when Highest. Together with Satyrical Epigrams on each by
yᵉ Author of yᵉ S-Sea Ballad.' The same heading is repeated on the other
print but the Bubbles are different. The Epigrams appear also on the set of
Bubble playing-cards which are possibly the last pack of satirical cards.[1]

---

[1] Historical and instructional cards continued, but these were no longer polemical or topical.
There were playing-cards on Byng [3370] in 1756, but no set has survived.

(There is also a quite different Dutch set.) The English set is interesting, each card concerned with an actual promotion, with a little picture—realistic or symbolical—and four lines of satirical verse. For instance the eight of spades is 'Puckles Machine', an effective-looking machine-gun and its operator—the 'Epigram':

> A rare invention to Destroy the Crowd,
> Of Fools at home instead of Foes abroad
> Fear not my Freinds, this Terrible Machine,
> They're only Wounded that have Shares therein.

The other pair of prints—in broadside form—give a still more comprehensive survey of Bubbles: again both have the same title, *The Bubblers Medley or a Sketch of the Times Being Europes Memorial for the Year 1720*, and both contain, arranged in the manner of medleys, copies of Bubble prints, Dutch and English, some probably designed for the medley, with a setting of other engravings sold by Bowles, including a playing-card. In each there is a famous Bubble broadside; on one [1610] is 'Bubble Poem', headed by a group of speculators in front of Garraway's, the words are from Swift's *The South Sea Bubble* (80 lines out of 228). On the other [1611] besides much other verse is 'A South Sea Ballad', the song sung in the London streets with much effect from the late summer of 1720. This is headed by another view of speculators in Change Alley—a lucky one goes first to the Herald's Office to get a coat of arms, 'and then in quest of a title'. An unlucky one tears his hair: 'Self Wife and Children all Undone.' In the first medley is a view of the Mint Coffee House crowded with defaulters (an excellent view of a coffee house interior); one says, 'And I sold a Bear of 500000, but Stock rising whipt over here and will never pay the Difference.' The Stock Exchange bear was at first, not the speculator but the stock—the skin sold before the bear was caught. The Mint in Southwark was a liberty which, as a place of sanctuary, was the resort of desperate characters.

Hogarth's pair of Bubble prints belong to 1721 and were many times reprinted during the century. *The Lottery* [1730] is an allegory without allusion to recent events, a satire on national credit, the mania for gambling and the State Lotteries. These began in 1709, although in 1698 lotteries had been prohibited as common nuisances. The other, though within the general convention of Bubble prints with its fantastic mixture of allegory and realism, differs from them in several ways: *An Emblematic Print on the South Sea Scheme* [Pl. 20 a] has no allusions to specific bubbles: the ruin of trade and of the City of London are attributed to the corruption of the times and the malign and fiendish power of money. The setting is between the base of the Monument on the right and Guildhall on the left, indicated by a figure of Gog (or Magog) on a balcony; in the middle distance is a merry-go-round in action and in the distance, St. Paul's. From the balcony hangs a mutilated figure of Fortune from which the Devil scythes off fragments for the eager throng below. Among the crowd Hogarth has introduced personal caricatures: a dwarfish and deformed Alexander Pope rifles the pockets of a fat man with a child's hornbook hanging at his belt who is supposed to be Gay—a South Sea loser (he invested £1,000, saw it rise to a nominal value of £20,000 and vanish), while Pope had been lucky. The inscription on the Monument attributing the fire of 1666 to the Papists has been altered: 'This Monument was erected in memory of the destruction of the City by the South Sea in 1720.' Two giant foxes on the pedestal look down at the scene below, where Trade is a dying woman, Honesty is being broken on the wheel, and Honour is being scourged by Villainy—figures deriving from designs by Callot. There are other incidents: women eagerly crowd into a building topped by antlers to raffle for husbands with their 'Lottery fortunes'. A Jew, a Catholic priest, and a dissenting minister crouch over a game of hustle cap—a form of pitch and toss—their religious differences forgotten:

> . . . Thus when the Shepherds are at play,
>     Their flocks must surely go astray
>     The woful Cause yᵗ in these Times,
>     Honour, & Honesty are Crimes,
>     That publickly are punish'd by
>     Self Interest, and Vilany;
>     So much for Monys magic power
> Guess at the Rest you find out more.

This connotes an attitude altogether different from Hogarth's incursion into politics more than thirty years later except that on both occasions he resents injury to trade. That it represents a considered point of view may perhaps be gathered from his 'Hieroglyphic Print', *Some of the Principal Inhabitants of yᵉ Moon* [Pl. 21], in 1724, a design in a circle as if seen through a telescope. This is one of the most striking examples of persons constructed of appropriate or symbolical objects, composites as they were afterwards called. Monarchy, Episcopacy, and Law are derided. The Monarch's face is a coin (a crown piece), he wears a pantomime crown, a collar of bubbles, and is spineless compared with the other two, and less regal than the bishop, the central figure who sits with one foot arrogantly on a stool, while the other is a cloven hoof. The bishop's face is a Jew's harp, that of the judge next him a mallet; the judge's foot rests on a Bible which is tied to a pump-handle, pumping coin into an episcopal chest, with its episcopal coat of arms, namely a knife and form. The pump-handle is attached also to the Jew's harp, regulating its note—money is all-powerful. A rope collar-wise round the judge's shoulders indicates his character; thus the three magnates respectively personify nullity, avarice and gluttony, cruelty. They are poised precariously above a platform resting on clouds and are flanked at a lower level by great officers of the Court and by two foppish persons of quality. The former are made of mirrors (with candle-sconces for arms) and firescreens—they are mere Court furniture. A tea-pot, goblet, fan, and hooped petticoat make up the lady whose companion consists of a wig and suit of clothes with a disk for face on which are armorial bearings. The figures have letters showing that Hogarth intended to supply an explanation. As it stands it is a bitter gibe at the hierarchy and the world of fashion. The context was the sense of national decadence and widespread but unfathomed corruption which was the aftermath of the South Sea débâcle.

The inordinate rise of South Sea stock had started with attempts to pay off the National Debt by juggling State obligations from one fund to another, with corrupt profits and bribes for the highly placed—Ministers and the King's mistresses. To the public it was a gigantic swindle. When Walpole was called in to restore credit (though we now know he did not in fact do so)[1] his retraint of vindictiveness and policy of compromise and moderation were extremely unwelcome to those who thirsted for blood. From the outset of his career as chief Minister he was charged with the corrupt protection of the guilty. He was nicknamed 'the Screen'; insulting paragraphs appeared in the papers and were embodied in prints. These Screen prints begin the long series of attacks on the Ministry in power which were the main theme of political caricature up to the fall of the Coalition in 1783 and always tended to recur. By convention Ministers and their supporters were placemen and venal exploiters of the public, while the Opposition were patriots—the Ins and the Outs indeed were known as the parties of Corruption and Opposition; this was the old anti-thesis between Court and Country that had been so potent a slogan be-tween 1667 and 1681, and was deeply rooted in the ancient tradition of the over-great subject. Walpole's methods provided ample material for this

[1] J. H. Plumb, *Sir Robert Walpole*, 1956, ch. viii.

Opposition propaganda which was the more formidable because ministerial propaganda was always attacked as venal, so that public opinion was normally anti-ministerial and liable to be stampeded into violence.

The South Sea incident which especially inflamed the public was the absconding of Knight the cashier in January 1721, taking with him a book credited with the blackest secrets. At the instigation of the British Resident in Brussels he was arrested and imprisoned in Antwerp; the Brabanters, relying on an ancient privilege, refused to give him up, and he soon escaped. This was alleged and believed to be a put-up affair to protect the guilty, managed by Walpole and paid for by the King's mistress, the Duchess of Kendal. On 4 March a libellous mock advertisement appeared in the *Post Boy*: 'To be sold, A Large Commodious Skreen, something the worse for wear.'[1] Other papers took up and expanded the notion. Walpole was 'Robert Skreen' in the *Daily Post* on the 27th. The *London Journal* in the same month elaborated the idea in a paragraph engraved on one of the Screen prints, together with more threats and insults: *A True Picture of the Famous* SKREEN *describ'd in the London Journal, No. 85* [Pl. 20 *b*]. On a tall screen with several leaves are pictures (compared with those on the shield of Achilles) representing the crimes and the punishments with which Walpole is charged and menaced. He is threatened with the fate of the de Witts—murder by the mob—as well as with Tower Hill; there are allusions to brazen effrontery (Friar Bacon's Brazen Head) and bribe-taking. Sheltering behind the screen but revealed by cast shadows are Walpole himself and other guilty men and women. On the wall is a map of Antwerp. Doggerel below the design gives 'Advice':

> . . . Remember Gaviston: on Spencer [Despenser] think;
> The Cup is full and somebody must drink:
> Justice and Vengeance is the common Cry,
> Guilt makes it terrible to live or die,
> To palliate Roguery never more be seen,
> They're doubly Guilty whom y<sup>e</sup> Guilty Screen.

*The Brabant Skreen* [1712] was an even more elaborately explicit attack, and the verses, quoted from the *London Journal*, No. 92, appeal to the King to rid himself of a traitor:

> Let no curs't Traitor tho of High Degree
> Eclipse the Beams of Sacred Majesty! . . .

On the screen are eight incriminating scenes and on the wall is a picture

---

[1] See C. D. Realey, *Early Opposition to Sir Robert Walpole*, 1931.

of the 'Joyful Entry' (*Joyeuse Entrée* to Antwerp 1514, origin of the Brabanters' privileges under the Empire).

At the beginning and the end of his career Walpole was threatened with the fate of Piers Gaveston and in 1742 the Screen theme of 1721 was revived. Both the Screen prints of 1721 were closely copied by a plagiarist, a sign of popularity. A cruder attack on Knight was also copied in a second print and given still wider circulation by its reproduction in woodcut for two successive numbers of the *Weekly Journal or British Gazetteer*. This is *Lucipher's New Row-Barge* [Pl. 10 *b*] in which devils take the fugitive cashier to the gaping mouth of Hell. Two lines of the inscription convey its tenor: 'Impov'rish Thousands by some Publick Fraud, / And worship Intrest as your only God.'

The screen was a convenient device for attacking Walpole without risky explicitness—a precaution soon dropped. It figures in an interesting print on the general election of 1722, *The Prevailing Candidate, or the Election carried by Bribery and the Devil* [1717]. On each of seven leaves of the screen is the date of one of the years of the late Parliament, each with its reprehensible enactment. These include the Septennial Act and the 'Act to indemnify S.S. V. . . . .ns' (Villains). Emerging from the screen—that is, dispatched by Walpole—and escorted by the Devil, is the candidate. He holds a money bag and takes the hand of a 'Knave . . . who has pow'r to command / All the Votes in the Corporation'. The knave is shackled by a chain; his conscience-stricken wife is reassured by a parson who 'avers brib'ry no Sin, / Since mony's a family blessing'. Two boys attend the candidate, one proffers a wooden shoe, emblem of French slavery. On 31 March, when the election was in full swing, this was advertised in the *Post Boy* with two other prints: 'Britannia stript by a Villain to which is added the true phiz of a late Member.' Both are on the same plate [1720–1], the Villain being a South Sea Director who gives Britannia a small purse and makes off for 'a distant Shore' with a large one; the 'late Member', depicted as Punch, has ruined the nation. Walpole was repeatedly Punch in later prints.

But the nation was clearly not ruined; prosperity and peace with Walpole's policy of conciliating his adversaries produced a period of calm after the excitements of 1721–2 when the Opposition had deluged the country with pamphlets and newspapers, and there had been close co-operation between newspapers and print-shops. In the placid interval the art of graphic satire advanced; its range was extended to ridicule the taste of the town, foreign musicians, the opera, the theatre, masquerades, topics which became part of the caricaturist's repertory. In 1726 came one of those sensations that from time to time invaded the print-shops—the controversy over Mary Tofts, who professed to have given birth to rabbits. In all this, Hogarth's prints stand out, and he produced one of a number of satires on the amazing credulity of the medical profession. The lighter touch of these social satires gradually influenced the political cartoon.

At the end of 1726 the birth of the weekly *Craftsman* was a sign that the halcyon period would end. There were reports of the imminent fall of Walpole and when George I died suddenly in June 1727 a new Ministry was expected. The elections were carried on with much animosity and disorder and there were seditious ballads, but the only surviving election print has no personal allusions. *Ready Mony the prevailing Candidate, or the Humours of an Election* [1798] is a commentary on the usual conduct of a country election; bribes, kisses for the elector's wife, chairing the member, with verses elaborating the contrast between the obsequious candidate and the arrogant elected person, a theme recurring in prints for more than a century.

Not till 1730 do pictorial thrusts at Walpole approach the animosity of 1721, although the *Craftsman* had been ruthlessly attacking his foreign policy and of course charging him with corruption. An ostensible panegyric in the form of a monument with figures, ironical in its extravagance, is clearly bitter denigration. In form and title it echoes a satire on the despicable Francis Charteris, classic eighteenth-century profligate, just convicted of rape. *To the Glory of the R$^t$ Hon$^{ble}$. S$^r$ Robert Walpole* [1842] is a companion print to *To the Glory of Colonel Don Francisco, upon his delivery out of Goal* [1841]. On a second state some inscriptions are altered to leave no doubt of the print's hostile intention.[1] It was copied as part of the more savage campaign of 1741–2 [2500].

Next year the essays in the *Craftsman* were reissued in seven volumes, each with a satirical frontispiece. All these were reprinted together on a single sheet [1822], headed *Robin's Game or Seven's the Main. Being An Explanation of Caleb D'Anver's Seven Egyptian Hieroglyphicks Prefixed to the Seven Volumnes of the Craftsman*, with the motto, *Jacta est Alea*. This was the folding plate to (and title of) a shilling pamphlet 'containing a Key to the State Hieroglyphicks and a description of the Seven Volumes . . . with Remarks thereon', the whole edition being too dear 'to be every Body's

---

[1] Stephens interprets the first state as praise of Walpole: 'BOBBY the *Screen*' (among others) was attacked for the very unpopular pardon to Charteris; *Ballad on Colonel Francisco Rape-Master General* . . .: M. Percival, *Walpole Ballads*, Oxford, 1918, p. 35.

Money', and the 'Enigmatical Frontispieces . . . set it above the ordinary Reader's Understanding'. The so-called explanations are elaborate interpretations, ostensibly speculative—insults only slightly veiled. The composite plate was also published separately as a large broadside, the title altered to *Robin's Reign . . .* [1822].

One of these designs (pl. to vol. v) is the first pictorial attack on Walpole's foreign policy, using the ancient theme of the balance. Walpole, 'a pitiful dirty looking scoundrel', completely subservient to Cardinal Fleury, throws appeasing documents into his scale to be hopelessly outweighed by French emblems of sovereignty and sea-power. The Gallic Cock crows on the back of the sleeping British Lion, a recurrent device of the cartoonist. In another design (pl. to vol. iii) there is a printing press, the first of many pictorial tributes to this palladium of liberty. 'I hope there will be no attempt to construe my Explanations as Libels', ran the introduction. But proceedings were taken: *Robin's Game* together with a play, *The Fall of Mortimer*, and a ballad, *The Chelsea Monarch or Money Rules All*, were presented by the Middlesex Grand Jury in July 1731 as 'false, infamous, scandalous, seditious and treasonable libels'.[1] Since the second revival, by Wilkes, of this old play was to have dire consequences, something must be said of it here. Walpole had already figured as Gaveston; the comparison with Mortimer was still more venomous: each the favourite of a queen consort, the fate of one is prophesied for the other. The lines, with seditious alterations from the original, seemed horribly pat and were received with dismaying applause:

> Tis full three years since *Mortimer* began
> To lord it over us by the Queen's vile Favour . . .
> In this short space, he and his brother Devil [Horatio Walpole]
> Have made, undone, new fram'd, shuffled and tost
> The antient Customs of our native Soil
> So very often that the Kingdom staggers
> Under the heavy Burthen of the Charge. [Act i, sc. i.]

With the Excise scheme of 1733 graphic satire was fully established as a standing instrument of propaganda. Popular agitation reached a new climax, which, though probably less than in the Popish Plot frenzy, perhaps than in the Sacheverell ferment, was geared more explicitly to party politics. Popular clamour against some ministerial measure or project is a recurrent theme of eighteenth-century politics. Hungry Outs eager to

---

[1] Percival, op. cit., pp. xx–xxi, 50.

supplant the Ins carried on the art and craft of agitation in newspapers, ballads, prints, and by organized petitioning and other devices, always fomented by cries of Liberty in danger. That famous slogan, 'Liberty and Property and No Excise', was first heard in 1733. To the Opposition who had been hammering at Walpole ('King Bob', 'Robin', 'Blue String', 'Volpone', and the like) as an arrogant Colossus, enemy of trade, a source of corruption, and himself in corrupt subservience to France, the Excise scheme was a godsend. It was also a menace. If carried, the country gentlemen would be propitiated by the reduction of the Land Tax, trade would be encouraged to the greater glory of Walpole. The word Excise—hated instrument of the Interregnum—was enough to set the agitation going. By a legerdemain which is apparent in the prints people were induced to believe that the excise—limited to wine and tobacco, the duty being transferred from customs—would become a General Excise, that an army of excise officers (actually 126 for the whole of England) would be a new 'standing army' with access to every house at any time, and that the result would be slavery and wooden shoes.

Ballads and prints were used to create the myth of the Excise Monster. *Britannia Excisa* [1936], a ballad attributed to Pulteney, was illustrated in woodcut with one of the long succession of many-headed monsters of English political folklore. A scaly creature, blend of hydra, medieval dragon, and Beast of Revelation, with webbed wings and the claws of a bird of prey, draws Walpole's coach, turning one of its seven heads to vomit coins into his lap, while the others gulp at the necessities of life— a leg of mutton, a sheep, a tankard, a goblet, a tobacco pipe. At the bonfires which celebrated the withdrawal of the Bill an Excise dragon was burnt:

> Your Liberties, Properties, now are secur'd,
> Which late were in Danger of being immur'd;
> The *Merchants* and *Vintners* their Trade may pursue,
> And not dread the Plague of a Raskally Crew.
>           For no new EXCISE,
>           With five hundred Eyes,
> Shall henceforth your Wives or your Daughters surprize
> For if they had Licence to gage all your *Stocks*
> May also pretend to gage under their Smocks.

In this display of propaganda and agitation some familiar devices of the cartoonist made a seemingly first appearance. Liberty with her cap and spear was to establish herself by stages during the Seven Years War, the

Wilkite disturbances, and the dispute with America. (After this she seldom appears, the cap and spear become emblems in their own right—or
occasional attributes of Britannia.) She appears first in an Excise print
(her cap is still a hat in the Dutch convention); together with Trade (a merchant holding a ship) she attends maypole rejoicings at the defeat of
Excise in *The Noble Stand: Or the Glorious CCIIII* . . . [1921]—the large
minority (204–265) that voted against the motion for the Bill.

One of the most interesting of the prints is *Excise in Triumph* [Pl. 22].
Walpole is a fat exciseman enthroned on a barrel and drawn by an
emaciated British Lion, yoked, and shod with wooden shoes, but expressing
angry resentment, an excellent example of the noble creature's capacity
for registering emotion. Walpole's truck passes over a document—Magna
Charta, reduced to infamy. One of the new standing army rides a mutilated
unicorn which walks beside the Lion, while others are drawn up behind.
Excise prints were adapted to fans; on one fan leaf (only a fragment survives) Walpole is compared to Wolsey: 'Wolsey and his Successor here in
one behold. Both served their Masters, both their Country sold' [1925].

Every phase of the uproar is illustrated—the large minority against the
Bill, the City petitioners escorted by a mob, and Walpole's unlucky comment (always remembered against him) that they were 'sturdy beggars';
the rejoicings, the bonfires, the burning in effigy. The 'Progress' of some
*bête noire* from lowly beginnings to undeserved eminence and final retribution, in a sequence of little scenes is a device still alive. It was inevitably used against Napoleon; the first example in these prints is *R–b–n's
Progress in Eight Scenes* . . . [1938], probably inspired by Hogarth's *Rake's
Progress*;[1] this begins with his criminal ambition and ends with Excise:
precariously poised on a pyramid he scatters bribes, while his effigy hangs
over a bonfire.

Even Walpole's favourable reception in Norfolk was elaborately ridiculed, first in *Fog's Journal* (28 July), then in a ballad, and finally in a print
[1931] on which the ballad is quoted, a good example of the close relationship between these instruments of propaganda. Walpole as a quack doctor,
his brother Horatio beside him as his zany, enters Norwich in his gig (the
quack was the eighteenth-century embodiment of riches got by humbug
and chicane). He holds three papers: 'Excise', 'A Cure for Religion', 'A
Cure for Trade'. The zany proclaims his master's feats; the mob retort,
'that's nothing he has cur'd a whole Bench of Bishops of Religion'; '. . .
Why he has almost cur'd a whole Nation of their Trade.'

[1] See below, p. 113.

The bishop was still, and long remained, a target for satire; indeed, the attitude of the prints to the Church and the clergy is a sort of gauge of currents of opinion. The line of attack was very different from that of the seventeenth century; he is no Tantivy-Tory or Popish prelate, but an ambitious worldling and a subservient tool of Walpole—arrogant, pompous, overfed. In 1731 there was an incident that evoked an outburst of ridicule. Archbishop Wake was reported ill: a broadside ballad illustrated with a woodcut described the competition for the succession: *First Oars to L—b—th; or, who strives for Preferment* [2867];[1] according to the *Craftsman* two hawkers were arrested for selling it. Three bishops, each in a Thames wherry (sculler), race each other across the river. The rivals are Hoadley (Salisbury), Gibson (London), Blackburne (York). Similar engravings of the race were sold separately, and verses relate the outcome: 'The man whose place each thought to take / Is yet alive and still a WAKE.' There were similar satires and prints when Wake died (in 1737) and again when Archbishop Potter died (in 1747).

The ancient theme of the pluralist inevitably recurs. In 1737 Archbishop Wake, book in hand, drives *An Ass Loaded with* (Church)[2] *Preferments* [2269] turning away from a poor kneeling parson. The ass (with the head of Wake's son-in-law) has panniers laden with church offices including the 'Sine-cure of Bray'. He is contrasted with 'Good antient Pastors'; today, 'A supple Conscience and a Front of Brass / For highest Honours fits the heaviest Ass.' *The Pluralist* [Pl. 23] in 1744 is in the classic form of a cleric grabbing at churches: having placed hands and feet on four, he looks greedily at a fifth: 'For what can Priestly Avarice aswage? . . . Let Curates drudge the lazy Drone to serve. . . .'

In 1736 there was an attempt, well-intentioned but unfortunate, to check the appalling evil of gin. Three prints are noteworthy as the first of the satires on gin and beer which recurrently spotlight the social and political environment. Nothing afterwards was to approach them, or the agitation they illustrate, for levity and brutality in the face of tragedy (except that in 1751 one was reprinted). Gin, cheap, fiery, lethal, was distilled anywhere, sold anywhere in the most brutalizing conditions. Repeated protests from magistrates on the devastation caused led at last to action, futile in 1729, drastic in 1736 with a Gin Act intended to stop the retailing of gin altogether, by a prohibitive duty and a retailer's

---

[1] Stevens has misdated the print 1747; M. Percival shows that the date is May 1731: op. cit., p. 54.
[2] Depicted.

licence of £50. It was violently attacked in Parliament by Pulteney and the Patriots, was passed but was defeated by the distillers and the London mob. On the date that the Act was to take effect retail dealers draped their signs with black and organized mock lyings in State and funeral processions for 'Madam Geneva' or 'Mrs. Gin'. Hence *The Funeral Procession of Madam Geneva* . . . [2277] which is dedicated by 'a Lover of Trade' to 'those Melancholly Sufferers the Distillers'. This is a parish funeral; the chief mourner is one Loddy, an almost naked beggar and a familiar character; distillers follow, and in front ragged women drink and fight. In *The Lamentable Fall of Madam Geneva* [2278] she is dead drunk and prostrate, with bottle and glass. Though the spirit is entirely different this foreshadows Hogarth's contrast between gin and beer in 1751. One of the burlesqued monuments (made out of the implements of distilling) beloved by cartoonists is depicted in *To the Mortal Memory of Madam Geneva* . . . [Pl. 24]. She was the 'kind comfort of the starving Poor', to quote from verses engraved below another print: 'Queen Gin: for whom they'd Sacrifice / Their Shirts, or Smocks, nay both their Eyes' [2278]. The theme of all these prints is that gin alone could produce that absolute (and degraded) drunkenness which was the only solace of the very poor who could not afford beer. Behind the agitation were the interests of publicans, farmers, and landlords, and the opportunity to attack Walpole. Of course Madam Geneva was not dead. She survived, at first under ironically defiant names—'Parliament Brandy', 'Strip-me-naked', 'The Last Shift', 'Cholick Water', and the like. Then openly, after gin riots ('No Gin, No King') and a war on informers.

Pictorial attack on the reigning sovereign is, so far, exceptional : as a rule Ministers can do no right, Kings, little wrong, a convention that makes exceptions noteworthy. George II was unpopular in 1737; his fits of rage, when he would kick his hat about, were well known. *Æneas in a Storm* [2326] shows the King's ship tempest-tost, while Britannia waits his return to England from Hanover; one of the winds in the clouds is kicking a hat. Much more disrespectful is *The Festival of the Golden Rump* [2327] in the same year. This is one of those prints deriving from the frequent 'dreams' and 'visions' dear to the *Craftsman* and other papers, in which the more elaborate fantasies of the Opposition wits were embodied. It is based on 'The Vision of the Golden Rump' in *Common Sense or the Englishman's Journal* (written by Lord Chesterfield and others) for 19 March: the King is a 'pagod' on an altar, a satyr with a golden rump; his high priestess (the Queen) tried to appease him 'when he lifted

up his cloven hoof to correct his domesticks'. Walpole is his chief magician
in a robe embroidered with the words 'Auri sacra Fames'. The Order of
the Bath (instituted in 1725) is also ridiculed in the text and in the print,
which is unbelievably gross. Disrespect could hardly go farther and one
must suppose that the authors were emboldened by the support of the
Prince, then enjoying popularity at his father's expense. Disrespect was
again displayed in 1738, in *Solomon in his Glory* [2348] where George II
dallies with Madame Walmoden, the sceptre falling from his hand, while
a pugdog plays with his mourning hatband for Queen Caroline, whose
portrait is on the wall.

Ever since 1731 grievances against Spain had been piling up, with a
swelling stream of anti-Walpole propaganda and a growing demand for
war. This increasingly appears in the prints from 1737 and only a few out
of very many can be noticed here. *Slavery* [2355, *c.* 1738], inscribed 'To
the Worthy and most injur'd Merchants of Great Britain', is noteworthy
for the first Shakespeare quotation: John of Gaunt's speech in *Richard II*
from 'This fortress built by Nature for herself' to '. . . bound in with
shame / With inky-blots & rotten parchment bonds'—very apt to Walpole's hated treaties and the Convention of Pardo. A Spaniard drives four
Britons in a plough, while Walpole forces the British Lion to follow; in
the middle distance another Spaniard cuts off Jenkins's ear, while a Spanish ship fires at an unresisting vessel. The famous ear appears repeatedly,
for instance in another scene by the sea which adorns a song with music:
*The Present State of Little Britain* [2335*],

> Britons where is your great Magnanimity, where's your boasted Courage
> flown (*bis*)
> Quite perverted to Pu-si-la-ni-mi-ty, Scarce to call your Souls your own
> (*bis*).

Britannia sits on a canon which is inscribed 'Open my lips', words from
what was then known as 'Cromwell's device'; the canon speaks: 'O Lord
open thou my Lips and my Mouth shall show forth thy Praise.' Inland,
a Spaniard cuts off the ear of the kneeling Jenkins, and stuffs a paper,
'Convention', down his throat—an attack on Walpole's bitterly resented
attempt to settle mutual grievances by negotiation.

Hostilities with Spain produced the usual exasperation with the Dutch.
*Hocus Pocus, or the Political Jugglers* [2419], dated 8 October 1739 (war
was declared on 29 October), contains typical complaints of selfish neutrality: a Dutchman rifles the pockets of an Englishman who is fighting with

a Spaniard, while a pug (Holland) runs off with the bone for which two other dogs are fighting. And again in the same print, 'Sly Hogan takes a neutral course / Yet helps yᵉ Spaniards with his stores.' The same theme is that of a crude street ballad, *The Whimsical Age or the Political Jugglers*,[1] where the three dogs and the bone reappear:

> Mynheer would have little to do,
> But cunningly crys out forbariance sir,
> He's nought but the gelt in his view,
> While England and spain are at variance sir.

The declaration of war did nothing to lessen the frenzied distrust of Walpole. In 1740 the coming general election loomed over politics, moving the Opposition to further flights of propaganda, and the print-sellers took full advantage of the public mood. Campaigning prints were produced on both sides, remarkable for a kind of sophistication that was new. *The Stature of a Great Man or the English Colossus* [Pl. 25], published in March, is a bold design and the first direct illustration of a passage from Shakespeare. Walpole 'doth bestride the Narrow World', with the familiar quotation from *Julius Caesar* engraved below; the 'dear Brutus' of the original becomes 'dear P . . . . . .y' (Pulteney). As usual Walpole is accused of subservience to Fleury, preventing the ships from fighting, destroying trade, raiding the sinking fund, and so on. The design illustrates the developing art of the cartoon. *The Cardinal in the Dumps* [2454] demands mention for its recognition of Anglo-French rivalry on the American continent, normally outside the cartoonist's horizon till the eve of the Seven Years War. Fleury and Walpole are both dismayed at Vernon's capture of Portobello; the former says, 'G—d, he'll take all our Aquisitions in America.' 'The Head of the Colossus' is on a pole.

The theme of Walpole as 'Prime Minister', an office, alien to the Constitution, which he had assumed, and for which, with other things, he deserved the axe, was prominent in 1740. It was implicit in the *Colossus*, more explicit in *The Cardinal . . .*, the direct thesis of the *Life and Death of Pierce Gaveston . . . Grand Favorite and Prime Minister To that Unfortunate Prince, Edward II . . . With Political Remarks by way of Caution to all Crowned Heads and Evil Ministers . . .* [2462]. The 'caution' was enforced by a frontispiece by George Bickham (who also published the book). Walpole, without his wig, stands by a block, holding a dying confession on which the word 'Corruption' is legible; a soldier stands by to represent the standing army.

---

[1] M. Percival, op. cit., pp. 158–61.

With the pending election, pro-Walpole propaganda makes a first appearance in two prints of 1740. One is yet another appeal to history: in *The Patriot-Statesman* [2459] Burghley conducts Walpole ('like *Burleigh*, shining with victorious Rays') to the temple of Fame; they are under the protection of Pallas, who drives away Envy, Discord, &c. This heads a broadside where the comparison of the two statesmen is seriously elaborated in a speech against faction put into the mouth of Elizabeth. Different editions and states, well worn, show that this was widely circulated: it can hardly have been effective against the general belief that the glorious past was being betrayed, and that all praise of Ministers was venal. Johnson's *London* (in 1738) expresses the mood of the time:

> Struck with the seat that gave Eliza birth,
> We kneel and kiss the consecrated earth,
> In pleasing dreams the blissful age renew,
> And call Britannia's glories back to view,
> Behold her cross triumphant on the main,
> The guard of commerce and the dread of Spain,
> Ere masquerades debauched, excise opprest,
> Or English honour grew a standing jest

And:

> Here let those reign whom pensions can incite
> To vote a patriot black, a courtier white,
> Explain their country's dear-bought rights away,
> And plead for pirates in the face of day.

In its day, *London* was a (Tory) political pamphlet. Another appeal to the age of Elizabeth was the reprinting, in January 1740, of the *Double Deliveraunce* [Pl. 3], that is, of the version of 1689, with the title *Spayne and Rome defeated* [2456].

The other ministerial effort was a defence of the Walpolean system in the guise of an attack on the *Craftsman*; the editor, Nicholas Amhurst, 'Caleb D'Anvers', is a tinker, crying, 'Constitutions to mend', the first of a line of political tinkers who damage the pot with every patch. Here is another instance of newspaper, print, and ballad in co-operation: in February the theme was broached in the *Daily Gazetteer*, which advertised the print in June: *The Itinerant Handy-Craftsman, or Caleb Turn'd Tinker* [2448]. A ballad followed, *The Tinker Turn'd Politician; or Caleb's Metamorphosis,*[1] and finally fourteen stanzas of the ballad were printed in the *Gazetteer* in March 1741. The theme was that the Place Bills, Bribery Bill,

[1] M. Percival, op. cit., p. 198.

&c., of the past fifty years were harmful tinkering with the Constitution. Lines from *Hudibras* on the print point the moral:

> Faults still they find with That or This
> And something always is amiss;
> As if Government was intended
> For nothing else but to be mended.

The *Craftsman* retorted that the 'tinkering' could be harmful only to the 'constitution of a Particular Ministry'.

This was shadow-boxing compared with the grand crisis of 13 February 1741, when a motion, 'the Motion', for the removal of Walpole from his Majesty's presence and councils for ever was made in both Houses. The tale of his misdeeds was a rehearsal of familiar accusations. This had been foreshadowed in the winter by a large and important print, *The Evil Genius of England in Several Scenes relating to the War* [2418], dated 6 December and still advertised on 24 February. The high hopes of Opposition were dashed by the Minister's unexpectedly large majority; 290 to 106 in the Commons, 108 to 59 in the Lords. The Walpolean triumph was celebrated in a famous print, *The Motion* [Pl. 26], which produced a sequence of prints and counter-prints, forming one of the peaks of English pictorial polemics. It is noteworthy too for the first full use of a device that at once became popular; the verse explanation is in the patter of a Savoyard raree-showman, admirably suited to the fantasies of propaganda.[1] This elaborate print, using the coach allegory with a new realism and with a topographical setting, the buildings of Whitehall, was advertised in the *Gazetteer* on 21 February. Sandys (who made the motion in the Commons) drops a Place Bill, dismayed at the reckless driving of the Duke of Argyll (whose speech in seconding Carteret's motion in the Lords had been impolitically violent). At Argyll's feet crouches a 'Spaniel curr', Bubb Dodington; the passenger, Carteret, cries, 'Let me get out:' Pulteney in the foreground wheels off a barrow-load of 'Patriot' propaganda, leading 'de Puppies by de Nose', first of many illustrations of this metaphor. The verses begin:

> Who be dat de Box do sit on?
> Tis John, de Hero of *North-Britain*
> Who out of Place, does Place-men spit on
> Doodle Doodle do

---

[1] It probably derived from ballads. Cf. *The Raree-Show-Man. Or His Box and Magick Lanthorn Expos'd* ... and *The Englishman's Answer to the Magick Lanthorn*. Madden Collection, Cambridge University Lib., III, nos. 1606, 1537. *The Raree Showman* is depicted in *The First Heat of the European Race* [2333]; his first appearance (as Charles II) was in 1681; see pp. 56–57.

They end:

> So Sirs, we have shewn you all de *Hero's*
> Who put you together by the Ear-os,
> And frighten you so with groundless Fear-o's
> > Doodle . . .

*The Motion* also encouraged a fashion for the characterization of individuals in a way that was new: Lyttelton is described: 'Who be dat astride de Pony / So long, so lank, so lean and bony.' Published at 3*d.*, *The Motion* was clearly subsidized, the usual price being 6*d.*, or perhaps a shilling. A woodcut version was 'sold by all the Booksellers of London and Westminster' and the design was adapted to a fan mount. A similar design [2478] is attributed to Gravelot, and may well be the original version; in this there is a riverside setting; evidently Walpole's house at Chelsea. It is one of the rare prints that can be ascribed to ministerial inspiration at the highest level. 'Tell me dear now', Horace Walpole wrote to Conway from Florence ('extremely diverted' by it), 'who made the design, and who took the likenesses, they are admirable. . . .'[1]

The print reflects the situation: the Walpolean elation and the momentary dejection of Opposition. But as the text of the famous motion served to point and concentrate election propaganda, so the print gave opportunities to the Opposition artists. The war of pictures was at its height in March and had ended by the dissolution of Parliament on 27 April. It was seemingly an affair of the initiated: M.P.s, journalists, political clubs, and coffee houses. *The Motion* was followed by *The Grounds*, *The Motive*, *The Protest*, and *The Reason* (for the Motion),[2] all setting out the case against Sir Robert: placemen, bribery, peculation, servile bishops, taxes, excise, standing army, the Gin Act, damage to trade and manufactures. There are attacks on Ralph Freeman, editor of the *Gazetteer*[3] called 'the Court Evil' (from Henry Fielding's paper, the *Champion*). In *The Grounds* Walpole's son Robert (Volpone Junior) drives the 'Money Press', a massive chest on wheels drawn by yoked placemen, which crushes 'Liberty', 'Honesty', 'Trade', and 'Manufactures'. Volpone stands on the chest, making coins pour into it by slashing at the body of his child, 'Sinking Fund'. He is 'de Grand Projector of Great Britain'. Verse 14:

> Who be de Groupes of Swordsmen, Gownsmen, and other dat escort him?
> Dey be his Creatures in de State, Church, Army and Revenue, dat court him
> For as dey depend on him, dey must needs support him.

---

[1] *Letters*, ed. Toynbee, i. 96 (25 Mar. 1741); was the author George Townshend? See below, p. 115.     [2] 2484, 2485, 2488, 2491.     [3] Cf. Johnson's definition, p. 2.

The other prints are on similar lines, each with special items of interest. *The Negotiator's* [2463], 'a brave gallante show', published in March, belongs to the same set, but is concerned with foreign affairs in a complicated way; George II and Charles Albert, who was claiming the Austrian Succession, are on a see-saw among the other powers; Frederick tramples on Silesia; 'Bohemia' (Maria Theresa) weeps. Walpole, with one foot in a grave—that is, tottering to his fall—clings to a pacifist policy and begs the bellicose Philip of Spain to listen to the (ostensibly) peace-loving Fleury.

The Walpolean counter-prints attack the Opposition leaders and their Press. In *The Political Libertines, or Motion upon Motion* [2490] Pulteney leads *The Champion* by the nose, that is, Henry Fielding who is further identified by holding his play, 'Pasquin'. In *The Funeral of Faction* [2487] who 'dy'd of a disappointment on feb yᵉ 13, 1741', the procession is led by Caleb D'Anvers (Amhurst) with his 'Craftsman' banner. Other newspapermen follow with their papers, including the *Champion* and the *Daily Post*. They carry Faction to 'the Family Vault', the tomb of Wat Tyler, Jack Straw, Jack Cade, and Kett. On a memorial stone are the figures by which the famous motion was defeated. The important point is made (in verses which by exception are not the showman's) that the defeat has dashed the hopes of 'Perkin' in 'Old England'. In *The Acquital* [2486] Pulteney and others impotently throw their darts at Walpole; these are 'Want of Place', 'Want of Pension', 'Resentment', 'Sham Patriotism', and the like. And in the more allegorical *Truth and Moderation* [2489] of 21 April the crowd of assailants is led by 'Vain Conceit'. Ministerial printshop propaganda of this kind is rare.

With the Dissolution there was a slackening of prints until the new Parliament met on 1 December, and the more sophisticated personalities cease, but during the interval there were some interesting satires on foreign affairs. The sensation of the election was the defiance of the Court in the supposedly safe Westminster, by Admiral Vernon and a Patriot colleague. This was the first of the famous Westminster elections where Opposition challenged potent ministerial interests with the cry that they represented the 'Sense of the People', and where both sides could command powerful mobs. George Bickham dedicated the first of many prints of the Covent Garden hustings [2497] 'to the brave Admiral Vernon, and his worthy Colleague': they are for 'the Glory of Britain'—their opponents for 'Excise'. Nevertheless, the Court prevailed, but the closing of the poll under the protection of a party of Guards gave opportunity for an election petition, carried against Walpole by a majority of two. In the new election two Patriots were unopposed; two exulting broadsides followed. In *The Triumph of Justice* [2501], dedicated to 'the Independent Electors of Westminster', the Prince of Wales presides over Walpole's tomb, and in *The Banner of Liberty* [2505], an illustration to the text of the election petition, Liberty drives away Slavery.

Walpole's fall is celebrated with exulting prints. Like Laud, and in the traditional manner, he disgorges his spoils in *The Political Vomit for the Ease of Britain* [2531], a print with a Dutch copy. And in *Brother Robert under his Last Purgation* [2533] a vision foretells his execution, which, seemingly, was now no longer merely visionary. In *From One House to Another* [2536] 'Sir Blew String' is driven by Justice to the Lords: 'The Country claims its due, Protection's vain.' But doubts soon prevail. The Patriots are now Placemen or would-be Placemen, and in *The Promotion* [2535] Walpole laughs at the distribution of offices and honours. The demand for vengeance was general: the populace held him guilty of the crimes so often stressed in newspapers, ballads, and prints. But proof was lacking. Had he robbed the Sinking Fund for himself? Had he given treasonous orders to admirals? Would the Screen operate again, as after the South Sea? A secret committee of 21 was appointed at last to investigate and a ballad in April voices fears and hopes: *The Secret Committee*:[1]

> In great expectation
> Thus prays the whole *Nation*
> No Screen in the SECRET COMMITTEE.

Pictorially, Walpole's career as Minister begins and ends with 'The Screen'. Four prints on this theme in 1742 are extant. First [2539], Walpole as Punch exults at the defeat by two votes on 9 March of the first motion for a secret committee; a picture on the screen anticipates his imprisonment and death; among the many allusions to national grievances is the first on the hard lot of the half-pay officer while commissions were given to boys. Shameful episodes are displayed on a tall folding screen in two other prints. *The Screen* [2540] has the sub-title, 'A New Screen for an Old one', and its advertisement in the *London Evening Post* announces that 'The Old Screen' in 1721 [Pl. 20 *b*] is 'to be had'. Walpole (now Lord Orford) behind the screen, is still Punch, pulling the strings of puppet M.P.s; Pulteney, 'Dear William', is informed:

> ... He was the *Punch* at first you saw;
> He gives the other Puppets Law,

---

[1] Percival, op. cit., pp. 180–2.

And by his secret Strings he still
Governs the others as he will;
And all the Difference that is known.
You only *hear another Tone:*
The *Puppet Man*,—behind the *Screen*,
Is the same man,—although not seen.

(Quoted on the print from the *London Evening Post*.)

In *The Night Visit, or the Relapse: With the Pranks of Bob Fox the Jugler* [2559] twenty-three charges against Lord Orford are depicted on the screen. In front, George II consults him on the management of his Ministers: 'Mix and divide them' is the reply. The King's protection of the fallen Minister is symbolized in *Touch me not; or B—bs Defiance* [2551], a Janus-head of Walpole and the King is seen as if in a glass; the former defies Justice herself: 'Touch me, Madam, if you dare.'

> . . . I and the King the haughty W—lsey cry'd,
> And All yᵉ Malice of his Foes defy'd;
> But R——n, haughtier still (t'evade Disaster)
> Cries, Touch me if you can,—and not my M——r.

The fabric of misrepresentation and exaggeration built up by propaganda and given visual substance in the prints led naturally to clamour for Walpole's punishment, for comprehensive Place Bills, for 'no standing armies' and (inconsistently) for vigorous conduct of the war; it led of course to anger with the new placemen and ex-Patriots. Some of this was directed against Pulteney. But it was manifested also in a flurry of Radicalism: popular constituencies, led by London, sent instructions to their members demanding the things they had been led to expect. They ordered them to vote for the punishment of Walpole, for shorter Parliaments, against decay of trade, and also against the export of wool, and so on. These instructions are the subject of *London's Conduct stands the Test* . . . [2577] in which unresponsive M.P.s rely on 'lesser Boroughs' and are double-faced; there is a 'Ministerial Forge' where a smith is hammering out the 'Lie of the Day', articles are being prepared for 'the Gazetteer', and instruments of oppression are stored for future use: 'Tax Skrews', 'Tax Bridles', 'Law Pincers', 'Hanover Bridles', and the like. A counter-print followed on 30 November, *Bristol and Nottingham against London: or the Funeral of City Faction* [2570], more defiant than propandist, and adapted from *The Funeral of Faction*; the tomb is the same, the newspaper banners are the same. A satyr burns the London Instructions in a bonfire, Discord flies off, Walpole laughs and his supporters shout derisively, 'Impeachers ha ha', 'Instructors ha ha'.

Disillusionment was complete. It is impossible here to follow the prints on the ministerial shufflings of the next few years. These were mainly anti-ministerial, but the Opposition was not sufficiently powerful to whip up popular clamour. One development must be noted—Pitt's growing importance. He makes a first appearance among the noisy clamourers for office in *The Claims of the Broad Bottoms* [3579] dated 1 March 1743; he hopes 'to be puff'd into something by and by. . . . Am I not an Orator? Make me Secretary at War.' His public repute, the occasional breaks in the popularity that was so vital to his policy and career, are vividly illuminated. His first achievement of office in 1746, with a consequent volte-face on the Hanover question, evoked violent attacks, summarized in a ballad by Hanbury Williams, *The Unembarrassed Countenance*.

> He bellow'd and roar'd at the Troops of Hanover . . .
> That no man was honest who gave them a vote . . .
>
> But nature had given him ne'er to be Harrass'd
> An unfeeling heart, and a front unembarrass'd.

The gibes of the song are repeated in *This is the Unembarrassed Countenance or, an Irish Post Face* [2854]—Pitt had just been appointed joint Vice-Treasurer of Ireland.

A main cause of discontent was the disappointing course of the war, and the use of Hanoverian troops. Dettingen brought this to a head—the English fight, and fast—Hanoverians rest, and feast—such is the theme of two prints [2583-4] on *The H—v—n Confectioner General*, that is, Baron Ilten, general of the Hanoverians, who was accused of preventing the Guards from following up the victory. In the second, George II, as the White Horse of Hanover, rides the fainting British Lion, who complains that he is starving on 'bon pour Nicole', a bitter catch phrase connoting the contemptuous words of a Frenchman on giving bread to his horse, Nicole, while the English troops were without it. Ilten lurks behind a tree; the English pursue the French, the Hanoverians are stationary: 'We will not be commanded by ye English.' Lord Marischal, the Jacobite, sent a similar print to an unknown correspondent, saying that it was widely circulated in England. He explains allusions to 'starve donc' and 'bon pour Nicole' as things which 'vraies ou fausses, font un grand effet sur le peuple'.[1] These anti-Hanoverian prints were in effect Jacobitish propaganda—perhaps Jacobite productions.

The reactions evoked by the Forty-five are vividly illustrated, with No Popery as the leading theme, especially at first, and much is made of the supposed threat to abbey lands. *The Invasion, or Perkins Triumph* [2636] is 'a Protestant Print. Inscrib'd to all true Lovers of their Religion & Liberty', and is an adaptation of an anti-Sacheverell print of 1710, *Needs Must when the Devil Drives*. As before 'Perkin' (now Perkin II) is in the coach; as before, two of the horses are 'Passive Obedience' and 'Non-Resistance'; the others are 'Superstition', 'Rebellion', 'Hereditary Right', 'Arbitrary Power'. Perkin holds a mask, sign that his *Declaration* (in which he declared himself 'utterly averse to all persecution') is a snare. The King of France drives, with the Pope as postilion; behind, as footmen, are the Devil and two monks. A monk carries the banner of the Inquisition, another superintends the burning of a heretic. A band of Scots follow the coach with the banner of Slavery and Wooden Shoes. The coach drives over Britannia, who drops her purse and other emblems of Property, and also over personifications of Religion (with a Bible), and Law (with Magna Charta). The verses, in the *Eikon*-Sacheverell pattern, conclude:

Our Laws, Religion, Liberties, a Prey
To Gallic Fury and Tyrannic Sway,
Our Lands to dronish Monks and Fryars given,
Who make a Mammon Merchandise of Heaven,
These lively Emblems grace our Poignant Print,
If these are nothing—the Devil's in't.

A more poignant attempt to curdle Protestant blood followed in October, *The Procession, or the Popes Nursling riding in Triumph* [2658]. Perkin and the Pope are drawn in a car by asses, wolves, and tigers; Louis XV drives, shouting, 'Universal Monarchy'; the Bourbon menace is combined with ultra-Protestant propaganda at its most extreme. A Spaniard shouts, 'Gibraltar and P. Mahon is ours'; others cry, 'Tame the Proud Britons', 'The Trade of the World is ours', 'Cape Breton restor'd' (it had just been taken from France). There are many other items, and emblems of 'Popish Errors Rage and Infernal Cruelty' include 'Bulls and Indulgences Fines Tortures Excommunications Death by Fire and Sword'. All the Church lands are to be reclaimed. But in the background is a view of York Minster, with a regiment of parsons led by Archbishop Herring, who

[1] Quoted from the *Stuart Papers* (4 Nov. 1743), Mahon, *History of England*, 1858, iii, appendix, p. xiii.

has discarded mitre and robes for military dress. (On news of Prestonpans Herring had convened the county and set on foot an association of volunteers.) In a patriotic print, *The Mitred Champion: or, the Church Militant* [2634], he is dressed (like Archbishop Williams in 1642) half as soldier, half as bishop; exclaiming 'Religion! Liberty! My Country', he leads a body of armed clerics, with an officer who shouts 'King George and ye Church of England for ever'. But this was travestied in a counter-print [2635] with the words of the militant Herring altered to 'My (Mitre),[1] my Lands, My Gold, Church'. The armed clergy lack enthusiasm; one says, 'I'll be Vicar of Bray still'; another, 'I've 12 Children but no lands'. The apathy of the volunteers is illustrated in *Briton's Association Against the Pope's Bulls* [2661]. The Pretender leads from Edinburgh a herd of bulls snorting out 'Excommunications, Indulgences, Massacres, Jure Divino, Decretals'. A medallion of Henry VIII has the legend 'Ho ho abby lands again'. The print is bisected by the river Tweed, with Jacobites marching on Scottish soil. Neptune, saying 'the true Spirit of Liberty', presents Britannia with a palm of victory. Soldiers are marching north, some prepared to fight, but one says, 'I wont go out of ye Parish'; another, 'Agod I'd go five miles to fight', and the chaplain complains, 'I wish they'd go to Dinner'.

All the post-rebellion Jacobite prints—quite a number from 1746 to 1750—attack the Duke of Cumberland. In December 1746 he is *The Butcher* [Pl. 27] in a caricature 'taken from ye Sign of a Butcher in ye Butcher Row'—one of those prints of persons constructed of appropriate objects. Actually, it is adapted from a print of a butcher [2470], one of a set of such composite figures. There is a symbolical border with satyr's head, and fire-brands, in the background are blazing buildings, and the figure is given a military dress. It is constructed of an ox on its hindlegs, with the head of a calf; the body is a butcher's tray, in one hand is a cleaver, in the other a slaughterer's axe—as in the original. But on the soldier's tunic is a star and an epaulette formed of butcher's hooks (anticipating Napoleon's famous emblematical epaulette[2]). The verses, with omissions and one significant alteration, are as on the original; they end:

> His axe, Knives, Clever, is prepar'd for fight,
> And Death & Slaughter are his sole delight
> Thus arm'd he Terror all arod doth* spread
> Had he not borrow'd from a Calf his Head.
>                     (* 'would' in original.)

---

[1] Depicted.                                        [2] See *E.P.C. 1793–1832*, Pl. 57.

The favourite approach is to contrast the Duke and the Pretender. A sequence of prints and counter-prints—though which is print and which counter-print we can only guess—may begin with a loyalist one, *The agreeable Contrast between the British Hero, and the Italian Fugitive* [2832]. Cumberland and Britannia address the Pretender, who sits reading: she says, 'Vain Tool, behold here at thy Feet / Your broken Hopes and Cullodens Defeat.' A Jacobite manifesto followed (or preceded) this: *The Agreeable Contrast. Shews that a Greyhound is more agreeable than an Elephant, & a Genteel personage More agreeably Pleasing than a Clumsey one* . . . [2833]. The graceful Chevalier, who turns to admire Flora Macdonald, is accompanied by a greyhound, while Cumberland's corpulence is set off by an elephant; the Duke, who has a butcher's knife and apron, deserts 'a town trollop'.

A climax of Jacobitism is expressed in a print without date or title [2834]. The Pretender, in Highland dress, stands with a cap of Liberty beside him, behind are a tent and Scottish soldiers; a lamb stands on a wolf. Cumberland holds a bloody axe and is surrounded with emblems of savagery; the crown falls from a plant which is probably intended for a turnip, emblem of Hanover. Britannia sits between them holding a balance in which 'Mercy' outweighs 'Butchery'. Below is Hamlet's speech to the Queen, beginning, 'Look here upon this Picture and on this', abridged, and adapted to 'two Princes', instead of two brothers. Another savagely Jacobite print (in 1749) was suggested by a gift of wild animals from Maria Theresa to Cumberland. In *The Prodigal Son. or; the Brute among the Beasts; to feed Swine* [3014], Cumberland sits near a horned owl wearing a Garter ribbon, which stands on a human heart and a skull inscribed 'Col . . . .n' (Culloden). A huge goat and a boar symbolize the Duke's character; a draggled British Lion is in a cage. The food—'like my own'— that the Duke chooses for his beasts is blood. The Prince of Wales is 'y$^e$ hornified owl' (seemingly an early allusion to Bute and the Princess), the Chevalier is the 'Lyon of England' who will 'chase to y$^e$ Forest y$^e$ bloodhounds again'.

Meanwhile, the peacemakers at Aix-la-Chapelle incurred the customary dispraise. The most obnoxious proviso was for the return to France of Cape Breton, 'the people's darling acquisition', with the humiliating condition that two hostages were to be given for its surrender. Among the prints on the negotiators and the terms two stand out. *Tempora mutantur, et Nos mutamur in illis* [3015] in December 1748 is one of those bitter comparisons with the glorious past. A Frenchman points to the two hostages:

'Dis for de Glory of de Grand Monarch.' A plenipotentiary, presumably Lord Sandwich, says, 'Dam Posterity I'll get Money'; he has stabbed the British Lion and the Hanoverian Horse is licking its blood, while the Gallic Cock crows; a 'poor distressed Sailor' begs from a defeatist admiral. At these shocking sights Cromwell, Henry V, and Edward III rise from their graves to say: 'Was it for this I sought the Lord and Fought'; 'Agincourt's forgot'; 'And Creci likewise'.

The Contrast 1749 [3028] satirizes the grand display of fireworks in the Green Park to celebrate the peace. The comparison is between the disgruntled Englishman who has got 'No Money, with Fireworks', and the elated Dutchman who has 'Money, with Commerce'. They face each other, one with empty pockets and a burnt-out pavilion behind him (a casualty of the display), the other with over-full pockets and with sunlit ships in the background. The Dutchman jeers: 'Myn Heer You have been at War what have you got?' In the public mind the Dutch had been laggards in war, intent always on their seaborne trade. This traditional attitude had been vividly expressed in The Benefit of Neutrality [2665],[1] dated 26 December 1745. A cow represents Power; an Englishman tries to pull it away by the tail from a Frenchman and a Spaniard who have seized it by the horns, while an unregarded Dutchman sits quietly milking: 'A neutral Cur, who sees the Fray / Steals in and bears the Bone away.'

During the political stagnation of the mid-eighteenth century, Opposition functioned feebly under the patronage of the Prince of Wales (till his death in 1751). The prints register discontent ranging from disgruntlement to Jacobite rancour. Modish folly, connoting national decadence, was symbolized in a fashionable toy: the *pantin*, a manikin suspended on a string with movable arms and legs (a similar symbolism was given to another toy some forty years later).[2] A languidly fashionable company dangle these objects in Pantin à la Mode [3017], a print with cautionary verses: Britain aspired like Rome to excel 'in Arts and Arms', 'Till Gallic Influence / Bid Foppery rise, and turn'd the Scale of Sense'. *Folly Triumphant . . .* [3068] is a broadside in a similar vein with attacks on (alleged) imbecilities: 'Folly, playing with his *Pantin*, in his Triumphal Car, drawn by a *Butterfly*, and a *Locust*, Emblems of Pride and Poverty.' The follies include the firework display in the Green Park, the new Mansion House, Westminster Bridge with its defective arch and

---

[1] Probably the origin of an important print of 1778; see below, pp. 153–4.
[2] The bandelure or *émigrette* (the yo-yo of the twentieth century), supposed occupation of *émigrés* at Coblentz.

foreign (Swiss) architect, as well as the grand hoax of the century, the Bottle Conjuror[1] which was the subject of many prints and for at least seventy years a recurrent symbol for political humbug.

[1] An advertisement (11 Jan. 1749, *General Advertiser, &c.*) that a man would, among other marvels, get into a quart bottle at the Haymarket Theatre attracted crowds; it was a hoax by the Duke of Montagu to test public credulity. Cf. p. 148.

# V

## FROM PEACE TO WAR

WITH the sudden death of the Prince of Wales in 1751, Opposition almost ceased to exist, but in 1753 the calm was broken by one of those storms against the Ministry of the day, blown up against the Pelhams by agitation against the Act for permitting the naturalization of foreign Jews. 'No Jews, no wooden shoes', was the slogan. Bishops who had voted for the Bill were assailed as Deists, and, with its other supporters, alleged to have been heavily bribed. The many prints on this burning question display the facets of a peculiarly crude manifestation of anti-semitism. A general election was imminent, and the Act, passed in June, was repealed in December. In *Vox Populi Vox Dei, or the Jew Act Repealed* [3202] Christianity is menaced by a 'Mob of Jews & Deists', and by a bishop who holds a bribe of £1,000. The verses begin, 'God's Word declares the Jews a Vagrant race.' On the eve of the election Henry Pelham died: in *His Arrival at his Country Retirement & Reception* [3264] he enters Hell, greeted by predecessors and demons; his crimes, and above all the Jew Act, are greater than those of the other villains: Walpole, Wolsey, Judge Jeffreys, and Machiavelli.

The Jew Act and its slogans echoed through the elections, and even cost some candidates their seats, notoriously in London and Oxfordshire (as the prints record). But ministerial influence was of course all-powerful, and in *The Compleat Vermin-catcher of G— B—n, or the old Trap new baited* [3269], published at the beginning of the elections in April 1754, Newcastle, who had succeeded his brother, fishes down the chimney of the House of Commons; his line is baited with 'Titles, Bribes, Places, Pensions, Secret Commissions, Army, Navy, Excise'. Eager aspirants hasten from all quarters.

Impending war, after the uneasy peace, soon dominated the scene. In *The Grand Monarque in a Fright; or, the British Lion roused from his Lethargy* [3284], dated 4 April 1755, it is clear that this is an American crisis, with the Ohio Valley in dispute, and that the West and East Indies are involved. Newcastle feebly listens to the blandishments of the Governor of Canada, de la Jonquière, who begs him to drug and pacify the awaking Lion. Louis is double-faced, making apparent concessions while ordering his Minister to use the chain of forts on the Ohio to drive off the Lion. Verses begin: 'France trembles at the British Lion's Roar / And Lewis' treach'rus Wiles deceive no more.' In June competition for the Ohio Valley is again the theme of *The American Moose-Deer, or away to the River Ohio* [3280].

Eve-of-war hostilities are the subject of a pair of prints by Boitard (a Frenchman), *British Rights maintained; or French Ambition dismantled* [3331] and *British Resentment, or the French fairly coopt in Louisbourg* [3332], one published in August, the other in September, and both reflecting the premature rejoicings and exaggerated hopes caused by the small engagement off Newfoundland under Boscawen. In both, Mars and Neptune aid Britain and the Lion worsts the Cock. In the first Britannia holds the staff and cap of Liberty; her Lion plants its paws on feathers stripped from the Cock, and these include Ohio and Quebec. The 'Genius of France' laments: 'Ave Maria que ferons nous! after our Massacres, and Persecutions, Must Heretics possess this promis'd Land. . . .'A falling star is inscribed 'Universal Monarchy—ha! ha! ha'. In the second, Britannia, listening to 'the complaints of her injured Americans, receives them into her protection': two noble savages kneel at her feet. The Cock disgorges French positions including Niagara, Crown Point, and Ohio, but not Quebec. A dismayed Frenchman watches a canon inscribed with 'Cromwell's Device'.

In *Half-Peace* [3334] and *Half-War* [3335] published in November the note has altered. In one, while France is eager to fight, an Englishman relies on treaties, and his sword is padlocked by the Hanoverian Horse. In the other, an Englishman tries to snatch Nova Scotia from a Frenchman who threatens to retaliate in Germany. Backwardness in fighting the French in America is the theme of *Oliver Cromwell's Ghost* [3340]. His portrait heads a broadside in which his spirit protests to the dithering Ministry and recites the exploits of Admiral Blake.

With the formal declaration of war on 18 May 1756 and the disasters that followed there was a swelling demand for the dismissal of the Ministry and the appointment of Pitt, embodiment of the discontents, antipathies, and aspirations of the country. In the crescendo of indignation prints multiplied as never before—they are literally to be counted in hundreds. The new development of 'cards' began in the summer, and George Townshend embarked on a campaign of 'caricaturas' published by Darly, a joint enterprise against the Ministry.[1] The political rebus—the pictograph

[1] See pp. 115–17.

letter—sprang into popularity, a device for combining the lampoon, the print, and the puzzle. The main themes are a corrupt, treacherous, and inept Ministry, the loss of Minorca, the employment in England of two regiments of mercenaries—Hessians and Hanoverians—instead of a national militia, the poisonous effects of French luxuries: 'A vain, luxurious and selfish EFFEMINACY' was the chief cause, according to 'Estimate Brown', of national degeneracy and misfortunes, in the book that went through seven editions in 1757.[1]

Ministers were caricatured, sometimes as animals—Henry Fox almost always with a fox's head and brush denoting craftiness—Newcastle was often a goose or an old woman, sometimes an ass, the dupe of Fox, and misled by his own sinister and all-powerful secretary, Andrew Stone. The first of the 'cards' is *The Pillars of the State* [Pl. 28a] by Townshend. Newcastle and Fox face each other, both wearing fleur-de-lis badges; behind each is a gallows and from this pair of 'pillars' hangs a chain supporting an inverted ship with the Gallic Cock crowing on its keel; 'Gallus so near' is a punning allusion to their French predilections and their coming fate. A favourite quotation from the *Beggar's Opera*, in a seemingly first appearance—'Brother Brother; we are both in the Wrong'—shows that they are a pair of thieves. Ministers were also the Knaves of a pack of cards; Newcastle, Spades, is *Mons$^r$ Dupe* [3504]; Fox, Hearts, is *Mons$^r$ Surecard* [3506], cunning and subtle; fleurs-de-lis grow at the feet of both. Anson, the gambler, is Diamonds, with a die in his hand [3535]; and Hardwicke, the Chancellor, is Clubs, *Null Marriage* [3522] with a bag of French gold, and pilloried also for his Marriage Act (which stopped some notorious abuses from irregular and unlicensed marriages). In the same series of prints he was also *The Vulture* [3502], preying on the vitals of the nation, an enemy of Liberty, Loyalty, and Justice. But Anson and Hardwicke are subsidiary villains, far less frequently attacked than Fox and Newcastle—the main theme of the cards is condemnation of these two as knave and fool [Pl. 28b], or fox and goose.

The national anger expressed in these and very many other prints went deeper than the inflated fury against Walpole, and this is recognized in *Poor Robin's Prophecy* [3383]. Sir Robert's apparition terrifies the timid Newcastle in one of the many rebuses. His words are in 'Hieroglyphick Characters' and in verse which ends 'When things are so bad that they can't be well worse / You'll wish for poor Robin who so oft you did Curse'. The comment, added in 1757, 'A Remonstrance of a deceased

[1] *An Estimate of the Manners and Principles of the Times*, 1757.

Minister to a People whose Complaints were rather numerous than well founded.' Another 'Hieroglyphick' (rebus) is *Oliver Cromwells Speach to the Ass & Fox 1756* [3508], an item in the Cromwell legend:

Those men that love their King & Country should not let Knaves or Fools govern, but let the Axe & Halter reward their maleadministration. Suffer not the French to frighten you, but arm your Militia, let them be your defence and be to 'em as I was. . . . I made them fear and the Dutch too. Liberty was then secur'd and no treason traitors suffer'd to rule. . . . I was a great Rogue to be sure but I had a head for it. You are such silly monkeys that you can not slip your necks out of the noose. . . .

*Hengist & Horsa* [3346], title of one of Darly's cards, repeats the names given to the two regiments of mercenaries, Hessians and Hanoverians, imported as a defence against France. They reflect the blackest suspicions against Ministers, who were thought to have raised this 'standing army' as a protection for themselves against national indignation. Hence the unusual excursion into fifth-century history for a parallel in the Saxon invaders who came to aid the Britons and stayed to pillage and conquer. Ministers watch their victim, the weeping Britannia, threatened by two German soldiers: 'These Foreign Friends will bleed me to death Oh! my Country. . . .' The popular demand was for a national militia as a 'constitutional' force which would be a protection against a standing army.

Between June 1756 and the following March, when he was executed, Byng is the subject of over fifty prints, almost all savagely abusive. Squibs, lampoons, and ballads abounded, and were collected into a volume of *Bungiana*. A popular street ballad is typical:

> Draw nigh, my good folks, whilst to you I sing,
> Great Blakeney betrayed by Newcastle and Byng.
> Before, such a story ne'er has been told;
> We're bought all my friends, by shining French gold.
> > To the block with Newcastle, and the yard arm with Byng
> > Tar a rara ra ra ra ra ra ra ras ring.

Newcastle, trembling for himself, did his best to concentrate anger on the Admiral and pressed for his immediate trial and execution. Opposition groups at once began to blame Ministers and were eager to prove Byng's guilt in order to discredit them for his appointment. Mass emotions were stirred and placards were posted in London 'Hang Byng or look to your King'. Most of the prints are concerned with the joint guilt of Ministers and Admiral. The former were accused of selling Minorca to the French, as in a rebus, *A Letter from an Auctioneer in Town to his Friend in the Country*

[3356]; other places will soon be cheaply disposed of; by exception Byng is not mentioned. *Byng Return'd; or the Council of Expedients* [3367] is an indictment ranging over a variety of subjects: guilt is fixed on the Ministry in four historical pictures of betrayals to France. Besides 'Portmahon' (Minorca) are 'Boulogne betray'd by the E. of Warwick in the Reign of Edward the 6th' (at the peace of 1550), 'Calais betray'd by the Council in the Reign of Queen Mary', 'Dunkirk sold by the Council in the Reign of Cha$^s$ the 2$^d$'. Sovereigns are ostentatiously exempted from blame and this corresponds to the seeming popularity with cartoonists of George II, despite Pitt's alliance with Leicester House and the Princess Dowager. One of Darly's cards is *Optimus* [3537], the King's head crowned with laurel, with the inscription 'Britons behold the best of Kings'.

Accusations of luxury—peculiarly applicable to Newcastle with his extravagance and his famous and indispensable cook—were no mere garnish to the more concrete crimes: it was alleged that Ministers were reluctant to resist France for fear of being cut off from French imports. In *Birdlime for Bunglers, or the French way of Catching Fools* [3434] a Frenchman scatters bait for Ministers to scramble for, money and tickets inscribed 'Cooks, Valets, Dancers, Fiddlers', while he holds 'bird cages', that is, scourges and wooden shoes. Newcastle has a bag of '8,000,000', a sum often repeated in the prints and connoting money 'well nigh sunk the last year and not any material service done the Kingdom, but loading the Nation with heavy Taxes' [3479]. Anson, the ruined gambler, rushes forward, tied to an E. O. (roulette) table which he overturns, and Byng lies crushed under the avidly competing Ministers. Irreligion and frivolity in high places are stressed in an emblematical print foretelling national ruin, *Britannia in Distress under a Tott'ring Fabrick with a Cumberous Load* [Pl. 30], an elaborate indictment of Ministers. These 'Degenerate Britons' pull down the Pillars of the State, a fabric already breaking under a burden of pensioned parasites; the ropes they use are 'Minorca Lost, America Neglected, Trade not Protected'. 'Manufacturers in the Dumps' are seated on the ground.

These and very many more prints of the summer and autumn merge with those of the autumn and winter illustrating the growing inevitability of Pitt's appointment, as first Fox and then Newcastle resigned and Pitt would agree to no coalition with either. In *The Fox in the Pit* [3399], Fox, a fox carrying a goose inscribed '8,000,000', has been chased into a pit by a man on a horse inscribed 'Integrity', who shouts 'Justice'; the goose cries, 'I'm in Tophet.' The pit was 'designed by Nature to destroy every thing of a crafty or subtle disposition'. A generation later the same play on words was used for the sons of Pitt and Fox. Pitt's career introduces a new conception to graphic satire—the Patriot Minister.

Tributes to Pitt soon gave way to satires on the confusion that followed his dismissal in April. Byng had been sacrificed,[1] despite Pitt's support for a motion that the verdict should be laid before the House. The chief bugbears in this interregnum were Fox and Cumberland. It may be noted here that no one goes through such violent alternations of favour and disfavour as Cumberland, and no one but Bute is more consistently dispraised than Fox. A famous print after Townshend appeared in April, deriding Fox's attempt to form a Ministry, *The Recruiting Serjeant, or Brittanniais Happy Prospect* [3581]. Fox calls for 'Gentlemen Voluntiers willing to serve under Military Government'; his drummer boy is Welbore Ellis (called by Horace Walpole Fox's jackal). The recruits are Lord Sandwich with a cricket bat, the fat Bubb Dodington in a coat patterned with fleurs-de-lis, and Lord Winchilsea carrying a rudder.[2] The grotesque patron of this group is Cumberland, posturing absurdly in a little temple topped by the Hanoverian Horse which tramples on Britannia. He had precipitated Pitt's fall by refusing to accept the command in Hanover while he was Minister.

Fox's intrigues are the subject of *Guy Vaux the 2ᵈ* [Pl. 29 a] (16 December 1756) where a fox advances conspiratorially on the House of Commons; this is an adaptation from the *Double Deliveraunce* of 1621, an anticipation of 'Guy Vaux' prints of his son Charles a generation later. Charles Fox, one of the most caricatured of English politicians, made his first appearance in 1757, aged eight, in two prints: his father had secured for his sons a reversion to a lucrative sinecure held by Bubb Dodington. In *The Sturdy Beggar* [Pl. 29 b], Stephen, the elder fox-cub, asks, 'Daddy won't he die soon, Sir', And Charles adds, 'He's too fat to live long.' Oddly prophetic is *The Bawd of the Nation or the Way to Grow Rich* [3636], in which Fox, while distributing honours to the grief of Honour (personified), encourages his children in reckless extravagance: Stephen pours money through a gridiron, while Charles begs 'Let me try'.

[1] Byng's monument in the church of Southill is inscribed: 'To the perpetual Disgrace of Publick Justice, The Honourable John Byng, Esq. Admiral of the Blue, Fell a Martyr to political Persecution, March 14, in the Year, 1757, when Bravery and Loyalty were insufficient Securities for the Life and Honour of a Naval Officer.' Transcribed by Boswell, *Life of Johnson*, Oxford, i, 1934, p. 315.

[2] It is a strange fact that two of these figures, Winchilsea and Dodington, are apparently copied from drawings by Hogarth in the manuscript of *The Analysis of Beauty* published 1753, which seems to decide the question of priority.

During the negotiations behind the scenes while gold boxes were raining
upon Pitt there were by exception one or two anti-Pitt satires. One made a
sensation; it is interesting as an example of the political print inspired by a
leading actor in the drama and intended to influence events; and remarkable too for its inside knowledge and its insolence. This is *The Treaty or
Shabears[1] Administration* [3608] published on 1 June. Newcastle sits on a
turnstile, one of whose four arms is tied to a table on which is a royal crown.
Pitt and Temple ('Gawkee') bow obsequiously to the Duke, while Bute
attitudinizes; standing behind is a young man wearing a Garter ribbon.
The point is made clear in the verses:

> See Gawkee & P——t how they Sue for a place,
> See, perch'd on a turnstile his unsteady Grace, . . .
> See a blue ribbon'd, silly, proud, son of a W——e,
> See a strutting Scotch Peer, of whom I could say more.
> Then see in the corner a strong hempen string
> That Shall hang the Vile D— if he leave his good K—.

In later states of the print an attempt was made to show that the young
man—clearly the Prince of Wales—was Newcastle's nephew Lord Lincoln.
'I enclose a most extraordinary print', Walpole wrote to Mann. 'Mr. Fox
has found a caricaturist equal to George Townshend, and who manages
royal personages with at least as little ceremony.'[2] The facts behind the
print were that Bute was taking the chief part in the difficult task of bringing Newcastle and Pitt together, playing on the Duke's dread of a Fox–
Cumberland coalition and his desire to be on terms with the future—that
is to be *persona grata* at Leicester House. The imputation against the
Prince's mother reflects the rumour—indeed belief—that Bute was her
lover; admittedly there was no evidence for this, it was assumed in order
to explain his favour at Leicester House.[3] The scandal was to be inflated
and exploited to a monstrous degree.

Another Foxite print was an attempt to ridicule the presentation of the
Freedom of the City to Pitt and Legge; in *Will Quixote and his Squire
going in triumph to the City* [3598] they drive together like mountebanks
in an ornate and canopied coach; the scene is the Strand with Temple Bar
in the distance. A bystander says, 'No, by G—d, wee are glad you are out.'
It is a strange coincidence that in a Foxite print of 1784 the younger Pitt

---

[1] John Shebbeare, a pamphleteer and hack partisan who 'made a pious resolution of writing
himself into a place or the pillory'. *Walpole Letters*, ed. Toynbee, iv. 26.

[2] *Letters*, ed. Toynbee, Oxford, iv. 58 (June 1757).

[3] *Letters from George III to Lord Bute, 1756–1766*, ed. R. Sedgwick, 1939, show that it was
not the Princess but her son who was infatuated with the tutor.

was caricatured making a mock-triumphal procession to receive the Freedom of the City in another gold box.

During the great coalition polemical caricature slackened, with the two chief *bêtes noires*, Newcastle and Fox, protected by Pitt's prestige, and in the years of victory it almost ceased. But not at first. Despondency verging on despair was the climate of 1757. The prevailing mood on the eve of Pitt's appointment is well summarized in a print called *Without* [3605]; twelve little scenes of national and ministerial sins and shortcomings have captions with a blank to be filled with the word 'Without'. A king obscured by clouds is 'Supreme Majesty [Without] Power' (a good illustration of the popular view of the 'Glorious Constitution'). Others are 'Bishops [Without] Religion', 'Commanders [Without] Abilities', 'Colonies [Without] Protection'. Ships and armies are idle, trade languishes, the poor starve. 'We are no longer a nation', wrote Chesterfield on 4 July, 'I never yet saw so dreadful a prospect.' And this was before Cumberland's German fiasco, for which he was pilloried by (among others) Townshend, his former aide-de-camp: as *The Terror of France 1757* [3610] he runs from Marshal d'Estrées across the Weser, crying, 'Oh for my Recruiting Serjeant [Fox] with more men and money.' In the mock procession of *The Triumph of Cæsar* [3615] he has ruined Prussia and destroyed British interests in America, all for the sake of Hanover and to the treasonous delight of Newcastle and Fox.

In the autumn there was another failure, the return of General Mordaunt from the expedition to Rochefort. This disappointment of high hopes is expressed in *Change of Diet. A Ballad: being a Sequel to the Roast Beef of Old England* [3628]; the verses are illustrated by a kitchen interior, with a French cook gorging on beef and an Englishman spitting out frogs. 'Rule Britannia' burns in the grate and a picture of a frog and an ox is inscribed, 'Sic transit Britanniæ Gloria'. The refrain is 'O! le Soupe maigre de Fransa / O! de French Fricassees & Ragout.' Mordaunt is blamed, and there is another contrast between past and present:

> When our Edwards & Henries sate on the Throne,
> The Grand Monarque trembled, whene'er they did frown;
> As Agincourt, Poictiers & Cressy must own.

This expresses a basic sentiment, characteristic of a time when Fielding's 'Roast Beef of Old England'[1] was a sort of national anthem, sung in the gallery between the acts of the play. It should be compared with Hogarth's

---

[1] In *The Grub Street Opera*, 1731.

two invasion prints of the same year. A similar shocking reversal of the Englishman's rights and privileges was depicted in 1801 [9714]. The *mystique* of roast beef is strikingly illustrated in caricatures, but usually in a vein of anti-Gallican complacency.

Among the many attacks on General Mordaunt and the Duke there was one savage thrust at Pitt, a bitter sequel to *Will Quixote and His Squire*, and presumably Foxite propaganda. This is *England's Benifit Night Or Pyt & Boxes put Together* [3640]. A Frenchman obsequiously presents Pitt with the Freedom of Rochefort, another does the same to Legge; and both promise their best endeavours in the service of France. The British Lion growls, 'Oh! how I am Decieved by Those Two false Prophets Curst, Damn'd & Decietfull men my Eyes are now Open'd.'

Blame for British generals was soon succeeded by praise for Prussian victories and the glorification of Frederick as the Protestant hero. In *The Difference* [3671], dated 1758, Prussian victories are contrasted with British humiliation; the cap of Liberty crowned with laurel has been transported to Prussia. Frederick taunts a degraded Britannia with failure at Rochefort, while England is given up to 'Mammon'. Once again 'heros defunct' rise from the grave to record their indignation—they are Raleigh, Cromwell, and Drake.

There are also a few prints on the situation in Europe not primarily concerned with English politics. *The Cricket Players of Europe*, June 1757 [2506, 3591], is the first cricket field cartoon—there are not many. Maria Theresa bowls, Frederick of Prussia bats, Louis XV prepares to catch him out; the 'She Bear', a fat Empress Elizabeth, rushes towards Maria Theresa, saying, '. . . if you are tired I will bowl for you.' Turkey as well as other European powers, not all easy to identify, have their roles. The umpires (both dishonest) are Spain and Holland, the latter as usual a self-regarding neutral, and the issue is highly doubtful. One of the many 'Balance' prints shows the outcome; in *The Ballance turnd: or the Russian Cat-arse-trophy* [3675] dated October 1758, the Kings of Prussia and England—'Value against Number'—completely outweigh a scale overcrowded with 'The Unnatural Confederates', despite the furtive attempts of Holland to pull it down; the King of Poland and the Tsarina are falling. This is a tribute to Frederick's defeat of the Russians at Zorndorf in August.

Victory in Europe is the subject of *The Court Cards of 1759, or Hearts is Trump & has Won the Game* [3699]. The twelve cards are in two lines, red above, black below. George II, 'Optimus' as before, is King of Hearts,

saying to his Knave, Pitt, ' I've won the Game My Dear Will & care not an
Ace for Europe.' Pitt, who holds the cap of Liberty on a staff, answers,
' My Liege You've Hearts enough left yet for another Rubber.' The Queen
of Hearts is Britannia; King, Queen, and Knave of Diamonds are Frederick II, the City of London, and Ferdinand of Brunswick. The black suits,
France, Austria, Poland, admit that they are beaten. The Knave of Spades
is Holland: 'I never play but I cheat.' The Knave of Clubs, Marshal de
Belleisle, says, 'We can play no more I've no more Cards or Counters.' He
was taken prisoner at Minden.

This is the only good-humoured allusion to the battle. There are many
Minden prints, all concerned with the failure of Lord George Sackville
(afterwards Germain), in command of the British cavalry, to obey the
order to charge. It was the situation at Dettingen in reverse, and another
example of the unfortunate consequences of Anglo-Hanoverian jealousies.
The clamour against Sackville recalled that against Byng, but was less bedevilled with politics (in fact he was protected by the Court). In *The
Cowardly Soldier, & the Runaway Ghost* [3687] he and Byng's ghost meet
on the field of Minden. In later prints in which Germain appears, and
there are many, he is never mentioned without some cruel allusion to the
battle.

For the moment the topic was thrust aside by more resounding victories.
On 16 October news reached London of the capture of Quebec. Then came
Hawke's victory at Quiberon Bay on 20 November, celebrated in (for instance) *Britons Glory, or Admiral Hawke Triumphant* [3688]. *The Grand
Fair at Versaile, or France in a Consternation* [3679] illustrates in seven
little scenes a French squib on both calamities : the deeds of Joan of Arc
are contrasted with the fatal influence of Mme de Pompadour. The squib
is engraved below: 'Batteaux plats à vendre / Soldats à louer / Ministre
à pendre / Generaux à rouer / O France! la Sexe Femelle / Fit toujours ton
destinée / Ton bonheur vint d'une Pucelle, / Ton Malheur vient d'une
Catin.' Horace Walpole supplied an English version—the last two lines:

> O France! still your fate you may lay at Pitt's door;
> You were sav'd by a Maid, and undone by a ——.[1]

The situation in Europe is the subject of *1760* [3745], a confused survey
in which Frederick controls the Russian Bear, Maria Theresa falls, saying,
'I have crackt my Crown . . .', France begs Spain for aid and the British
Lion insults the Gallic Cock. This was explained as indicating 'the com-

---

[1] *Letters*, ed. Toynbee, Oxford, iv. 305.

mon Humbugg of confederate Nations, who having almost exhausted their
Blood and Treasure in the support of a destructive War, are yet resolved
to persist, tho' they expose their Shame and Weakness to their very enemies'. Thus the reign ended in a blaze of glory, with Pitt at the zenith of
his reputation.

# VI

## HOGARTH AND ENGLISH CARICATURE—
## MID-CENTURY DEVELOPMENTS

ONLY in the last three decades of the century was the transformation from the emblematical print to the political caricature complete. The engraving, complicated and sometimes cryptic, seldom comic, conceived in black and white and heavily cross-hatched, had been succeeded by a bold design, immediately striking to the eye, intended (usually) to amuse, and sold plain or coloured but commonly coloured. But important progress towards this development was made in the mid-century. The changes are associated, first with Hogarth, who has been called the father of English caricature (paradoxical as this seems for one who disparaged caricature). Secondly, with the amateur, who introduced the Italian art of *caricatura*. Thirdly, there was the enterprise of print-sellers who took advantage of political turmoil and amateur talent. There were also some interesting developments of imagery.

Hogarth's influence was fundamental. In his own satirical and humorous masterpieces he painted and then engraved—to use his own words—'the customs, manners, fashions, characters and Humours of the present age'.[1] These great sequences raised the standards of engraving and the prestige of the print; they were raised also by 'Hogarth's Act', the Act he obtained in 1735 for securing to engravers copyright in their designs and protecting them from victimization by print-sellers. Despite loopholes, this revolutionized the status of the engraver and was to the ultimate advantage of the print-seller, since prints became an important British export.

The impact of personal caricature, introduced from Italy, at first as a fashionable art practised by the virtuosi and their friends, was not welcomed by Hogarth—adversary of connoisseurs. Arthur Pond, virtuoso, artist, and picture dealer, etched twenty-five caricature portraits after Ghezzi and others from 1736 to 1747. And in 1743 Hogarth published his *Characters & Caricaturas* [2591], 'Being perpetually plagued from the mistakes made among the illiterate by the similarities in the sound of the words. . . .' (Here one remembers that in 1732 Hogarth had 'made a

---

[1] Joseph Burke, *William Hogarth. The Analysis of Beauty*, Oxford, 1955, p. 208.

Characateur' of a Billingsgate porter.[1]) 'Caricatura' is represented by
heads by Ghezzi, Annibale Caracci, and Leonardo, all copied from etchings by Pond. For 'Character' Hogarth copied heads from Raphael's cartoons and from his own *Marriage à la Mode*. 'For a further explanation of
the Difference', he inscribed on the plate, 'See ye Preface to Joh Andrews.'
Here Fielding had distinguished between the 'comic history painting' of
his friend Hogarth, whose true excellence consisted in 'the exactest copying of nature', and caricatura, with 'all distortions and exaggerations . . .
within its proper province'. The distinction was vital to Hogarth, disparaged by jealous rivals—'the whole nest of phiz-mongers'—who had
taught their friends to run down his men's portraits as 'charicatures'. And
his expressive realism was not to be confounded with the crudities of
caricaturists. His own 'manner of designing' he called 'the Comic and
Moral'.

But caricature and the burlesque were destined to transform the
emblematical print, and here the amateur made his contribution with
drawing that was incorrect and expressive, an art superbly practised by
Max Beerbohm. It was an amateur, George Townshend, afterwards Mar-
quis, who in 1756 introduced caricature into political satires (though
there had been earlier approaches to this); his vein was ribaldry and
buffoonery. It was natural that Hogarth, both as craftsman and artist,
should think little of such productions.

The print-sellers (in 1756) used the words 'Character' and 'Caricatura'
indiscriminately for collections of prints by Townshend and others, and
in 1758 Hogarth returned to the distinction with *The Bench* [3662]. He
elaborated his thesis in a long inscription which begins, 'There are hardly
any two things more essentially different. . . .' His own comment on this
print was, 'I have ever considered the knowledge of character, either high
or low, to be the most sublime part of the art of painting or sculpture, and
caricatura as the lowest; indeed as much so as the wild attempts of children—yet so it is, that the two words from being similar in sound are often
confounded.'[2] (It would seem rather that no firm line can be drawn
between the two, his own *Portrait of John Wilkes Esquire* [Pl. 36]
might be taken as a superb example of either: Hogarth called it 'The
Monster Caricatura that so sorely gall'd . . . the Heaven born Wilkes'.)
An ironical dedication of a later state of *The Bench* to the 'Honble Coll.

[1] *Hogarth's Peregrination*, ed. Charles Mitchell, Oxford, 1952, p. 3.
[2] Quoted, Nichols, *Anecdotes of William Hogarth*, 1833, pp. 66–67. See J. Burke, *William Hogarth. The Analysis of Beauty*, Oxford, 1955, pp. li–lii.

T . . . s . . . d' implies contempt, or perhaps resentment for plates attacking himself, attributed (doubtfully) to Townshend.

Hogarth practised most of the categories into which the satiric prints of his day can be classed, and gave an impetus to the comic in doing so. These prints are a small part of his *œuvre* but important in the development of English graphic satire. The well-established form of burlesque heraldry is assimilated to caricature in *The Undertakers Arms, or a Consultation of Physicians* [2299], in 1736, a satire on notorious quacks (with portraits) and on the medical profession. The travesty of the picture was to be brilliantly applied to politics by Gillray: Hogarth introduced the genre in England in 1725 with his parody [1764] of Kent's altar-piece in St. Clement Danes, where it had been violently attacked as a Jacobite manifesto: 'a popish paultry Piece of Trumpery' containing a portrait of 'the wife of the Pensioner of the Whore of Babylon'.[1] He ridicules both the protest and his enemy Kent in his elaborate joke: 'Tis not the Pretender's Wife and Children as some weak bretheren imagine . . . Nor St Cecilia as the Connoisseurs believe, but a Choir of Angells playing in Consort.' And in his *Paul before Felix* [3173], in 1751, 'Designed in the rediculous Manber of Rembrant', he burlesqued the Dutch masters and parodied his own attempt at the grand manner, the *Paul before Felix* painted for Lincoln's Inn Hall. *The five Orders of Perriwigs* . . . [3812] in 1761 was a satire on 'Athenian' Stuart's forthcoming *Antiquities of Athens Measured and Delineated* . . ., and ridicules antiquarians and their learned and costly publications, the heads ranging from portraits (a flattering one of the Queen) to caricature. What an admirable example of the emblematical print and the *singerie* is *The Tailpiece to the Artist's Catalogue* [3809] with the affected ape-connoisseur watering the dead work of the dead masters.

These jokes are not political. Until *The Times* in 1762 his political plates were scarcely polemical. The emblematical South Sea prints of 1721 are more the work of a moralist than a politician; the same could be said of the hieroglyphical fantasy of 1724. After 1724 none of his prints conforms to the anti-ministerial convention. On the contrary. After the appearance of *The Rake's Progress*[2] in 1735, Hogarth was pressed 'by the Patriots in Opposition to Sir Robert Walpole to design a series of prints, to be intitled *The Statesman's Progress*, but he, scorning to prostitute his art to the purposes of faction, rejected their offer.'[3] Horace Walpole in his *Anec-*

---

[1] *A Letter from a Parishioner . . . to the . . . Bishop of London*, 1725.

[2] Here Hogarth seems to have given birth to a phrase: *The Oxford Dictionary of Quotations* attributes 'rake's progress' to Thackeray (*Pendennis*).

[3] Hawkins, *Life of Johnson*, 1787, p. 500 n. Cf. p. 83.

*dotes of Painting* calls this 'a very lucrative offer that was made to engage him in a set of prints against the head of a Court party'. He refused. In 1735 he had expressed his gratitude for Hogarth's Act in an emblematical tribute to the British Constitution: he published the plate of a royal crown irradiating a group of coronets, mitres, the bag of the Great Seal, the mace, the Speaker's hat, &c., with the Act itself and a long inscription beginning, 'In humble and grateful Acknowledgement of the Grace and Goodness of the Legislature. . . .' Hogarth was exceptional (in 1735) in being 'a warm partisan of George II'.[1] The story of the King's displeasure at the artist's treatment of his Guards in *The March to Finchley* is probably apocryphal.[2]

The classic expression of the time-honoured John Bullish contrast between English beef and liberty, and French *soupe-maigre* and slavery, is *The Gate of Calais. O the Roast Beef of Old England* [3050], with political allusions in the refugee Highlander and the degraded Irishman in the French service. 'To sum up all', he wrote, 'poverty, slavery, and innate insolence, covered with an affectation of politeness, give you even here a true picture of the manners of the whole nation.' Caricature intrudes on character in the persons of the fat friar and the lean cook: 'I meant to display to my own countrymen the striking difference between the food, priests, soldiers etc. of the two nations. . . .' This was in 1749, and reflects feelings roused by 1745. The contrast was given a more direct political application in 1756: the two plates of *The Invasion* [3446, 3454] are the antithesis of the voluble pessimism and defeatism of that year. Hogarth advertised them in March and again in September (in the full spate of anti-Byng satires): 'Two prints desin'd and etch'd by William Hogarth. One representing the preparations on the French Coast for an intended Invasion, the other, a View of the Preparations making in England in order to oppose the wicked Design of our Enemies: Proper to be stuck up in publick places, both in Town and Country, at this juncture'—and we may be sure they were stuck up, and at other junctures—in 1759, before Quiberon, for instance. In one there is a sledge-load of Popish furniture ('trumpery'): instruments of torture, gibbet, &c., a figure of 'St. Antoni' and a 'Plan pour un Monastere dans Black Friars à Londres'. An officer roasts frogs spitted on his sword, pointing to a flag: 'Vengeance et le Bon Bier et Bon Beuf de Angleterre.' In the other [Pl. 31], British soldiers and a sailor amuse themselves in a carefree way outside an inn while a sergeant measures a recruit; one of them is drawing on the wall a caricature of the

---

[1] Boswell, *Life of Johnson*, Oxford, 1934, i. 146.
[2] R. B. Becket, *Hogarth*, 1949, p. 18.

French King holding sword and gibbet. The inscriptions are the quint-
essence of the patriotism of the day: lines from James Thomson's *Rule
Britannia*, and a young fifer playing 'God save Great George our King'
(then a novelty): verses by Garrick end:

> Britons to arms! and let em come, . . .
> No Power can stand the deadly Stroke
> That's given from Hands & Hearts of Oak
> With Liberty to back em.

This is in the vein of patriotic prints of 1803: it was as much opposed
to the political satires of 1756 as *The Times* was to those of 1762. More
could not be said.

The well-known *Beer Street* [3126] and *Gin Lane* [3136] in 1751 were
political in the sense that they were produced to support a ministerial
measure against the unlimited sale of gin (which was in fact a turning-
point), while other prints attacked the Act as they did that of 1736. 'Bear
St and Gin Lane were done when the dredfull consequences of gin drinking was at its height', he wrote in his Autobiographical Notes. The four
prints of *The Election* are a generalized satire on election brutality and
corruption, in which both sides are involved—no longer Whig and Tory
but 'Old Interest' and 'New Interest'. Money is poured out from the
Treasury, it is true, but that was a commonplace. The series is seemingly
a protest not only against the conduct of elections, but against senseless
party rancour and meaningless slogans, a theme that underlies some of his
other prints. That the intention was not anti-ministerial is shown also by
the dedications, the first (in 1755) to the hated Henry Fox. Hogarth's political prints of 1762–3 and the imbroglio with Wilkes are part of the history
of the time, to be considered in their context.

The acknowledged share of the amateur in the cartoon began in 1756[1]—
the joint enterprise of George Townshend, Matthew Darly (who was
artist, print-seller, drawing-master, and designer of *chinoiserie* decorations
and furniture), and his wife Mary, also an artist and a print-seller. She
taught etching and caricature, and in 1763 published a little guide to the
art (engraved by herself),[2] in which she included examples of the work of
her pupils and clients, among whom was Townshend. At first in partner-
ship with one Edwards, Mat Darly began in August 1756 to publish a new

[1] A reference to Townshend in the *Public Advertiser*, 5 June 1765, may imply that he was
credited with *The Motion* (see p. 90). At that time he was only 18, but there is something in the
design which suggests that it may have been based on a drawing by him; especially in view of
the close association of Walpoles and Townshends. George Townshend's step-grandmother was
Walpole's favourite sister. [2] Copy in B.M. Print Room.

form of political print; this was the 'card', a small design about 2½ by 4 inches on pasteboard, convenient for sending by post in the manner of a picture postcard. Cards were sold at 6d., and had a great vogue; sometimes they were original designs, sometimes reduced versions of larger prints. The size made them relatively free from over-elaboration and they were generally humorous. They began as part of the campaign against Newcastle and Fox. Horace Walpole attributed the invention to George Townshend, who certainly designed the first of the series: 'A new species of this manufacture [satiric prints] now first appeared, invented by George Townshend; they were caricaturas on cards. The original one, which had amazing vent, was of Newcastle and Fox, looking at each other, and crying, with Peachum in the *Beggar's Opera*, 'Brother, Brother we are both in the wrong'.[1] Townshend's etching for this is in Mary Darly's book. Elaborated as *The Pillars of the State* [Pl. 28 a] it begins the series. A comparison with the 'Pillars of the State' in *Britannia in Distress* [Pl. 30] spotlights the contrast between the old school and the new.

The Darlys gave a longer life to the cards by reprinting them in little volumes as *A Political & Satyrical History* . . . first, of the years 1756–7 and then in a succession of books of which there was a bewildering number of editions and volumes up to 1766, as well as imitations and piracies (one called *England's Remembrancer*) by other publishers. In this way many prints circulated in a number of versions: in their original form (either a large print or a card or sometimes both), in one of Darly's volumes with added comments (reprinted with additions from year to year) and again in a rival series. In these books the term caricature for political print became established. At first, in 1756, caricatura was used for the person depicted, almost at once for the print itself, and caricature very soon replaced caricatura.

The work of the amateur was essential to the enterprise—a source of prestige and inside information as well as of pupils. A volume for 1756–60 contains 'An Explanatory Key to every Print: rendering the whole full and significant', and professes to be 'Drawn and Etch'd by some of the most eminent Parties interested therein'. In a volume published in 1763 the imprint was followed by 'Where Sketches or Hints, sent Post Paid, will have due Honour shewn them'. Some of the sketches and hints, usually anonymous, sent to print-sellers in Gillray's day have survived; probably from Darly's time onwards they were never negligible. The publication line of an illustrated broadside against Bute continues,

[1] *Memoirs of the Reign of George II*, ii. 68. See above, p. 101.

'who returns the unknown Author Thanks for the Above, and shall be greatly obliged to him for any future Favours of the same kind'.

Mary Darly's book was intended for the amateur; following Hogarth, she begins with the 'Difference between Character and Caricature':

'Caricature is the burlesque of Character, or an exaggeration of nature, when not very pleasing, it's a manner of drawing that was, and still is, held in great esteem by the Italians and French, some of our Nobility and Gentry at this time do equal if not excel anything that ever has been done in any other Country, tis a diverting species of designing, and will certainly keep those that practise it out of the hipps or Vapours, and that it may have that effect on her Friends is the wish of M<sup>y</sup> Darly.

The innovations of Townshend and the Darly's were a response to political rancour; developments in imagery followed. Britannia and the British Lion had already expressed almost every conceivable change of mood and fortune. Both were commonly subjected to injury and insult, not stopping at murder. Britannia had acquired the cap and staff of Liberty as occasional attributes—but in general only to be deprived of them. Occasionally the Lion personifies the King—displacing the Hanoverian Horse, which had several times reflected George II's unpopularity and sometimes stands for George III. The first mention of John Bull in the prints seems to be in 1756 [3467], when Andrew Stone sells by auction 'all the valuable effects of John Bull Me[rchant] . . . leaving of Trade', Minorca having 'cost Mr Bull a great deal of money'. This is a long time-lag from Arbuthnot's invention of John Bull.[1] Here, in 1756, John Bull is England, and it is not for a considerable time that he acquires his secondary character of typical Englishman—though some equivalent to Sawney, Teague (Paddy was later), and Taffy was clearly needed—supplied sometimes by 'Jack English' (as in 3829), once by 'Will' [4008], a seeming tribute to Pitt, and once, perspicaciously, by 'Jack Afterthought' [4020]. In 1757 [3548] Britannia, brutally murdered, was 'the Lady of John Bull Esq<sup>r</sup>' (a relationship which occasionally recurs). After this John does not reappear in the prints till 1762, and then always in connexion with the peace negotiations. He appears when caricature and the comic are encroaching on allegory and symbol, for which Britannia is more suitable. He is first depicted (previously he had been only mentioned) in an imitation of the inn sign, as *A Poor Man Loaded with Mischief or John Bull and his Sister*

---

[1] *Law is a Bottomless Pit, exemplified in the case of the Lord Strutt, John Bull, Nicholas Frog., and Lewis Baboon, who spent all they had in a Law Suit* [the War of the Spanish Succession], Mar. 1712. Rearranged with other John Bull pamphlets as *The History of John Bull* in *Miscellanies* (by Pope and Swift), 1727.

*Peg* [3904]—Peg being Scotland. An ox or bull long continued to be a symbol for John Bull, especially when slaughter or mutilation or murderous anger was to be depicted: this imagery dates seemingly from 1762: in the *Caledonian Slaughter-House or the Death of John Bull* [3907] Bute prepares to give 'the fatal blow'. It is interesting to note that in 1819 Wellington was depicted (by Cruikshank) as the Bull's executioner.[1] In *The Smithfield Bargain or Scotch Salesman* [3942] Bute hands over to France 'the English Bull' garlanded for sacrifice. In a complicated satire by Paul Sandby (without a title) against Bute, Hogarth, and others John Bull is a bull-headed man [3910]. In yet another on the approaching peace Bute shaves 'Master' Bull in a barber's shop [3959]—the first of many political shavings (executed especially by and on Napoleon). 'The Bull-dog of England' is an animal appearing for the first time in 1762 [3987]. At this time, and for long afterwards, John Bull (like the British Lion) was occasionally the King, as in *The Three Roads to John Bull's Farm* [3926]. In *John Bull's House sett in Flames* [3890] the house is St. James's Palace, the incendiary is Bute. *A Catalogue of the Kitchen Furniture of John Bull Esqʳ leaving of House-keeping, now selling by Auction* [3990] is one of many satires on economies in the royal household.

A development which was to have a great influence on caricature was the use of colour. Every now and then among the mid-century prints there is a coloured impression. When or by whom the colour was applied we do not know, but from time to time a print is inscribed '6*d*. plain, 1*s*. coloured', or the like. The first examples known to me are a print of 1748 [3019] and two of 1750 [3086, 3091]; they remain rare during the fifties and sixties. In 1762 two volumes of *The British Antidote*[2] were advertised on a print [4004] at '10*s*. 6*d*. coloured, 5*s*. plain', but this was exceptional —single volumes are repeatedly advertised at 2*s*. 6*d*. with no mention of colour. The *Public Advertiser* (7 December 1762) adds to a list of the contents of the *Antidote*, 'The above prints may be had BUTIFULLY coloured, framed and glazed, or in a volume.'

While the cartoon was slowly altering, the old-fashioned explanation in verse was becoming less frequent—it was unsuited to the format of the card. The pictorial broadside in which the text was at least as important as the print continued to appear, but less often. The political ballad had become comparatively rare—supplanted by the newspaper. But it is characteristic of these prints that nothing was lost. Old symbols, old allegories, old forms were absorbed and adapted.

[1] See *E.P.C. 1793–1832*, Pl. 74.  [2] See p. 120.

# VII

## PITT, BUTE, AND GEORGE III

THE new reign opened with a loyal print, an apotheosis of the young
King enthroned among clouds: *Long live his Most Excellent Brit-
tanic Majesty, King George the Third, or Down with the Devil, Pope,
French King, and Pretender* [3732]; all are prostrate at his feet. But politics
soon intrude. The cartoonists expanded a penetrating epigram, attributed
to a physician's wife and current in December 1760: 'that the great
question was whether the King would burn in his Chamber *Scotch*-coal,
*Newcastle* Coal or *Pitt* Coal'. Hence, *The Quere? Which will give the best
heat to a British Constitution PITT: Newcastle or Scotch Coal* [3735].
Fires burn on three altars; Bute's fire, on 'a kind of new rais'd alter',
warms only Scots. On Pitt's is the motto which is his appellation in many
prints—*Pro Patria non sibi*. Newcastle's altar is inscribed *Pro sibi non patria*
and its fire was 'smother'd in the year 57, & is too much decay'd to break
out with Vigour . . . & never was universally esteem'd except by French
cooks & so not fit to be us'd'—a legend that does him less than justice.
Britannia's *Answer to the Quere* [3737], dated 1760, is a rebus: '. . . As my
King is a Briton born let no northern Hero or Frenchified sham Patriot
ever dare to separate our mutual love. . . .' She adds a list of 'Negatives':
'no Pitt no Money, no German Connections, no religious Humbug
[Whitefield, much attacked at this time and later], no German petticoat
Government, no more mercinary Foreign Generals, nor no [more] War
then is Necessary.' An unsophisticated but significant pronouncement.

Aversion to petticoat government and the Scots is also expressed in *The
Loyal Beasts, or Visionary Addressers. a Dream* [3740]. George III is 'a
youthfull lion' receiving addresses and homage; there are descriptive
verses but no names are given. Two at least are obvious. On the King's
right 'Is a most dreadful scottish bison', and crouching behind it is a
tigress, not mentioned in the verses, but clearly the King's mother—seemingly the first allusion in the new reign to her supposed relations with
Bute; later ones left nothing to the imagination. The elements of discord
are too clear, and the flames were blown up by controversies over the peace
negotiations and by Pitt's resignation. There is no trace in the prints of the
short-lived unpopularity that followed his acceptance of a pension, and a

barony for his wife—on the contrary. In *Merit Rewarded or Truth Triumph-ant* . . . [3814] the King begs Britannia to bestow '3000 p$^r$ Annum' on Pitt—a most unusual attitude to any pension; the famous letter to Alder-man Beckford, his chief supporter in the City, is quoted in full on a scroll held up by a winged figure: 'I resigned . . . in order not to remain re-sponsible for Measures, which I was no longer allowed to guide.'[1] A Spaniard muzzles the British Lion which is ridden by a fox—Henry Fox, who says, 'I ride now post to preferment. . . .' The Gallic Cock prepares to crow again and de Bussy, the French agent for peace negotiations, hands out bribes. The print is exceptional in being without a reference to Bute. Prints multiplied, almost all directed against Bute, and with insults to the Princess Dowager. Henry Fox's opinion (in 1762) that jealousy of Scots was the prime motive of opposition to the peace is supported by the prints:

> The Press is with more vehemence than I ever knew set to work against Ld Bute. And it would be very surprizing to see how quick & fiercely the fire spreads, but for the consideration that it is fed with great industry, & blown by a national pre-judice which is inveterate & universal. . . . A peace is thought necessary to Lord Bute: therefore a peace or any terms is exclaim'd against. But the true objections, his being a Scotchman & a Favourite, are avow'd, & on those articles is he most scurrilously accus'd . . . with as little disguise as ever faction wore boldly attack'd, & told of his intrigue with the Prss Dowr of Wales—[2]

All this is still more emphatically true of the prints, to whose influence there is much contemporary testimony.

The volume of the *Political & Satirical History* for the years 1761–3 in which 'cards' and other caricatures were reprinted, took the additional title *Displaying the Unhappy Influence of Scotch Prevalency*. . . . An imita-tion of this which appeared in 1762 and subsequently was called *British Antidote to Caledonian Poison*, and this again was imitated and followed by *The Scots Scourge*. . . . These little books contained, besides the prints, additional inflammatory comment. From 1761 to 1763 and after almost every print was primarily an attack on Bute,[3] sometimes with Fox as a secondary villain. Pitt—'English Will' or 'honest Will'—was Bute's anti-thesis and enemy.

The assault began with 'the Thane' as the lover of the Princess Dowager of Wales, the King's favourite, and thus the bestower of posts and pensions

---

[1] See p. 139.

[2] *Life and Letters of Lady Sarah Lennox, 1901*, i. 68 ('Lord Holland's Memoir . . .').

[3] For the contemporary attitude to Bute cf. Butterfield, *George III and the Historians*, 1957, pp. 45 ff.

to hordes of hungry barbarous Scots to the exclusion of the English. These insults continued, and sharpened the attacks on the peace negotiations: Bute is a Jacobite, with French interests at heart, the enemy of Liberty and Magna Charta. Then came a climax of rage over the Cider Tax, reviving the cry of 'Liberty, Property, and No Excise'. Wilkes and Churchill and a swarm of lesser libellers made these insults their own. Priorities are often doubtful, but very many prints anticipated Churchill's diatribe against the Scots—*The Prophecy of Famine*—probably also the *North Briton*, while others pay tribute to the paper and illustrate its gibes. Prints were largely responsible for the public opinion fostered by skilful propaganda which was the background of Wilkes's triumphs. Their importance is vividly illustrated by two famous plates, one by Hogarth in 1762, the other by his friend Benjamin Wilson in 1766. Only in the prints can we now recover the crescendo of abuse that assailed Bute—its effect on uninstructed opinion, the way in which these cries merged with 'Wilkes and Liberty', and these again with the slogans of the dispute with America.

It seems odd that the Ministry made almost no attempt at pictorial counter-propaganda, though there were ministerial journalists and pamphleteers (much abused in the prints). Speaking very roughly, there are extant some 400 prints against Bute—not counting all the copies and piracies—and only four on the other side; the uproar caused by the most famous, *The Times* (to be considered later), speaks for itself. *Britannia guided by Justice* [3865] is an openly Butite print which in the then state of opinion could have seemed merely laughable. Justice crowns Bute with laurels and he says that he values not 'the World's Cencure, as I am determin'd to Act with impartiality, with honour and with Honesty'. Any defence of the Ministry was written off as the work of 'hirelings', probably with truth—prints had to be popular to sell on their merits—or demerits. The second ministerial print (*c.* 1762), an attack on Pitt (Bute is not mentioned), was at once alleged to be paid for. This was *Sic Transit Gloria Mundi* [3913] in which he is charged with pride, popularity-mongering, 'changing sides', taxes, and the pension. It was copied for the *Antidote* with the mock signature 'Sawney Scott fecit' and the inscription: 'This Print was trumped up by Sejanus [Bute] and his party against the Great Commoner; whom they have placed on the Globe; blowing . . . bubbles of his Popularity; while the Mob below are sounding his Praise; on the right Side is a Figure modelling a Crown into a Commonwealth's Hat.' Indeed, as the *Briton* showed by being the incentive to the *North Briton*, ministerial propaganda was apt to provoke damaging retaliations. The fourth appeared in 1766.

*The Hungry Mob of Scriblers and Etchers* [Pl. 32] is an interesting though puzzling attack on Bute's propaganda. He scatters coin to an expectant crowd, one of whom is Samuel Johnson, holding (as in 3979) his pension of '300 Pr Ann.'. It is to be presumed that Smollett (of the *Briton*) and Murphy (of the *Auditor*) are there. Hogarth is an inconspicuous figure with an engraving tool, walking behind the more imposing Mat Darly who holds one of his most insolent prints, 'The Screen' [3825]. Is he—Darly, one of Bute's most inveterate enemies—there to defy Bute? And if so, can the parson be Churchill?—he is not unlike him. And have these 'Patriots' among the hirelings come to be bought off or to defy? The comment on the version in *The Scots Scourge* is, '. . . He got *this* a pension, and gave *that* a bribe. But his fortune can't silence the ill-natur'd Tribe.'[1]

It is also remarkable, if perhaps natural, that print-sellers as such were not prosecuted for seditious libel. Doubtless the worst prints were too scurrilously obscene to be brought into court or given publicity, but they may have had their influence on Press prosecutions, even on the famous proceedings against No. 45 of the *North Briton*. The *Antidote* challenged the law of libel and the pillory in its 'Humorous Explanation' of *Multum in parvo or a New Card for a Scotch Courtier* [4078]; the figures are 'Droll Caricatures going to receive the Reward due to their Merit; but, who they are, or where they are going, or for what they are going, we dont think it convenient to explain at present, as we have no great inclination to pass our Heads through a certain wooden Machine, invented by a set of arbitrary Men, to punish all those who are wiser than themselves.' Some characters in this print are indeed obscure, but they include Bute, a he-goat wearing a boot, riding a she-goat (the Princess), and their destination is Hell.

In the attacks on Bute history was called in. He was compared with the murdered 'Rhezzio' (Rizzio), reputed lover of Mary Queen of Scots, in, for instance, *The Scotch Colossus* . . . [3939]; like Walpole, he was Sejanus— favourite and tyrant. He was Macbeth, 'a favourite who murdered his master' [3897]. In *An Antidote by Carr for C-l-d-n* [Caledonian] *Impurities* [3845] Sir Robert Carr, favourite of James I, rises from the grave holding axe and halter to say (incorrectly), 'These were my doom for

---

[1] Nichols lists the plate among the attacks on Hogarth for *The Times*, but in another of those attacks, *The Fire of Faction* [3955], in which Hogarth blows up the fire with bellows, the fuel includes not only *The Times*, *The Briton*, and the *Auditor*, but the *Hungry Mob*.

Ad-lt-y, Oppression, Injustice. . . .' In *The Highland Seer, or the Political Vision* [3867], Bute starts from the Princess's bed to hear the warnings of five ghosts. First is Roger Mortimer: 'Let not ambitious Love they Heart ensnare/Lest thou the Fate of Mortimer should share.' The others are William (i.e. Peter) des Roches, Bishop of Winchester, Hubert de Burgh, Simon de Montfort, and Elizabeth's Earl of Essex. They illustrate some odd historical notions as well as the hatred attaching to a favourite. The design is headed by lines beginning:

> Is there a Curse on human kind
> So pestilent, at once, to Prince and People,
> As the base servile Vermin of a Court.

On his resignation, in *Sawney below Stairs* [4048], one of the many Charon prints, Bute is welcomed in Hades by Roger Mortimer, Wolsey, Walpole (because of Excise), Sejanus, the two 'Spencers' (Despensers), and Count Bruhl, the allegedly treasonous Minister of Maria Theresa.

The punning symbol for Bute was the jack boot, and this often contains two little figures, the Princess and her supposed lover. A typical print, and an example of the Townshend manner, is *The Loaded Boot . . .* [Pl. 33], drawn by White Horse and zebra, that is, by the King and Queen. The Princess's symbol was the petticoat, usually of tartan, and the emblem of petticoat government. These two objects became fuel for many bonfires. A new device to give verisimilitude to slander was the 'transparency', a device ascribed to Townshend, a print so folded that one design was superimposed on another, which became visible, as part of the whole, when held to the light. Thus, what is behind a curtain [3824], or a screen [3825] or inside a tent is revealed. In *The Scotch Tent, or True Contrast* [3912] not only Bute and the Princess but George III are discovered, the King with a petticoat suspended over his head and holding a scroll, *amor vincit omnia*. They are engaged upon a 'Scotch & French Scheme . . . to hurt King and Country' which the Duke of Cumberland swears to resist. All three are crudely scurrilous and all have been attributed to George Townshend. It seems astonishing that the last was openly advertised as published by Mary Darly.

The famous road from Scotland to England is the scene of *We are all a comeing, or Scotch Coal for ever* [3823]. Hungry aspirants crowd a public coach, others ride or drive or plod on foot. There is the inevitable joke about the 'scotch fiddle' or the itch (scabies) which was to be worked hard sixty years later to deride George IV's highly successful visit to Scotland.

The reduced version of the print in the *Political & Satirical History* is
described as 'a droll caricature of the Expeditions of the Locusts to the
English Canaan which (they cry'd out) flow'd with Milk and Brimstone'
[a cure for scabies]. There is a sequel, *We are all Come, or Scotch Coal
burns longer than Pitt or Newcastle Coal* [3858]. A lucky Scot who has
waxed fat in England holds up a sign to his countrymen, the root of a tree
entwined with thistles and supporting a big irradiated boot, 'the root of all
evil'. In this scene of rejoicing the Scots make inflammatory remarks, as,
'They say we shall have all the places of Profit & the English may go
starve': 'Let em send the English to Canada . . .' (a gibe at the peace—
Canada was represented as a very bad bargain).

No terms could have been acceptable when it was reiterated that Bute
and Bedford were betraying the country to France, and peace was 'the
approaching ignominious event'.[1] Bute was allegedly a Jacobite, and, or,
bribed, Bedford selfishly intent on a reduction of the Land Tax. This was
'The Peace (but not of God) which passeth all Understanding' [3926]. A
gross attack on Bute called *Gisbal, Lord of Hebron* [3848] is inscribed (on
reduced versions in the *Political & Satirical History*), 'This is the Man
that eas'd Brittain of a War, which, if continued must have finally ruin'd
our Enemies, 'tis to him we owe our happy disunion, the Excise, extended
Œconomy, &c. &c. &.' In *The Congress; or, a Device to lower the Land-tax*
[3887] Bute marches under 'the Standard of England'—a petticoat and a
boot—and hands over to a Frenchman 'Guadelupe, Martinico, &c &c &c
&c &c &c', saying, 'Tak aw again Mounseir, and gie us back what ye
please.' The other gives back 'Barren Canada' and 'Part of Newfoundland', adding, '. . . Now tank de grand Monarque for his royale
bountee.'

To personify the Beast of *Revelation* was reserved for the most execrated
of *bêtes noires*. In a print of December 1762, *The Vision or the M—n—st—l
Monster* [3983], Bute was described in a parody of Biblical language (a
form of humour that became very popular): '. . . I saw a Beast rise up out
of the Sea from the North, and many who were Sons of Corruption
worshipped yᵉ Beast. . . .' Pictorially, the creature does not conform to
the canon—he has not seven heads, but a dog's head wearing a Scots bonnet
and an earl's coronet. He is a hideous dragon with webbed wings, claws,
scaly neck, and three tails. One leg is a fox which devours a soldier (Henry
Fox was Paymaster), the other is a goose (the Duke of Bedford as peace
negotiator). The monster devours Britannia and Habeas Corpus and tears

---

[1] *London Evening Post*, 16–18 Sept. 1762.

at Magna Charta. An imp, Hogarth, is preparing to paint a flattering portrait of the monster, one of many attacks for *The Times*.

A further stage, if that were possible, in anti-Bute clamour was reached with the budget (22 March) and the introduction of a Cider Tax. The cry of 'Liberty, Property, and No Excise' was renewed, and there was a fresh outbreak of bonfires in which boot and petticoat were burned. As in 1733, but with even less excuse, the tax was represented (pictorially) as a general excise. The print-sellers battened on the new topic and the anti-Excise propaganda was loud, libellous, and long-drawn-out. One print must suffice here—not typical of the others, but an interesting example of the emblematical figure made of appropriate objects—*An Exciseman made out of y^e Necessaries of Life now Tax'd* ... [Pl. 34] has the head of a knave in a pack of cards and is made up of taxed objects; a setting sun, 'Light', connotes the Window Tax, and the ground at the exciseman's feet represents the Land Tax. This is seemingly the first of the innumerable prints on the general burden of taxation.

Bute quailed before the storm of abuse and resigned on 8 April, despite his unshaken majority. For many years he remained a political bogy: the favourite, the personification of 'secret influence'. This widely held belief lost all touch with reality from 1765, but persisted as part of the Whig doctrine of an attempt by George III to regain the power of the Crown and subvert the Constitution by ruling through 'King's Friends' and so by-pass the Cabinet. All this is fully illustrated and exaggerated in the prints, where Bute remains a prime villain throughout the war with America—indeed for about thirty years.[1] The note was set as soon as he resigned in a print with a title highly disrespectful to the King: *The S—— Puppitt Shew or the whole Play of King Solomon the Wise* [4049]. Bute and the Devil are on the stage, drawing back a curtain to display a row of puppets among whom are the King and his mother. Bute says, 'Tho I am out it's known for Certain,/I prompt 'em still behind the Curtain.' The King: 'War is no more & Smileing Peace/Shall Taxes thro the Land encrease.'

Bute's resignation was quickly followed by the unfortunate proceedings against Wilkes and the printers for No. 45 of the *North Briton*, the opening of the vendetta between the King and Wilkes which had followed the vendetta of Wilkes against Bute, to whom he attributed his failure to become either ambassador to Constantinople or Governor of Canada. But

---

[1] In *The National Assembly or Meeting of the Three Estates* [7623] in 1790 by Dent, where King, Lords and Commons are travestied as animals, with George III as 'The King of the Beasts'; Bute is prominent as 'The Secret Beast'.

first, to consider the related topic of the treatment of the King in the prints, a by-product of the attitude to Bute and the Princess. There are a few indications of popularity in 1760, but commonly, from 1761, George III is represented as weak and stupid. Occasional identification with the British Lion or John Bull is not a suspension of blame. In *The State Ballance or Political See-Saw* [3843] the King and his mother (with a big boot in her lap) sink, while Pitt and Newcastle rise, though Cumberland in the middle tries to 'Preserve the Equilibrium'. George holds a map of Scotland showing 'Bute I', and says,'Tho they have blinded me yet I find I am sinking in national Esteem'; Britannia lies prostrate, her cap of Liberty has fallen off. Bute drives the Princess in *The Triumphal Car or Scota's—— Victory 1762* [3846], while the King, personification of Folly, stands behind as footman, holding a rattle and a fool's cap and saying, 'I am nobody.' They drive over Magna Charta, Trade, and Laws. In *The Masquerade; or the Political Bagpiper* [3880] Bute and the Princess sit on the throne while the King stands by, playing the Scotch fiddle; in the version in *The Political & Satyrical History* he says,'I'll play any tune you bid me', while Bute remarks, 'He's as soft as wax. . . .' With unpopularity for George III goes praise for George II and for the King's father and uncle, Frederick and Cumberland, who are popular as enemies of Bute, and are 'Sons of Great George' [3907]. The King is blinded by his mother who holds her fan before his eyes and asks 'dear Sawney' for a pinch of snuff—that is 'Scotch Snuff with French Opium' [3927]. As *The Four Nonparells* [3934] King, Queen, Princess, and Bute dance round a maypole to a Highlander's piping. This is on a verse broadside which openly derides the King:

> The first Nonparell, grown so famous of late,
> Renown'd for his Wisdom, in matters of State;
> In Politicks skilfull, in Judgment so Sound,
> There's none can excel him search all yᵉ World round.

This is in the vein of ironic toasts in the City to Wit, Beauty, Virtue, and Honour, that is, to King, Queen, Princess, and Bute.[1]

The old grindstone theme was called in, and in *Scotch Impudence or the Northern Grinder* [3938] Bute drags the King towards the stone. One of many indications that the King was expected to rule as well as reign is *The Tenant's Complaint to David Simple, of Noodle Hall, Esqʳ* [4021] in which no less than fifteen tenants state their grievances; these are interesting but

---

[1] Walpole, *Memoirs of the reign of George III*, 1945, i. 274.

too long to quote here. The squire (George III) answers, 'you know good people, I don't trouble myself about my Estate, I leave the management to my Stewards & Clerks, if they supply me with mony that's sufficient'. He holds by the hand a fat little boy—the future George IV— and in his arms is the infant Frederick. 'Leo Britannicus' is clearly the King in *The Lyon Entranced* [3922] where the Lion, dead or doped, lies in state with Britannia as chief mourner, but only in the *Antidote* version is this made obvious by an 'Explanation': 'When Princes suffer themselves to be thrown into an inglorious Lethargy by the Arts of designing Favourites, it is a certain Sign the D——n is plac'd upon a weak Foundation.' In 'a curious caricature card', *The Lion made Ridiculous by Sawney & Jenny* [3962], the Lion is on his hindlegs wearing a petticoat, jack boots, and a Scots cap topped by a fleur-de-lis, while the Princess holds a thistle and Bute leads him by the nose. This was openly published by Mary Darly. *John a Boot's Asses* [3979] is a daring satire which by exception is without imprint—but it was openly copied for the *Scots Scourge*; Bute rides an ass, the Princess; tied to its tail is a second ass, blindfolded, to represent the King. A climax of insult, also copied for the *Scots Scourge*, was reached in *The Opposition* [4036]; the British Lion with the head of a mule (the King) drags a cartload of Englishmen uphill. Bute, riding a she-goat, the Princess, is one of a group pulling at the Lion's rein, while another group pull in the opposite direction. One of the latter says, 'Tis an obstinate Creature, he'll be guided by none, but that d——d Scotchman, & his villainous gang': another says, 'I'm tired with pulling, so he may go to Hell his own way.' One of the men in the cart remarks, 'If yᵉ Cart overturns I hope ye Animal that draws it may break his neck in yᵉ fall.' Here, by exception (till much later) the King is charged not with weakness but obstinacy: verses begin, 'Some say he's a Lion & some say a mule,/But most people say he's an obstinate fool.'

Most of these prints were attacks on the peace negotiations of 1762; most contain gross insults to the King's mother. In others she was the chief target. She was, for instance, *The Wanton Widow* [3851]; in 1769 she was the Queen in *Hamlet* directing Bute to pour poison into her sleeping son's ear [4329]. These flights are related to a theme with which Wilkes was especially connected; the identification of Bute with Roger Mortimer, lover of Isabella, Queen of Edward II, thereby comparing the Princess to a queen who had murdered her husband and ruled England with her lover. This was elaborated, broadened, and coarsened in the prints, but it was exploited also (perhaps first) by Wilkes in No. 5 of the *North Briton* in

July 1762. He followed this up in March by republishing the old play used against Walpole, *The Fall of Mortimer*, with a dedication to Bute: '. . . wherever the name of Roger Mortimer shall be mentioned, that of Bute will follow to the latest time. . . . I wish you my Lord the most exquisite pleasures under the Cyprian myrtle. . . .' George had learned (in 1756) of the calumnies against his mother, and he wrote to Bute: 'They have also treated my Mother in a cruel manner (which I shall never forget nor forgive to the day of my death. . . ). I do therefore here in the presence of Our Almighy Lord promise that I will remember the insults, and never will forgive anyone who shall venture to speak disrespectfully of her.'[1] Is it surprising that the young, inexperienced King was obsessed by hatred of Wilkes, or that his Ministers struck at the *North Briton* at the first opportunity, given by No. 45 (25 April 1763), with its remarks on the untruthfulness of the King's Speech on the peace, though this was blamed on the Minister (no longer Bute but Grenville). It was not one of Wilkes's most effective squibs. Is it not probable that the dominant motive was revenge for No. 5 and desire to stop the stream of insult against Bute and the Princess?[2] The use of General Warrants made Wilkes a martyr of Liberty and started a sequence of great issues. But before this Wilkes had embarked on a vendetta against Hogarth for his print *The Times* [Pl. 35].

Hogarth threw his bombshell, the third of the four Butite prints, on 7 September, 1762, and it duly exploded to his own damage. It was similar in spirit to the attack on Pitt (*Sic Transit Gloria Mundi*), but far more comprehensive and thoroughgoing—a protest against warmongering and demagogy, against factious attacks on the negotiators of the peace. The complicated design is filled with emblematical details, but the main theme is clear. A street is in flames, the flames of war and faction; one set of people try to put out the fire, others blow it up and obstruct the firemen. Incidentally, there is an excellent view of a contemporary fire-engine, fed by hose and buckets and worked by pumping. The chief fireman, whose badge, a crown and G.R., indicates the King, stands on the engine, directing a jet of water at a blazing terrestrial globe, the sign of the nearest burning house. The other houses also have signs, a fleur-de-lis, an eagle, and so on, to identify the countries at war. Scotsmen, one being Bute, are among the firemen. Newcastle furiously drives a wheelbarrow at the hose

---

[1] *Letters from George III to Lord Bute, 1756–1766*, ed. R. Sedgwick, 1939, p. 3.
[2] The dismissal of the Grenville-Bedford Ministry in 1765 for their insult to the Princess in excluding her from the Regency Bill seems to support this.

and the legs of a Scot, his barrow is heaped with *North Britons* and *Monitors*—fuel for the fire. Standing on the stilts of popularity and surrounded by a clamouring mob among whom are three adoring Aldermen, is Pitt, blowing at the blazing globe with bellows. A millstone, marked '3000£ per annum' (the pension) hangs from his neck. Across the way is the 'Temple Coffee House'; Lord Temple, Pitt's brother-in-law and Wilkes's patron, with a blank face (to suggest his unpredictable and factious disposition), squirts water at the King's back from a window. From the attic windows, and very small in scale (to show that they are garretteers, or insignificant literary hacks), Wilkes and Churchill also aim their squirts at the King. In the foreground Frederick of Prussia plays the fiddle, delighting in the conflagration, regardless of his wretched subjects who surround him, having fled from a burning house; one is a dying woman with a new-born infant. As a pendant to this group is a contented Dutchman, fat with the spoils of neutral trade. A dove with an olive branch flies above the clouds and flames. There are other details, including a building with a number of emblematical sign-boards, some obscure; on one is a picture of soldiers—evidently the militia—marching to the tune of 'the Norfolk jig' and signed 'G. T. fecit'. In this, according to Wilkes,[1] Hogarth 'vents his spleen upon Mr George Townshend and the gentlemen of Norfolk'. Townshend (like Pitt) had been an uncompromising advocate of the Militia Bill: attempts to levy the Militia had caused riots. *The Times* seems to be a counter-print to *John Bull's House sett in Flames* [3890]; St. James's Palace is burning, Bute, the incendiary, escapes in a shirt, and Pitt works the engine.

The uproar caused by *The Times* shows the importance of cartoons, especially one by Hogarth. It reflects also the enormity of his challenge to public opinion. Wilkes devoted a whole number—17—of the *North Briton* to a vicious attack. The cartoonists outdid themselves in elaborate pictorial invective; among them was Hogarth's old enemy Paul Sandby. At least thirteen vengeful prints rapidly followed *The Times*, most of which appeared again in versions made for the *Political & Satirical History* and the *Antidote*. In Sandby's *The Boot & the Blockhead* [3977] Hogarth, feebly passionate, protests to Churchill against the *North Briton* article. 'This Caricature', runs the explanation to Darly's version, 'shews the exaltation of a Scotch Blockhead, which infatuated the greatest droll genius in the World to fall down and worship and even daub his own Character to whitewash the Black Boot; and forgot himself so far as to aim at injuring the most

---

[1] *North Briton*, No. 17.

exalted *English* Patriot that ever was, till the bold and honest North Briton nipped him in the Bud. But they say he has Scotch fitts at intervals.' In *Tit for Tat* . . . [3978] there are more of the customary insults to Bute and the Princess. Hogarth is at his easel painting a big irradiated boot, and has defaced a portrait of Pitt 'by order of my L——'; he says, 'any thing for money. I'll gild this Scotch Sign & make it look Glorious, & I'll daub the other sign to efface its Beauty & make it as black as a Jack Boot.' His 'Line of Beauty' (theme of his *Analysis of Beauty*) is ridiculed, and in other prints becomes the line of 'Buty' or 'Booty'. He is *The Butefyer* [3971] and he is credited with a pension of £300 a year. The foundation for this was his office (contemptuously derided by Wilkes) of 'Serjeant Painter of all the King's Works' at a fee of £10 a year, which, 'one way or another', was worth, he said, £200 a year. He got it in 1757 on the death of his brother-in-law. His own explanation of his motives carries conviction. He had lost money by an illness, and the war abroad and 'contentions at home' had interfered with the sale of his prints. So it was necessary to 'do some timed thing' (cash in on the mania for political prints): 'this produce the Print call The Times the subject of which tended to Peace and unanimity and so put the opposers of this humane purpose in a light which gave offence to the Fomenters of distruction in the minds of the people. . . .'[1] Surely one of the least successful attempts at peace and unanimity ever made.

All this time the cartoonists had paid little attention to Wilkes—the *North Briton* was associated not with him but with Churchill—which must have galled one so avid of notoriety. 'I am excellently pourtrayed in Saturday's *Briton*', he wrote to his publisher (29 August 1762). 'Why do not the print-shops take me . . . I am an incomparable subject for a print. . . .'[2] It was not till the affair of General Warrants that the cry 'Wilkes and Liberty' was heard. Here Hogarth struck back. On the second appearance in Westminster Hall before Chief Justice Pratt (6 May) Hogarth made the sketch for the famous portrait, *John Wilkes Esqʳ Drawn from the Life, and Etch'd in Aquafortis* [Pl. 36]; beside the Patriot are two numbers of the *North Briton*, 17 and 45; Wilkes is the embodiment of Mephistophelean cunning and impudent demagogy and for the first time the cap and staff of Liberty are sardonic symbols. This was a portrait, as Hogarth wrote, 'done as like as I could as to feature at the same time some indication of his mind, [it] fully answerd my purpose the ridiculous was

---

[1] Joseph Burke, *Wm. Hogarth. The Analysis of Beauty*, Oxford, 1955, p. 221.
[2] G. Nobbe, *The North Briton, A Study on Political Propaganda*, New York, 1939, p. 85.

apparent to every Eye a Brutus a saviour of his country with such an aspect
was [so] arrant a Joke that it set every body else a laughing gauld him and his
adherents to death. . . .'[1] A copper-plate printer told Nichols that nearly
4,000 impressions were worked off in a few weeks. The papers were, as
Hogarth said, 'stufft with evectives' (invectives). Wilkes reprinted No. 17
and added a caricature portrait of 'William Hogarth Esq[r], Cut in Wood,
from the Life' [4053]. Churchill published his verse satire, *The Epistle to
William Hogarth*:

> Lurking, most ruffian-like, behind a screen,
> So plac'd all things to see, himself unseen,
> Virtue, with due contempt, saw Hogarth stand,
> The murd'rous pencil in his palsied hand.

Hogarth retorted with *The Bruiser, C. Churchill (once the Rev[d]) in the
Character of a Russian Hercules, Regaling Himself after having Kill'd the
Monster Caricatura that so Sorely Gall'd his Virtuous Friend, the Heaven
born Wilkes* [4084]. Besides the caricature of Churchill as a bear clutching
a tankard of porter and a knotted club, there was added in the two final
states (not often reproduced) a tiny picture (on the palette) in which
Hogarth renews his attack on Pitt: against a pyramidal tomb is a reclining
statue of Pitt flanked by Gog and Magog, the Guildhall giants, one of
whom holds a crown over the head of the City's idol. Hogarth stands in
the foreground flogging a dancing bear, Churchill, and holding a rope
attached to a performing ape, Wilkes, which rides cock horse on the staff
of Liberty. Nine more cartoons (at least)[2] followed, attacking Hogarth,
with savage gibes at his wife and his work, for instance, *Tit for Tat or
W[m] Hogarth Esq[r] Principal Pannel Painter to his Majesty* [4054].

The fateful quarrel between Wilkes and the Ministry went on, with
Bute, now called Mortimer, as enemy in chief, though behind the curtain.
Until the Stamp Act controversy the cartoonists ignored Grenville. The
Wilkes affair produced two more *bêtes noires*, Sandwich and Chief Justice
Mansfield. One had already been caricatured by Townshend as a creature
of Fox (in *The Recruiting Serjeant*), the other (then Murray) had been
attacked in 1756–7 as Newcastle's Attorney General. But now both became
villains in their own right. Sandwich was execrated as Jemmy Twitcher
(in the *Beggar's Opera*) who had peached on his boon companion and

---

[1] Joseph Burke, op. cit., p. 221.

[2] With the thirteen that followed *The Times* this makes twenty-two in the British Museum,
not counting copies in the *Antidote* and the *Scots Scourge*. Mr. Peter Quennell estimates the
total at over twenty-five: *Hogarth's Progress*, 1955, p. 278.

fellow rake in the affair of the *Essay on Woman* (the privately printed parody which Walpole called 'bawdy and blasphemous to the last degree'). Mansfield got the sobriquet of Judge Jeffreys for the sentences on Wilkes and on John Williams who had reprinted No. 45 after it had been burnt by order of Parliament. All this is illustrated. *The Execution* [4066] is a striking print in which Sandwich, trampling on the muzzled British Lion, drags the manacled and half-naked Britannia by a noose round her neck; in his pocket is a paper, 'Blasphemy'; Fox, now Lord Holland, scatters bribes, treads on Magna Charta, and cries 'Twitch-her, Twitch-her Jemmy Twitcher'. Britannia's spear is broken, her shield half hidden by a huge Scottish thistle.

> What has Britannia left to hope
> When Graceless Twitcher pulls the rope?
> When old Corruption holds the bribe
> And Gold secures the venal tribe.

The pillorying of John Williams (14 February 1765) is the subject of a number of prints, including *The Pillory Triumphant* [4115]. In a scene in Palace Yard, Williams, under a 'Scotch Yoke', is protected by an angel. The jack boot and a Scots bonnet are being suspended from an improvised gibbet to the shouts of the 'sons of *Wilkes* and *Liberty*'. Williams had published some of the more savage anti-Bute prints and his imprint is on perhaps the most venomous anti-British cartoon of the whole American War.[1]

A different note is sounded in another print of 1765 when efforts were being made to induce Pitt to take office and so rid the King of Grenville. Pitt was at Hayes, suffering from gout and severe nervous irritation, and was being exacting and difficult. Therefore in May the King sent his uncle, Cumberland, to negotiate in person, but the overture, like others, ended in failure. This is the subject of *The Courier* [4121]. Cumberland gallops along 'The Road to Hays', towards Pitt's house, which is represented as a hovel; from the open door projects a huge gouty foot resting on a stool; a pair of crutches leans against the wall. The hovel has a sign, 'Popularity the Blown Bladder by W. P.' Behind Cumberland is another public house, with the sign of the Crown, proprietor 'I. Bull' (George III) and with the names M—d and B—e (for Mansfield and Bute). The hovel symbolizes Pitt's theatrical economies when he left office in 1761. Thus blame is distributed all round.

[1] *The Closet* [5470] in **1778.**

In July 1765, with Pitt still obdurate, Grenville was dismissed and the Rockingham Whigs came in. Their year of office was marked by one thing, the repeal of the Stamp Act, and this produced an outburst of important prints. This was the first issue between England and America to come before the public. In these prints the pattern of popular attitudes to the dispute and the war is already apparent. From first to last Bute is made responsible for 'stamping' and then for coercing America. The causes of the Colonies and of Wilkes are treated as one, with General Warrants and the Stamp Act as linked tyrannies. The prints illustrate the extent to which relations with the Colonies were bedevilled by Wilkes and Liberty.

Little attention was paid to the Act when it passed in March 1765, but reactions in America—'Non-Intercourse' and damage to trade—produced a demand for repeal. The agitation had much in common with other agitations—against Excise, against the Jew Act, and the Cider Tax. Like them it was promoted by vested interests, fomented by mobbing and cries of Liberty in danger, carried on by organized petitioning, backed up by Press propaganda and satirical prints. Like them it was successful. But there were important differences: the issues were far wider, the agitation was not anti-ministerial—Rockingham, in office, adopted the cause of repeal. And while the prints on the other agitations are unanimous, Stamp Act ones are not. In these prints America is personified for seemingly the first time, sometimes as a Red Indian in war-paint, or as a blend of Indian and Amazon, sometimes as a woman resembling Britannia (her mother) but younger and more buxom.

The first[1] Stamp Act print—one in which Grenville makes a first appearance—was advertised in October 1765, *The Great Financier, or British Œconomy for the Years 1763, 1764, 1766* [Pl. 37]. Grenville holds up a balance in which pettifogging economies are far outweighed by 'Debts 140 Millions'. Pitt is behind him, leaning on a crutch and saying, 'Conquests will ballance it'; he points to sacrifices of the peace, which Grenville drops to the ground: 'Guardalupe, Martinico, Havanna' as well as 'Newfoundland Fishery' and 'Philipines'. Behind Pitt is America, a suppliant Indian with a yoke on her neck inscribed 'Taxed without Representation'; she holds a bag of 'Dollars', saying, 'Commerce will outweigh it.' Behind her are tax collectors; one helps himself to dollars, saying, 'We must obey orders'; his companion answers, 'Dam'me Jack better pillage the French.' Grenville's servant, wearing a fool's cap inscribed 'Œconomy', drops

---

[1] F. G. Stephens thought *The Last Shift* [4118, n.d.] the first: I think it can hardly be earlier than 1775.

candle ends into the scale thereby robbing a hungry cat (economy was much disparaged as a Scottish failing carried out in the royal kitchens). On the right is a prison from which hang chains inscribed 'General Warrants'; Britannia sits dejectedly at the gate while Grenville's ape, wearing his master's collar, pulls away the stone on which she sits and breaks the spear from which her cap of Liberty has fallen. France and Spain rejoice. Ships are for sale, with brooms at the mast-heads, a usual item in Stamp Act prints.

*The Deplorable State of America or Sc—h Government* [4119] was advertised on 2 January, and some weeks earlier (11 November) in the *Boston Gazette*,[1] where there was a long description, an interesting example of the extension of this graphic propaganda to the Colonies. Britannia offers Pandora's box, the Stamp Act, to America (an Indian), the latter turns to Minerva: 'Secure Me, O, Goddess, for I abhor it as Death'; she answers, 'Take it not.' Liberty lies prostrate, menaced by a serpent emerging from a huge Scottish thistle. Mercury (commerce) flies off, saying to America, 'It is with Reluctance I leave ye.' In the sky is an irradiated boot to which the King of France proffers a bribe: 'Take this, and let thy banefull Influence be poured down upon them.' Ships of course are to be sold, and a gallows is prepared for 'Stamp Men' who find themselves compelled to rob or starve.

Two prints followed which deserve special attention; by a lucky chance we know how and why they were produced.[2] Both are by Benjamin Wilson, a leading, perhaps the leading, portrait painter of the day, who was making a large income and enjoyed the profitable patronage of the Duke of York. He was also an inventor and a F.R.S., and an etcher whose fake Rembrandts tricked 'certain artists and amateurs who imagined themselves to be connoisseurs'. Something well above the level of the ordinary satirical print might be expected. This is not so, but the success he achieved is remarkable. The first, in February, was produced, Wilson says, 'In order to please Lord Rockingham . . . who had promised to take care of him.' This was *The Tomb-Stone* [Pl. 38], commemorating Cumberland, go-between in the negotiations for the Ministry, who had died in October. 'Here lieth the Body of William Duke of Cumberland &c lamented by his Country, which he twice Sav'd. First . . . at the Battle of Culloden, and after by selecting a Ministry, out of those virtuous few, who gloriously withstood

---

[1] R. T. H. Halsey, 'Impolitical Prints', *Bulletin of the New York Public Library*, Nov. 1939.
[2] From the manuscript autobiography incorporated (against his instructions) in Randolph's *Life* of Wilson's son, Sir Robert Wilson, 1862.

General Warrants, American Stamps, Extensions of Excise—&c &c &c.'
Britannia and America flank the inscription, weeping figures in bas relief,
surrounded by military trophies. Bute—'Sejanus'—and his friends dance
exultantly on the lid of the sarcophagus; he is between Bedford and Grenville, from whose pockets hang 'Stamps', 'Reversions', 'Pensions', and
'Cyder Tax'. Dancing with them is a little dog in parson's dress—'Anti-
Sejanus'—who is held up by Sandwich. He is Dr. Scott, Sandwich's
chaplain, who had 'hackneyed his pen in support of the Stamps'. Bagpipe
music is provided by a bulky Scotch demon, a monster who is balanced on
the left by Lord Temple with a blank face as in *The Times*. He holds a
huge 'Oriflame' of discord and says to Grenville, 'Stamp away Brother.'
Others pilloried are Halifax (for General Warrants) and two bishops who
think it prudent to 'stay a little' before joining the dance. The print, says
Wilson, was 'very successful in its object' so that 'Mr. Edmund Burke
[then Rockingham's secretary] and Grey Cooper [Secretary to the Treasury]
pressed him much to try another political print'. Wilson responded with
*The Repeal, Or, the Funeral of Miss Americ– Stamp* [Pl. 39] published,
he says, within ten minutes of the repeal of the Act (8 March). Here
then is one of the very few prints known to have been officially inspired.
Its success was immediate and remarkable. Wilson states that in four days
he sold above 2,000 at a shilling apiece. He could not keep pace with the
demand and on the fifth day two pirated copies came out at half the price:
'credible persons' told him that 16,000 of these were sold. Actually, there
are four piracies in the British Museum, besides a reduced copy in the
*Antidote*. Seven versions were exhibited in the New York Public Library[1]
in November 1939. It was described in the newspapers and a long facetious
description is quoted in Benjamin Franklin's *Memoirs*. A funeral procession
makes its way towards a tomb inscribed 'Within this Family Vault; Lie
interred, it is to be hoped never to rise again, The Star Chamber Court,
Ship Money—Excise Money and all Imports without Parliament, The Act
de Hæritico [*sic*] Comburendo, Hearth Mon Gener Warrants And [a blank
for Miss Americ– Stamp] which tended to alienate the Affection of Englishmen to their Country.' Above the tomb two skulls of traitors (as those
displayed on Temple Bar) associate not only Bute but the Stamp Act with
Jacobitism. Anti-Sejanus heads the procession reading the burial service,
two legal *bêtes noires* follow, Wedderburn and Fletcher Norton, with black
processional flags decorated with 'Stamps'—a device of Scottish thistle

---

[1] Horace Walpole's copy of the print, now in the Library, has the names of the 'Mourners'
in his handwriting.

and Jacobite white rose. Grenville carries the infant's coffin, and is followed by the chief mourner, Bute—' Sejanus'. Next come Bedford and Temple, Halifax and Sandwich, and two bishops. Now that Non Intercourse is over, the Thames-side warehouses are open again, ships are ready to sail—the *Rockingham*, the *Grafton*, the *Conway*, named after those who had carried repeal. A big chest is being shipped containing 'a statue of Mr Pitt'.

Wilson's two prints embody the main points of the propaganda against the Stamp Act—the only American tax except the Tea Tax to be mentioned in the prints. They stress the firmly held delusions that Bute and his following were responsible for 'stamping' America, that the Stamp Act and General Warrants were linked tyrannies, and that the causes of America and Wilkes were one. (All this was developed with great virtuosity in later prints which treat the tax as if it were still valid and ignore the provision that the money was to be used only for the defence of America.) They were not propaganda for repeal—that issue was decided before they were published, but self-regarding panegyrics of the Ministry by an expectant.

The propaganda that prevailed against much contrary opinion was that of the commercial and industrial interests alarmed at the check to trade. To this was added the tireless lobbying of Benjamin Franklin to show 'that the Colonies cannot be forced to submit to the Stamp Act but at an Expence greater than the Profit'. He pointed his arguments by a famous cartoon 'invented' by himself and printed on cards on which he wrote his messages to 'Men in Power'. This was *Magna Britannia—Her Colonies Reduced*, engraved at the end of 1765 and used in the early weeks of 1766.[1] A mutilated Britannia has slipped from her globe, her amputated limbs lie beside her—they are Virginia and Pennsylvania (with a hand from which an olive branch has dropped), New York and New England, the last a leg from which a spear points at the helpless body. Her ships are for sale and a legend, *Date Obolum Belisario*, shows that she is destitute, reduced to beg for alms. Nothing suggests that this was ever for sale in England. None of the original cards has been traced, but in August 1768 an English copy was published without comment in Almon's *Political Register*: *The Colonies Reduced* and *Its Companion* [Pl. 40], a second design, to show the guilt of

---

[1] This account is based on Edwin Wolfe's article, 'Benjamin Franklin's Stamp Act cartoon', *Proceedings of the American Philosophical Society*, vol. xcix, pp. 388–96 (Dec. 1955). I am indebted to Mr. Lawrence Towner, editor of the *William and Mary Quarterly*, for information about this. Franklin wrote to his partner, David Hall, on 28 Feb.: 'I enclose you some of the cards on which I have lately wrote all my messages.' According to a contemporary inscription on the American version he also 'employ'd a Waiter to put one of them in each Mans hand as he entered the House the day> receding the great debate': op. cit., p. 390.

Bute, who stabs Britannia in the back and delivers her up to Spain: 'Now I shew you her Weakness you may strike Home.' Britannia threatens America who throws herself into the arms of Louis XV who will thus become 'King of de whole World'. A Dutchman runs off with her shipping trade.

Franklin's card was copied in America with a lengthy explanation, probably in 1767—perhaps later. It would have been appropriate to the Olive Branch Petition of 1775. A French version would seem to belong to the years of war with England (years covered by Franklin's residence at Passy)—or to the eve of war. A large Dutch adaptation, *Grande Bretagne mutilé ou horrible mais vraie répresentation* . . ., is similar in spirit to prints of 1780; an Englishman mourning the loss of his trade has been introduced.[1]

Just before *The Tomb-Stone*, one of the hitherto rare satires against Pitt had appeared, *The Colossus* [4162], in which he is attacked for his eloquent denunciations of the Stamp Act. This was advertised as 'A Character not a Carricature, called the Statesman in Stilts; or American Colossus. 'Tis true 'tis Pity, and Pity 'tis true. Shakespeare.' As in Hogarth's *The Times* Pitt is on stilts; one, 'Sedition', is hooked and extends over 'New York'; the other, 'Popularity', is planted in the City and among the merchants in the 'Royal Exchange'. One crutch, entwined with serpents, is over the House of Commons; the other is his 'Pension' and is among bubbles: 'Patriotism, M. Charta, Continental Connections, War, Peace, Gold Boxes, Minority, Majority.' Above Pitt's head is a 'Common-Wealth' hat. On an air-borne temple is Lord Temple, as Fame, blowing bubbles that fall and disappear: 'Publick Spirit, Honesty and Loyalty.'

Much more characteristic of Stamp Act prints is *The State of the Nation A.D. 1765* [4130, n.d.], a scene by the sea with Britannia weeping on the shoulder of an angry America, while Grenville rushes forward to enforce the Stamp Act but is stopped by Pitt, who holds the staff and cap of Liberty. Mansfield, directed by Bute, menaces Britannia, but is checked by Pratt who insists, 'No General Warrants.' In another scene by the sea, *Goody Bull or the Second Part of the Repeal* [4142, not by Wilson], Britannia (Mrs. Bull) resents the success of America: 'Oh the Hussy, She dares me to my Very face.' Pitt rebukes her—'Why you Old Devil, what have you a Mind to turn your Daughter a Drift.' Across the ocean is Pitt's statue: 'To the Memory of Will Pitt Esq[r] who Delivered America from Slavery by the repeal of the Stamp Act 1766. Honour Inv[t] Liberty fecit.'

[1] Cf. the French, Dutch, and American versions of an English cartoon of 1778, pp. 153-4.

Men surround the statue shouting for Pitt, for King George, and for Liberty and against Twitchers, Sejanuses, and anti-Sejanuses: 'Wilkes, England and America for ever.'

But for a short time, after Pitt had succeeded Rockingham, his American policy shared his own unpopularity and one or two of the many anti-Pitt prints are also anti-American. This was the Ministry which Pitt—now Chatham—intended to transcend party divisions by combining 'men in favour with the public' with 'men in favour at court'. His title, according to Horace Walpole, 'blasted all the affection which his country had borne to him, and which he had deserved so well. . . . The people . . . thought he had sold them for a title.'[1] The prints suggest that they thought he had sold them to Lord Bute. Thomas Hollis wrote to America on 1 October 1766 of 'the recent unparalleled prostitution of the once magnanimous and almost divine * * * * * * *, who now is totally lost in parchment and BUTISM'.[2]

There is a conventional tribute to Chatham and Pratt (now Camden) on their promotions, with attributes of Liberty and Justice, and figures of Fame and prostrate Envy. This is *Britannia's Glory* [4144]. There is a naïve print in which Chatham and Bute clasp hands before an enthroned Britannia: *Britannia's Affection for her Children or Envy Expos'd* [4157]— the fourth and last Butite print. Otherwise the chorus of dispraise is complete and prolonged. Chatham is *The Hypocrite unmaskd or the Double Pensioner* . . . [4146], supporting Bute on his shoulders; he has discarded his crutches and a hypocrite's mask. In *The Cat's Paw* [4148] Bute, a big monkey, forces a cat to pull chestnuts out of the fire. A royal crown over the fireplace is surmounted by thistles and white roses. By exception, Bute is omitted from *The Triumph of America* [Pl. 41]. Down a steep slope Chatham drives a Red Indian Amazon in a triumphal car, with his crutch, topped by a coronet, beside him. He lashes at the leaders who are about to plunge over a cliff from which Britannia has already fallen. His team are members of his oddly chosen Ministry, the leaders 'Crafty' (Shelburne—a first appearance) and 'Royal Oak' (Grafton, descendant of Charles II). The next pair are 'Weathercock, a fine showy horse' (Charles Townshend) and 'Surly' (Lord Northington). The wheelers are 'Prudence' (Conway) and 'Prerogative formerly known by the name of Liberty' (Pratt, now Camden, who as Pitt's Chancellor shared his unpopularity). The postilion (on Crafty) is an American Indian.

[1] *Memoirs of the Reign of George III*, 1845, ii. 358.
[2] *Memoirs of Thomas Hollis*, 1780, i. 340.

Another of the few anti-American prints is *The New Country Dance as Danced at C\*\*\*\*, July the 30th, 1766* [4147] advertised in September, and as the title shows a satire on Pitt's appointment. Courtiers and Ministers dance while George III plays the fiddle. Bute, dancing with the Princess, leads Chatham on a string. The latter, hobbling on a crutch, says to America, 'I stood staunch to your cause.' America, who is a half-naked young woman holding a bottle of 'Rum' (a unique attribute) answers, 'Yes we finely hum'd Old England.' Britannia has fallen awkwardly and says, 'I'll dance no longer if America takes the lead.' Wilkes is carried off to Paris by a witch on a broomstick. The many other characters include the Kings of France and Spain who announce their intentions of not fulfilling the obligations of the peace of Paris, now they have 'got a Friend at Court'. Another aspect of the reaction against Chatham is stressed in a rebus, a *Hieroglyphic Epistle from Beelzebub* . . . [4145]: 'Your pretended Poverty, Your selling your horses your acceptance of a Pension and now a Place and a Peerage, are Convincing Proofs of what vast Knowledge you have in men and things and indicates that no man can be a good Politician without thinking of himself . . .' (a gibe at the *Pro Patria non sibi* motto); Lord Bath (Pulteney), a fellow renegade, sends him greetings from Pandemonium.

The most interesting of this group of prints is a complicated and cruel satire advertised in March 1767, *P\*\*\* and Proteus, or a Political Flight to the Moon* [4163] with the sub-title *Mutatas dicere Formas* and the motto *Quem Deus vult perdere prius dementat*. Chatham is symbolized in a number of forms, first as a kite flying to the moon by a 'Via Lunatica', with Bute holding the string on which is a lantern inscribed 'Privilege' and 'Prerogative'. Inscriptions on the kite include 'as I do not guide I am not responsible' (a gibe at his letter to Beckford in 1761[1] which points to his present incapacity for affairs of State); 'A Project for annexing the Empire of the Moon to the Crown of . . . . . . .;' 'The Family Compact between the Sun and Moon discover'd' (his schemes of empire are derided). The King watches the kite with a half-witted stare, crying, 'Emperor of the Moon O la.' The papers on the kite's tail are 'Patriot, Post, Places, Pension, Peerage, Popularity'. Chatham is also a savage bull, and has knocked down his brother-in-law Lord Temple, and threatens Wilkes, who drops the staff and cap of Liberty. He is a cormorant swallowing 'Posts, Pensions, Titles' and emitting 'Grants, Bounties, Reversions, Dukes, Hard Taxes, Undigested Subsidies'. He is also a weeping crocodile, fawning on the King and saying, 'so good so gracious Hoh oh oh'. There is an inscription:

[1] See p. 120.

Sir! He can turn! and turn! and yet go on!
And turn again! and he can Weep Sir Weep
And be Obedient as you see, Obedient,
Very Obedient.

Thus was his grandiloquent respect for the Crown derided.

After a short spell of furious energy Chatham relapsed into what was then called suppressed gout, and might now be called manic depression, quite unable to leave his country house. At last he recovered sufficiently to press his resignation on the King, and in October 1768 Grafton became actual as well as nominal leader.

# VIII

## WILKES AND LIBERTY

A NEW phase in cartoon history began in 1767, the monthly magazine illustrated by satirical engravings; this succeeded the vogue for 'cards' and 'Political & Satyrical' histories. John Almon—journalist, bookseller, and militant Wilkite—started the fashion with his *Political Register* in May, the plates illustrating the more extreme contents or sometimes prudently left to speak for themselves. The *Oxford Magazine* followed in January 1768; it had a longer life and a gradual decline in acrimony. Two ephemeral and aggressive publications belong to 1768–70; the *Freeholders Magazine* and the *London Museum*; the old-established *London Magazine* introduced polemical prints. In the seventies other magazines appeared and disappeared, notably the *Westminster Magazine* in December 1772. The vogue passed, but from time to time, especially in the early nineteenth century, there were magazines in which folding caricature plates were an important feature.

For cartoonists politics continued to be aspects of Wilkes and Liberty with Bute as arch-villain; till after 1770 every incident of the Wilkes saga is illustrated: the Middlesex elections, the riots, the imprisonment, the feud between the City and Crown, Ministers, and Commons, the stirrings of Radicalism manifested in meetings, petitions, and Addresses. The Press was in one of its more violent phases with the *Letters of Junius* as the highlight of much pamphleteering. The context of fable and mass-emotion surrounding the important issues at stake is conveyed in the prints as nowhere else. Preoccupation with Bute became more fantastic than ever, and the thesis of a ministerial design to enslave both Britain and America gained ground. In the Colonies revolutionary unrest had been in conflict with much traditional loyalty to the Crown, but in 1768–9 the Americans received a barrage of inflammatory news about Wilkes which turned George III into a tyrant. The Sons of Liberty in America had fraternal relations with Wilkite organizations in England; Americans vied with the English in gifts to the prisoner during his comfortable sojourn in the King's Bench. It was in the summer of 1769 that the new township in Pennsylvania was called Wilkes-Barré in honour of Wilkes and Colonel Barré—defenders of the Colonial cause. 'The Wilkite thesis, that coercion

in the Colonies was the complement of a royal scheme to subvert Liberty
in the Motherland through "corruption" of Parliament, carried increasing
conviction in Boston, Philadelphia, Charleston and Williamsburg, as the
conflicts of the 1760's continued into the early 1770's.[1] In England cartoonists in the main still held to their picture of a blindfolded King.

After the repeal of the Stamp Act public interest in the Colonies waned,
despite increasing unrest in America, but prints illustrate the way in which
conflicts there were aspects of Wilkes and Liberty. They illuminate the
passions and propaganda (powerfully aided by ministerial ineptitude) by
which a vendetta between George III and his Ministers on one side and
Wilkes and Opposition groups on the other, was transformed into a great
constitutional issue, highly damaging to relations with the Colonies. In
June 1769 the *Political Register* produced twin designs: *What may be
doing Abroad—What is doing at Home* [4287]. The sovereigns of France,
Spain, Prussia, and Austria agree on the partition of Great Britain and
her possessions: George III weeps at the shameful consultations of his
Ministers on the Wilkes affair—both very far-fetched notions; one of
many crimes attributed to Grafton is 'The Reduceing of Boston by the
Military'—that is, the landing of troops after the riots of 1768.

*The Triumverate or Britannia in Distress* [4298] is a complicated allegorical fantasy on the petition of the Livery of London to the King on
5 July 1769. The Triumvirate are Grafton (enthroned), George III, and
Bute who holds the sceptre he has taken from the King. Britannia is in
chains, but America—an Indian in war paint—is escaping from slavery:
he has broken the yoke on his shoulders and tramples on the Stamp Act;
beside him are discarded wooden shoes, fetters, and a scourge. A symbolical procession approaches the throne in which Liberty is personified
by Wilkes and Fortitude by Alderman Beckford. In *The City Carriers*
[4296] on the same petition, an Alderman shouts, 'I feel for the wrongs of
America.'

A Wilkite print, *Political Electricity; or, An Historical & Prophetical
Print, in the Year 1770* [4422], is an emblematical design that in scope,
complications, explanations, and size ($22\frac{3}{4}$ by $15\frac{3}{4}$ in.) approaches more
nearly to *Magna Britannia Divisa*[2] than to contemporary prints—a last
flare-up it would seem of an obsolescent manner. Description is impossible.
There are thirty-one little designs, most of them linked by an 'electric
chain' which issues from Bute, who stands on the French coast and is

[1] Douglas Adair, 'The Stamp Act in Contemporary British Cartoons', *William and Mary
Quarterly*, Williamsburg, x. 539 (Oct. 1953).          [2] See pp. 26–28.

described as an 'electrical machine in yᵉ Character of Dʳ Franklin'. The chain crosses the Channel to the Princess Dowager beside whom stands the King as a button-maker, with a book beside him—'History of Charles, A Dissolution dangerous to the Crown.' Ministers dine off the British Lion. There are mobs protesting against wages at 5s. a week, beef 8d. a pound, corn 8s. a bushel. There is also a Wilkes and Liberty mob after the third Middlesex election. London is in flames and in ruins, 'alluding to yᵉ furious Distress and Anger of yᵉ Inhabitants occasioned by yᵉ late un-constitutional Proceedings of yᵉ Ministers'. Scene 24 is 'The City of London transferred to Boston' and described as 'the Coasts of America where yᵉ Inhabitants are Industrious in every Art to provide themselves with yᵉ Manufactures that Great Britain used to furnish them with, being constrained & drove as it were to Industry by yᵉ late Mi—l harsh Pro-ceedings, in forcing yᵉ Stamp & other Acts of Internal Taxes upon them contrary to yᵉ true Spirit of British policy, & which sooner or later this Country will rue yᵉ Imprudence of'.

In this 'Electrical Print' Chatham is still a lapsed Patriot, clogged by his pension and condemned for his attitude to Wilkes. The prints show little appreciation of his return in 1770 to violent opposition, but the *Political Register* published a tribute to the short-lived co-operation be-tween Opposition groups: *The Hydra* [4370] is an eight-headed beast (Bute, Mansfield, and others) attacking Britannia and itself attacked by Chatham (with his crutch), Temple, and Rockingham.

Two unfortunate happenings, skilfully exploited, inflamed the anti-Bute element in Wilkite emotion. During the riots outside the King's Bench prison (10 May, 1768) the troops were mobbed and stoned. A young man, one William Allen, was chased by three soldiers and eventually shot. In some form or other this incident appears in almost every Wilkite print—and all political prints were Wilkite. The soldiers happened to be Scottish, and the affair was represented as an attempt on British liberties, planned and directed by Bute, and carried out by Scots. The magistrate who read the riot act and gave the order to fire was execrated and tried for murder (which largely explains the supine conduct of the magistrates in the Gordon Riots). Again, during an election affray at Brentford, a Wilkite was killed in a quarrel with an Irish chairman; medical evidence that death was not due to the blow was not believed, and the incident was represented as a second deliberate murder followed by a royal pardon. Only the prints can give an idea of the way in which these things were inflated. Among very many cartoons are two called *The Scotch Triumph* [4195, 4228]. The

second was announced as 'A Satiric Scratch, in the Stile of Rembrandt,
. . . with the Representation of their amazing Exploits in St. George's
Fields, the Murder of the Innocent, and the Sacrifice of Liberty, by
Moloch; with some curious anecdotes'.[1] There are also two called *The
Scotch Victory* [4196–7]. The second [Pl. 42] is barbed by an unusual
realism, and is inscribed, 'To the E—l of [Bute, represented by a boot
under a petticoat], Protector of our Liberties . . . by L Junius Brutus.'
*Scotch Amusements* [4237] include the shooting of Allen and the *amours* of
Bute and the Princess.

In these prints there are frequent appeals to history. Cromwell's portrait is used as a threat of deposition or regicide. In *The Triumverate . . .*
of 1769 already mentioned, there are medallions of Cromwell, Charles II,
and James II; there is also a picture: Henry III 'forced by his Parliament
and People' to 'renew the Charters', while the Archbishop is 'denouncing
a terrible curse against all those who should violate the laws and alter the
Constitution of the Kingdom'. In *The Times. Pl. 2* [4243], the design is
headed by a medallion of Cromwell and on contrasted columns are the
names of Patriots and anti-Patriots: Hampden, Andrew Marvell, Algernon
Sidney, and Lord Russell (the last two executed for the Rye House Plot)
are contrasted with Carr (Somerset, favourite of James I), Buckingham,
Laud, and Macclesfield (the Chancellor impeached for corruption in 1725).
In *The Funeral of Freedom* [4288] are the tombs of those 'murdered' in
Wilkite riots; the gravedigger has thrown up the skulls of Charles I and
Cromwell. Such allusions were characteristic: Junius, in his *Letter to the
King*, warned him to profit by the fate of the Stuarts. The Address of the
City Livery presented by Beckford in March 1770 declared that the ex-
clusion of Wilkes from Parliament was an illegality 'more ruinous in its
consequences than the levying of Ship Money by Charles I or the dispens-
ing power exercised by James II'.

With all these menacing comparisons the Whig thesis of the King's
attempt to recover the powers of the Crown finds little if any countenance;
he is the victim of evil counsellors—Ministers of course, but pre-eminently
his mother and Bute. 'A New Song' for Wilkes's birthday in 1769 begins,
'Here's a Health to our King, lets rejoice drink and Sing, and may he grow
wiser and wiser; and may he grow wiser and wiser; and wise he'd now be,
were it not for a she, and a Damnable Scottish adviser.'[2] George III
is persistently attacked for neglecting the business of government when
he was in fact attending to the details of administration with industry and

---

[1] *Public Advertiser*, 13 June 1768.          [2] *Freeholder's Magazine*, 1769, p. 168.

tenacity. He neglects State affairs for his hobbies—button-making repeatedly—and farming, as in *Farmer G—e, Studying Wind and Weather*
[4883], in 1771, through the wrong end of a telescope.

1771 was a turning-point in cartoon history—a change of mood, a change
of scene, and a change in technique, which, as often seems to happen, coincides with other changes. Two new targets and the disappearance of an
old one contributed to the change. Lord North, 'Boreas' (who had succeeded Grafton in 1770), and Charles Fox, whose fortunes were to be so
dramatically linked, were discovered by the caricaturists in 1771. Early
in 1772 the Princess Dowager died. Prints had been largely responsible
for the hate that literally followed her to the grave in the insults of the mob.
'Satirical prints generally dispersed throughout the Kingdom in which her
Highness was not at all spared, inflamed the public mind.'[1] Legacies from
the past were Bute—completely outside politics for years—and the blasted
reputations of Sandwich (Jemmy Twitcher), Mansfield (Judge Jeffreys for
condemning Wilkes), and Germain (Minden),—all contributing to the
animosities that bedevilled the conflict with America.

The Wilkite turmoil was over. 'After a noted fermentation in the
nation', Burke wrote in July 1771, 'as remarkable a deadness and vapidity
has followed it.' The deadness withstood two crises that might have revived the fermentation. One was the quarrel of the Commons with Wilkes
and the City over the publication of Debates. Despite the importance of
the issue and the imprisonment in the Tower of the Lord Mayor and a
Wilkite Alderman and consequent riots, the public were more interested
in the quarrel between Wilkes and his friend Horne (afterwards Horne-
Tooke), carried on in the newspapers with reciprocal insults. In the prints
Horne is accused of being instigated by the Devil, by the Pope, by
Ministers (as he was by Junius), but the affair was clearly discreditable to
Wilkes, who was involved in other damaging quarrels. The situation was
correctly summed up in *Patriotic Meteors* [4887], a *London Magazine* plate
in October. Three heads with civic chains round their necks are being
drawn into gaping hippopotamus jaws—'The Gulf of Oblivion'. They are
Wilkes, Lord Mayor Crosby (the Patriot recently in the Tower), and
Alderman Bull, Wilkes's co-Sheriff. 'Wilkes is almost as dead as Sacheverell, though Sheriff,' wrote Walpole in December.[2]

The other crisis was the Falkland Islands affair. The Opposition
violently attacked the Ministry for corrupt subservience to Spain after the

[1] Walpole, *Last Journals*, 1910, 17 and n.
[2] *Letters*, ed. Toynbee, Oxford, viii. 122.

seizure of Port Egmont by the Governor of Buenos Ayres. Chatham led an attempt to rouse war fever against Spain and France, and indignation against the Ministry, in the way that had succeeded against Walpole. But Port Egmont was restored and the aggressor disavowed after successful diplomacy and naval preparations. All the prints were violently Oppositionist—it might be more true to say that they violently express memories of Walpole and 'the Ear' as they did again in 1790. Islands are 'to be given away—French Mistresses paid for conveying them.' In *Admiral Rodney before Carthagena* [4940] Glover's ballad, *Hosier's Ghost*, was quoted again, as in 1740 [2422]; he stands with his hands tied behind him: 'Nothing has its wealth defended / But my Orders—Not to Fight.' Another print demands notice because, after the Boston Tea-Party, it was copied by Paul Revere for an American magazine to show England humiliated by Spain: *Spanish Treatment at Carthagena* [4934] in the *London Magazine* for December 1771 is a purely imaginary scene of English sailors forced to labour on Spanish fortifications.

The old manner was strongly entrenched in the magazines. *The Young Heir among bad Councellors or the Lion betray'd* [4859], a December plate in the *Oxford Magazine*, recalls prints of 1762. The King is a lion, blindfolded and in chains; North, a dog with one leg in a jackboot (for Bute), gashes him with a barbed paw. In the foreground is a foppish and Frenchified fox-cub (Charles Fox) with one foot in a dice box, holding a muff and the ace of clubs, and looking through a single eyeglass. Two prints in a rather more modern manner reflect the change of scene. *The Politician* [Pl. 44] by S. H. Grimm is a caricature portrait of Lord North as a flabby and repulsive degenerate, sitting draped in a sheet, in the hands of a French hairdresser who whispers in his ear. He is dismayed at reminders of the Falkland Islands and menaced by a bust of Cromwell. There is a picture on the wall of Don Quixote tilting at a windmill. The other is *The Young Politician* [Pl. 45]. An elegant young man, with the head and brush of a fox, sits between two French hairdressers and tears up Magna Charta for curl-papers, looking with cynical langour in the glass held by a sinister-looking valet. He is the embodiment of the man of pleasure and the reckless enemy of Liberty, and it is easy to forget that this was Fox's reputation on his first astonishing impact on society and politics —when he was a Lord of the Treasury and an uncompromising enemy of Wilkes. He was also pre-eminently the man of fashion and the Macaroni as in *Charles James Cub Esq* [4811], a satirical portrait in the *Oxford Magazine* for May.

The transition that outmoded the emblematical print and prepared the way for Gillray and Rowlandson was due chiefly to Matthew Darly and his wife. From 1770 to 1777 or 1778 they dominate the print-selling world with caricatures in the newer manner, largely from the drawings of amateurs etched by themselves. (Bunbury was now the leading amateur, but he was soon lost to Darly.) In 1771–3 he published six sets (twenty-four in each) of single (occasionally double) satirical portraits, commonly known as Macaronies, which he reissued in volumes as *Caricatures, Macaronies and Characters* (the order of the words changed for different volumes). Macaroni was a new coterie word in 1764 for ultra-fashionable travelled young men, Italianate and Frenchified—the macaroni super-seded the beau and anticipated the dandy. From about 1770 for a few years the word was used widely and facetiously. It also connoted a new fashion in men's dress which succeeded the full-skirted coat and flapped waistcoat of the mid-eighteenth century and prepared the way for the plainer dress of the '80's, usually attributed to French Revolution fashions, but which had been introduced into France by the *Anglomanes* before the Revolution. Darly's Macaronies were personalities of the town in all classes: for in-stance the Duke of Grafton was 'The Turf Macaroni', Cosway the minia-ture painter, who was very small, was 'The Miniature Macaroni', Darly's shop was *The Macaroni Print Shop* [Pl. 43].[1] Darly followed these up with other series, larger and more elaborate, decorative and attractive, suitable for colour but usually found uncoloured. Their chief subjects were the follies of fashion—extravagant hairdressing and the like. But into these from 1777 political prints (pro-American) occasionally intruded. After 1781 his imprint disappears.

About 1773 Darly held an exhibition of caricatures (seemingly of original drawings), forerunner of the caricature exhibitions of London print-sellers. A catalogue has survived[2] and each entry (all are anonymous) is specified as by a Gentleman, a Lady, or an Artist: out of 233 exhibits 106 are by gentlemen, 74 by ladies, 27 by artists, 26 unspecified.

Darly thus prefaced his Macaroni volumes:

Comic Humour, Caricatures, &c In a Series of Drol Prints, consisting of Heads, Figures, Conversations and Satires upon the follies of the Age Design'd by several Ladies, Gentlemen and the most Humorous Artists &c. Pub^d by M Darly Engraver and Printseller at No. 39 . . . Strand, London, where Gentle-

---

[1] The window displays recognizable prints, including *The Fly-Catching Macaroni* [4695], Joseph Banks catching a butterfly, striding from the 'Arctick Circle' to the 'Antarctick Circle' (on his expedition with Solander).      [2] In the British Museum Print Room.

men and Ladies may have Copper plates prepared and Varnished for etching.
Ladies to whom the fumes of the Aqua Fortis are Noxious may have their Plates
carefully Bit, and proved, and may be attended to their own Houses, and have
ev'ry necessary instruction in any part of Engraving, Etching . . . &c,—Ladies
and Gentlemen sending their Designs may have them neatly etch'd and printed
for their own private amusement at the most reasonable rates, or if for publication, shall have ev'ry grateful return and acknowledgement for any Comic
Design. Descriptive hints in writing (not political) shall have due Honor shewn
'em & be immediately Drawn and Executed. . . .

The exclusion of politics is significant and altogether exceptional. (From
1756 to 1766 Darly had been the chief publisher of political prints—first
against Fox and Newcastle then against Bute.) The link between social
and political caricature is Charles Fox, the fox-cub, the Macaroni *par
excellence*, leader of fashion, and extravagant gambler. In the Darly series
he is *The Original Macaroni* [5010] dressed for a masquerade, and inscribed
'Tom Fool the First'—not a political gibe—'Tom Fools' with cap and
bells were conspicuous characters in the fashionable masquerades of 1772.
But he is the macaroni-politician of *The Senators*, a verse satire of 1772:

> By turns solicited by different plans
> Yet fix'd to none, Fox dresses, games, harangues:
> Where varying fashion leads the sportive band,
> And whim and folly bound it hand in hand,
> Behold him ambling through these flow'ry ways
> A model Macaroni, *A l'Anglaise*.

During the calm before the storm raised by the Boston Tea Party the
prints are anti-ministerial in a rather tired way, with George III still asleep
or blindfolded. The unpredictable transformations of Charles Fox from
reactionary to Patriot, and thence to insubordinate placeman (junior Lord
of the Treasury) are the context of *A Peep in the Garden at Hayes* [Pl. 46]
dated 1 May 1773, an imaginary but significant scene. Chatham (who was
not at Hayes), a gouty invalid, just risen from his wheeled chair, listens
with wary friendliness to Fox, who stands before him as if making terms
for a political alliance. This is by William Austin, a drawing-master rival
of Darly, and is a cartoon in the newer manner, without explanation. Not
so a print of 1774 on the deflation of Wilkes when he had become Lord
Mayor. In *The Two Jacks* [5245] he is 'Jack Minor', the bottle imp,
emerging from a bottle—that is, he is an impudent impostor.[1] 'Jack

---

[1] The bottle imp hoax contrived by the Duke of Montagu in 1749, the subject of several
prints [3022–7]. Cf. p. 99.

Major' is a diabolic Bute standing in a jackboot; there is a Wilkite mob of tiny labouring men, 'Waking dreamers', who have dreamed of fabulously cheap porter and bread and cry, 'down with the rates and taxes'. There are verses ending, 'Firm to his int'rest each with Zeal Abides / The Secret Motive gain on both their Sides.'

# IX

# FROM THE AMERICAN REVOLUTION TO THE COALITION

WITH the news of the Boston Tea Party, which reached London in January 1774, America absorbs the caricaturists. The prints not only reflect opinion but were weapons of war. In England as in America 'the Revolution was in the hearts and minds of the people'.[1] The struggle in England was against the minority in Parliament who identified the Colonial cause with their own opposition to the authority of the Crown. Being almost entirely anti-ministerial, the prints are naturally, though not exclusively, pro-American. Two contentions were highly comforting to the enemy: one, that it was impossible for Britain to win and the war would end not only in defeat but ruin. The other, that victory, if achieved, would mean the end of British liberty. These contentions are lavishly illustrated—explicitly and implicitly. There is also a recurring strain of No-Popery and anti-Episcopacy, under the combined influence of dissent and of the attitude of the bench of bishops to the war: the bigotry that exploded in the Gordon Riots had flourished on allegations against Bute (whose name was unfortunately Stuart) and attacks on the Quebec Act.

The prints of 1774–5 attack Bute, Mansfield, and Ministers for the 'Intolerable Acts' passed to punish (to quote the King's message to Parliament) 'the outrageous proceedings at Boston'. *The Able Doctor, or America Swallowing the Bitter Draught* [Pl. 47 a] was at once copied by Paul Revere for an American magazine, and often passes as the American print which it might well be. Mansfield holds down America, while Bute stands behind with a drawn sword, watched by the deeply interested Kings of France and Spain: North forces her to drink from a teapot, and Sandwich twitches up her skirts to peer; Britannia weeps. This attack on the Boston Port Bill was in the *London Magazine* (April 1774). *The Mitred Minuet* [5228], also in the *London Magazine*, attacks the Quebec Act; bishops, approving 'The Roman Religion', dance to the bagpipe music of Bute

---

[1] John Adams (President U.S.A. 1796–1800), quoted Schlesinger, *New Viewpoints in American History*, 1922, p. 162.

and are directed by North who is instigated by the Devil. This measure, 'dictated by an enlightened liberalism . . . to secure the loyalty of the French Canadians',[1] was classed with the 'Intolerable Acts' against Massachusetts, and, in England as in America, singled out for special condemnation, provoking a stream of No Popery propaganda. Chatham denounced it as 'a most cruel, oppressive and odious measure, tearing up justice and every good principle by the roots'.[2]

Two pleas for conciliation strike a quite exceptional note; both are mezzotints in the grand manner by John Dixon. In *The Oracle . . . Dedicated to Concord* [5225],[3] Time shows a magic-lantern view of the future to Britannia, Hibernia, Scotia, and America: they see Concord putting Discord to flight while Liberty and Plenty, Truth and Justice, walk together. The unprophetic scene was the basis of a well-known satirical engraving published in Paris in 1778 with English, German, and French titles: *The Tea-Tax-Tempest, or the Anglo-American Revolution* [5490].[4] The four women now personify the four quarters of the world; Time shows them a vision of an exploding teapot bringing defeat and ruin to Britain. In its turn this was adapted (in March 1783) in an English print [6190] with the painful allusions made more explicit. The lesson of Dixon's second print is that punitive measures will bring disaster: in *A Political Lesson* [5230], published in September, a horse, America, rears violently and has thrown its rider, whose head has broken a milestone: 'To Boston VI Miles'; a signpost points to Salem. (Owing to the Boston Port Act seaborne trade was transferred to Salem.)

Two prints followed attacking the coercion of Massachusetts, published just before news of the outbreak of hostilities at Lexington on 19 April. In *Virtual Representation. 1775* [5286], dated 1 April, Bute is a highwayman who aims a blunderbuss at America (by exception a man), while the Speake. of the House of Commons says, 'I give you that man's money for my use'; America retorts, 'I will not be robbed', and an English sailor hurries to his defence. Bute and the Speaker are egged on by a Frenchman and a monk with a cross and gibbet. Britannia, blinded, rushes towards 'the Pit prepared for others'. On the horizon are two contrasted towns, one in flames, the other flying a Union flag: 'The English Protestant Town

---

[1] Morison and Commager, *Growth of the American Republic*, New York, 1930, p. 21.
[2] *Parl. Hist.* xviii. 1402.
[3] Exhibited, Society of Arts, 1774.
[4] By Carl Guttenberg of Nuremberg. Described, *Mémoires secrets* (xii. 172–3), 27 Nov. 1778 (known in France as *Lettres de Bachaumont*, the first scribe being Louis Petit de Bachaumont).

of Boston', and 'The French Roman Catholick Town of Quebec'. The title of this fantastic attack on the Quebec Act derides the theory that the Colonists, like Britons without the franchise, were virtually represented in Parliament. In *The Scotch Butchery, Boston. 1775* [5287], advertised and described in the *London Chronicle* for 18 April, Boston is bombarded by 'English Ships with Scotch Commanders' to the satisfaction of Bute and Mansfield, 'Superintendants of the Butchery from the two great Slaughter Houses'. Scottish soldiers attack unarmed fugitives with bayonets, but English ones are 'Struck with horror and are dropping their arms'. Both prints are typical of the more violent pro-American propaganda, as, for instance, that of Wilkes's ex-friend Horne who advertised for subscriptions for the dependants of Americans killed at Lexington, who 'preferring death to slavery, were for that reason only inhumanly murdered'.[1] His manifesto has a pictorial counterpart in one of the very few prints on specific military operations, *The Retreat from Concord to Lexington of the Army of Wild Irish Asses Defeated by the Brave American Militia*,[2] a realistic view of houses burning and soldiers fighting and plundering. In *Bunkers Hill or the Blessed Effects of Family Quarrels* [5289] America, a Red Indian woman with tomahawk and scalping knife, is seized and threatened by Britannia, who is mortally stabbed in the back by France; Spain, striding across two hemispheres, slashes Britannia's shield.

Till the disasters of Saratoga and Trenton, 1776–7 were years of success for the British. The first of the few anti-American prints is *The Yankie Doodles Intrenchments near Boston 1776* [5329], ill drawn, badly produced, and without imprint; the 'Death or Liberty' men are ridiculed as unsoldierly incompetents and canting Puritans, devoted to 'Old Oliver's Cause / No Monarch or Laws'. The artist is under the impression that Israel Putnam (not Washington) was the Commander-in-Chief. This was in a vein never repeated: Washington, with one post-war exception, is a hero, Benedict Arnold an arch-traitor; the exploits of Paul Jones are celebrated in popular prints without a trace of condemnation.

In this civil strife the hate which war engenders and needs was not for the Americans, not even for continental enemies—Holland scarcely excepted. It found its targets chiefly at home. From 1775 to a peak in 1779–80 the prints register a crescendo of anti-ministerial violence, with a developing counter-trickle of resentment against the Patriots. *The Parricide.*

---

[1] For this he was sentenced (1777) to a year's imprisonment and £100 fine.
[2] In the John Carter Brown Library, Brown University, Providence, U.S.A.

*A Sketch of Modern Patriotism* [Pl. 47 *b*] in the *Westminster Magazine* (previously pro-American) was altogether exceptional in 1776. America, an Indian woman with tomahawk and dagger, attacks Britannia, directed by Wilkes and watched by members of the Opposition, including Chatham and a fox—Charles Fox—his first appearance as a Patriot. 'With an effrontery beyond example in any other age or nation, these men assume the name of Patriots . . . they bind the hands of the mother while they plant a dagger in the hands of the daughter.'

Many things combined to make North's Conciliatory Propositions (with which Commissioners were sent to America in April 1778) a crisis of opinion. They gave up all the original points at issue, stipulating only for political union, and, but for the French alliance, still ostensibly secret, would probably have been accepted.[1] They dismayed the extreme Patriots in America: 'more dangerous to our cause than ten thousand of their best troops'—so Governor Johnson of Maryland was warned when the terms were distributed from Howe's headquarters. The French, dreading a reconciliation above all things, impugned their good faith and represented them as England's recognition of defeat.[2] Their reception in England was all that her enemies could desire. The Opposition, who preached surrender, were dismayed at the possibility of conciliation achieved by North and Co. and in a way which—so they persuaded themselves—would increase the power of the Crown. They denounced the terms as specious and deceitful and poured scorn on the choice of Commissioners. Even some Whigs traduced the terms as humiliating, and, though there were those who welcomed them as 'the only means of getting out of the scrape we are in',[3] the prints are violently hostile. Any one of them might have served as enemy propaganda; at least two did, one of them to a sensational degree. Paradoxically, this was a plea for the more active conduct of the war and a traditional attack on Holland as a profiteering neutral.[4] It exactly illustrated the motives and hopes of France and Holland: the destruction of British trade leading (on mercantilist principles) to the crippling of Britain. This was the first of the prints on the Propositions, a plate to the *Westminster Magazine* for March, *A Picturesque View of the State of the Nation for February 1778* [Pl. 48]. British Commerce is 'a poor tame cow'; an American—'the American Congress'—saws off her horns 'which are her

[1] Morison and Commager, *op. cit.*, p. 96.
[2] P. G. Davidson, 'Whig Propagandists of the American Revolution', *American Hist. Rev.* Apr. 1934.
[3] *Lord Fife and his Factor*, ed. A. and H. Taylor, 1925, p. 105.
[4] Cf. p. 98.

natural defence and strength'; a Dutchman milks, a Frenchman and a Spaniard walk off, each with a bowl of milk. The sleeping British Lion is trampled on by a pug dog (Holland) and 'A Free Englishman in mourning' bewails his inability to rouse him. In the background the Howe brothers—the admiral and the general—sleep over their wine and punch in Philadelphia (evacuated in June 1778), 'out of sight of fleet and army, the flagship laid up and all the rest of the fleet invisible, nobody knows where'. The Howes (who are attacked in a number of prints) were much condemned at home and despised in America for inactivity. The points are stressed in an 'Explanation' which concludes that the 'proof' of the deplorable state of things is the abject character of the Propositions. Darly published an enlarged version:[1] *Poor Old England: Or the Bl—ss—d Fruits of a Wise Administration*, one of three which he advertised[2] as 'Impolitical Prints'—its use by the enemy shows how very impolitic it was. The design was also copied on Staffordshire pottery—a sure sign of popularity. Foreign copies[3] use the original explanation in the magazine, but omit all reference to the Propositions. A copy was published in America in 1778 'taken from an English copy'. A second American copy, attributed to Paul Revere, appeared in 1780 with the Howes transferred to New York—a correction not made in continental versions. Three French versions are extant (one the subject of a paragraph in the *Mémoires secrets* for 13 August 1778), besides an adaptation for a fan and another adaptation where the Frenchman tramples on a peacock, symbol of British pride. Five Dutch versions were exhibited in the New York Public Library in November 1939; in the British Museum there are four, besides a small copy in a composite sheet of 'Political Fables'. Two sequels, in 1781, carry on the story. First, in February, a naïve English print: *Mynheer Nic Frog's Lamentation: Or Dutch Milk a Fine Relish to British Sailors* [5830]: the Hollander, no longer neutral, mourns the loss of his ships. *York Town* [5859] is the triumphant Dutch retort: the cow is now moribund and feeds on thorns; the Dutchman carries off a heavy pail of milk, the Frenchman and the Spaniard have their smaller shares; the Englishman kneels in abject despair; the wounded Lion howls, hurt by the exploding 'American Tea Pot'. Obsequiously, the British approach America, who has thrown off her yoke and shackles; on the shore an American prepares exports for European ports; the British flagship is wrecked, the French fleet is near

[1] John Carter Brown Library.
[2] *Public Advertiser*, 1–3 May.
[3] See *B.M. Satires*, v. 285, 449–51; R. T. H. Halsey, 'Impolitical Prints', *Bulletin of the New York Public Library*, Nov. 1939.

the horizon. There could hardly be a better example of the international importance of pictorial propaganda than this sequence of prints, with its illustration of the deep concern for seaborne trade.

Darly's two other 'Impolitical Prints' were attacks on the Commissioners. In the first, *The Commissioners* [5473], each of the five makes a speech in character to a triumphant America, irradiated and enthroned on barrels and bales of tobacco, rice, and indigo destined for continental ports. Admiral Lord Howe: 'We have block'd up your ports, obstructed your trade, with the hope of starving ye & contrary to the Law of Nations compelld your sons to war against their Bretheren.' His brother the General says, 'We have ravaged your Lands, burnt your Towns, and caus'd your captive Heroes to perish, by Cold, pestilence & famine.' (Both Howes had refused to act as Commissioners.) And there is much more of the same sort.

A pair of pictograph letters (rebuses) published by Darly and dated 6 and 11 May sum up the situation facetiously: In *Britannia to America* the former holds out an olive branch and signs herself 'your Friend and Mother'. The answer, *America to her Mistaken Mother* [Pl. 49], is headed by a print of America as a Red Indian woman with flag and shield of stripes and stars, holding a fleur-de-lis for the French alliance. She begins,'you silly old woman that you have sent a lure to us is very plane', and ends, 'take home your ships [and] soldiers . . . leave me to myself as I am at age to know my own interests without your foolish advice & know that I shall always regard you & my Brothers as relations but not as friends. I am your grately injured Daughter America.'

Another Darly plate, *Folly on Both Sides or a View of the Political State of the Nation* (11 May),[1] has a quite exceptional lesson—that both the Ins and the Outs were contributing to disaster. The overladen State Car, driven by an outsize diabolical Bute, is bogged down by its burden of 'Pensions, Needless Expenditure, Civil List, National Debt, Placemen'; placemen, bishops, and King's Friends try to push it from the mire, since 'no work, no play'. The team of ministerial asses are assailed by ferocious Opposition curs; most only bark, but two bite savagely: Fox attacks Germain, Richmond tears at Sandwich; the barkers are an emaciated Wilkes with a fool's cap on his 'pole of Liberty', Burke, and four peers including Shelburne but not Rockingham. The Commissioners are flying to America with 'Sureties for Intreaties, Contrition, Reparations, Concessions'—bladders embodying 'The Hope or England's Last Shift'. There are small inset

---

[1] In the John Carter Brown Library. Photostat in the British Museum.

designs; in one the Devil superintends a seesaw with France and America safely uppermost and England about to fall into his net. Verses in a showman's patter point the moral—Ministers deceive the King with tales of victories—and so on. There is a French copy with a prose translation of the verses. The discomfiture of the Commissioners in America, where they were ridiculed and obstructed in every way, is the subject of a French print with an English title and a fictitious and ante-dated publication line but with French inscriptions, including 'le Lord Burthe couronné sur un ane.' 'Infortunez Anglois, à quoi vos Bills Conciliatoire [sic] ont-ils servis?' The mysterious Burthe is seemingly Lord North. This is *The Olive Reject<sup>d</sup> or the Yankees Revenge*.[1]

A typical misrepresentation of the Stamp Act characterizes the last belated print on the Commissioners, *The Curious Zebra* [Pl. 50] on 3 September. The names of the thirteen colonies are inscribed on the creature's stripes; four men compete for it, while the three Commissioners find their oats and hay rejected. Grenville (died 1770) saddles it with the Stamp Act: 'I say Saddle the Beast, She will be able to bear great burdens for plac—n and Pensioners.' 'Boreas' says, '. . . I hold the Reins and will never quit them till the Beast is Subdued' (an odd comment on his Propositions). Washington and a Frenchman pull at the tail: '. . . dis Zebra Vill look very pretty in my Menagerie.'

Moderation at last—and quite exceptionally—breaks in with a Darly plate in November: *The English and American Discovery, Brother, Brother We are Both in the Wrong*.[2] John Bull and Brother Jonathan sit together over pipe and glass in serious meditation; a picture on the wall of clasped hands points the moral.

Attacks on recruiting were effective anti-war propaganda. There are several. First, in 1775, when trade was booming, *Six-Pence A Day* [Pl. 51]: the calamities of a soldier and his family are contrasted with the prosperity of 'the lowest trades' (a chairman and a waggoner) who 'earn sufficient to enjoy the Comforts of life'. Even a little chimney-sweep's boy gets a shilling a day, and mocks the starving family. A personification of Famine and Death, ragged and skeleton-like, beckons to 'The Target' a tall, emaciated melancholy soldier, who is flanked by his protesting family— pregnant wife and hungry children; and the subscriptions for soldiers' comforts are bitterly derided. In 1779, when invasion seemed imminent and so-called loyalty regiments were being hurriedly raised, these were ridiculed and disparaged. The 85th regiment, raised in London, was de-

---

[1] *Collection de Vinck*, no. 1215.      [2] In the John Carter Brown Library.

rided in *The Terror of France or the Westminster Volunteers* [5552]; four extremely unsoldierly pairs with fixed bayonets are guyed in a quatrain, beginning, 'Can we Invasion dread, when Volunteers / Like these, propose to Fight the Gay Mounseers.' At this moment—26 August—the country was in danger: the combined French and Spanish fleets were in the Channel; 30,000 French troops were on the coast between Havre and St. Malo. Defeat is prophesied in *The Horse America, throwing his Master* [Pl. 52], dated 1 August 1779. George III is about to fall head-first from the plunging animal which he has maddened by a cruel scourge, to each lash of which is tied a sword, sabre, bayonet, scalping knife, or axe. A French officer walks towards the riderless horse.

In 1779–80 there is violent and increasing animosity to George III— a tyrant—'Sultan'—an oriental despot—through whose obstinacy the country is in danger of ruin. Commercial and industrial distress darkened the gloom; the agitation against the Catholic Relief Bill aggravated the hostility to the King. A savagely ironical *Birth-Day Ode* [5540] for 1779 is sophisticated; North is first violin, Sandwich performs with great vigour on kettle-drums, Germain on the oboe. The 'Full Chorus' ends: 'His Worth's the same in Jove's impartial Eyes / Who saves a sinking Empire, or destroys.'

*Mr. Trade & Family or ye State of the Nation* [5574] is dedicated by 'Thomas Tradeless' to 'his Excel^y. Gen^l Washington Pat. Pat^æ': A destitute man, with his starving wife and children, holds out his hat for alms: 'I was once a Capital Dealer but thro y^e Obstinacy of ONE MAN & y^e Villainy of many More—am reduced to Beggary.' Two owls on a dead tree say, 'Long live Sultan—as long as he lives, We shall never want ruin'd Towns & Villages.' (About this time several versions of a mezzotint bust portrait of George III in Turkish dress were published with ironical titles—*The Patriot*, or *Behold the Man*.) In another print with the same date, December 1779, *The Botching Taylor cutting his Cloth to cover a Button* [5573], the King (the button maker) sits crosslegged in a tailor's workroom, slashing his cloth—the United Kingdom—to pieces. Guided by Bute he is about to cut off Ireland; North holds 'North America'—already cut off; Sandwich has a 'Scheme for ruining the Navy'. Discarded scraps lie under the table, the 'Bill of Rights, Magna Charta, Remonstrances, Petitions', and so on. The Pope embraces the Pretender and both watch the besotted King with deep interest. There is a picture of the 'Flight to Egypt', the King and his family are on their way to Hanover; among the broadsides on the wall is one headed by crossed axes: 'Dr. Cromwell's effectual and only remedy for the King's evil', a gibe that verges on treason. The spirit of this print is that of a famous speech by Fox (24 November) with its menacing allusions to the fate of the Stuarts: 'When a nation was reduced to such a state of wretchedness . . . the people would inevitably take up arms and the first characters in the kingdom would be seen in their ranks' —a speech which the *Morning Post* stigmatized as a 'parliamentary invocation to rebellion'.[1] The publisher's name on the *Botching Taylor* may be fictitious, but another savage attack on the King was openly published by John Almon; in *The Allies—Par nobile Fratrûm*! [Pl. 53], 3 February 1780, George III shares a cannibal feast (on his American subjects) with an Indian brave. A very fat bishop hastens up to them followed by a sailor laden with 'Scalping Knives, Crucifixes, Tomahawks, Presents to Indians 96,000': 'The Party of Savages went out with orders not to spare Man Woman or Child. . . .' (Almon cites his own propagandist annual *The Remembrancer*.) The bishop is clearly Markham, much attacked for his attitude to the war, 'Archbishop Turpin' as Walpole called him; *General Sanguinaire Mark-ham* [5400] in a print of 1777, where he is the third Archbishop of York to be part-bishop, part-soldier, but he is treated more harshly than Williams or Herring. In *Review of the York Regiment* [Pl. 55] he leads a troop of soldier-clerics against Britannia (who wears a cap of Liberty): 'Please you Madam, for Mitres, Deaneries and Prebendaries, we will wade through an Ocean of Yanky Blood.'

In one of his earliest political plates, dated 10 February 1780, Gillray expressed the general contempt for the Ministry at the peak of the pressure against it. North, Sandwich, and Germain are *The State Tinkers* [Pl. 54], who break up a giant bowl, 'The National Kettle', under pretence of mending it. The King, in his oriental turban, looks on with a fatuous smile, directed by the delighted Bute.

Such prints reflect the spirit of near-revolution expressed in the vast movement of Associations and Petitions early in 1780 when the people were 'mad from virtue, and were bent on reforming and amending the Constitution on erroneous principles . . .'.[2] First came the famous Yorkshire meeting of 30 December with its project for radical parliamentary Reform, then Burke's Plan of Economical Reform to eliminate jobs and so curb the power of the Crown. These are the subject of approving prints, for instance, *Association or Public Virtue Displayed in a Contrasted View* [5638]

---

[1] *Parl. Hist.* xx. 1123–5. See Butterfield, *George III, Lord North and the People 1779–1780*, 1949, 166–7.

[2] Lord Hillsborough, debate of 14 Apr. 1780, quoted Butterfield, op. cit., pp. 327–8.

on 15 February, a complicated allegorical design. Britannia, robbed by
Bute of her staff and cap of Liberty, turns to the marching processions of
petitioners: 'Tis you alone my Friends who can revive my drooping Hopes
& save me from Distruction.' The ghost of Chatham, saying 'O Cleanse
yon Augean Stable', points to the House of Commons which is 'Ruled
by Powerful Influence' and placed near the King's Closet.

The success of Dunning's famous motion on the increasing power of
the Crown (6 April) is acclaimed in *Prerogative's Defeat or Liberty's
Triumph* [5659] on 20 April, anticipating a change of Ministry, peace with
America, understanding with Ireland. Aided by Fox, Dunning treads down
Bute and North, saying, 'I'll trample on Corruption's favourite Minions.'
America, a feathered Amazon, stands beside an armed Irish Volunteer;
one says, 'now we will treat with them'; the other, 'We are loyal but we
will be free.'

Nevertheless, supported by successes in America, North held on for
nearly two more years. The prints register a change of political climate;
Ministers of course are attacked, but the King is no longer a tyrant—there
are even indications of a return of popularity. The most obvious cause of
the reaction against the Opposition was the object lesson of the Gordon
Riots on the dangers of Associations and mass petitioning. But this is not
to be deduced from the prints which with one exception are pro-Protestant
Association. There were other reasons for the reaction. It is remarkable that
the Catholic Relief Act of 1778, the only measure on which the Ministry
and Opposition were agreed, should have been popularly regarded as an
outrage. That cartoons were part of the adroit propaganda of Lord George
Gordon's Protestant Association cannot be doubted. Highly significant
is *Sawney's Defence against the Beast, Whore, Pope, and Devil* [Pl. 56],
dated 1 April 1779, in which the organized and successful rioting in
Scotland against Catholic Relief is applauded in the familiar imagery
of the seventeenth century. John Bull is urged to imitate a Scottish
soldier—not now an emissary of Bute but a hero with a shield inscribed
'Begone Judas'. But John is helpless, tied hand and foot, and trampled
on by the Beast, led by George III, whose 'Plot' is resisted by Sawney.
The Pope absolves the King from his Coronation Oath,[1] of which so
much was to be heard—not quite its first appearance, it had been invoked

---

[1] Cf. *An Heroic Epistle to an Unfortunate Monarch*, 1779, pp. 195–8.
    Proceed, great Sir! and breaking all restraint,
    Embrace the *scarlet whore* and be a *Saint*.
    *Sworn* to maintain the establish'd Church advance
    The cross of Rome, the miracles of France.

against the Quebec Act. In *The Invisible Junto Dedicated to the Truly Honourable Lord George Gordon* [5671, n.d.] the King is compared with the wicked and idolatrous King Manasseh and is outweighed, in a pair of divinely held scales, by the Bible, 'Sidney on Government',[1] and the cap of Liberty. As *The Royal Ass* [5669] on 20 May 1780 he is led to Rome by Bute and Archbishop Markham, and as *The Mangy Whelp* [5670] he is taken there by 'Father Peters'—an echo of 1688 which probably points also to Lord Petre, head of the English Catholics. *The Ecclesiastical and Political State of the Nation* [5678] was timed to appear on the day of the mass meeting and march to Westminster (2 June) which started the Riots: urged on by the Pope and a swarm of devils, George III and North attack Protestantism and the Constitution. In other cartoons 'Protestant' themes infiltrate prints on the constitutional issues and vice versa.

After the Riots, as before, Gordon is the Protestant Hero; the stream of propaganda does not stop but is diverted to showing that the Protestant Association was blameless. (One print only, *Fanatacism Revived* [5685], impugns it.) The culprits are the underworld [5679], George III, the Papists; the Government are accused of using the riots to foster a military despotism [5683]; the Lord Mayor is ridiculed for what he called his 'temerity' (meaning his lamentable cowardice). On 10 June, the first day the shops ventured to open, appeared *A Priest at his Private Devotion* [5680]; George III is a monk, kneeling at an altar, having dishonoured both the Protestant Petition and the County petitions for Reform. Finally, Gordon and the Protestant Association were eulogized in a plate [5841] to a new edition of *Foxe's Martyrs*, attributing the riots to 'the mischievous Emissaries of the Papists', a view of Palace Yard and the Petitioners utterly unlike the disorderly scene on 2 June. It is emphatically not in Gordon Riots prints that the reaction—still slight—against the Opposition is to be traced.

In 1780 popular preoccupations—besides Constitutional Reform—were naval victories and swelling indignation against the Dutch as profiteering neutrals, both unfavourable to Opposition. A significant—though exceptional—print dated 27 February is *Opposition Defeated* [Pl. 57]; North, riding a bull—John Bull—damages enemies at home and abroad. The bull, trampling on France, Spain, and America, has fatally wounded

---

[1] This republican work was influential in America; cf. Caroline Robbins, 'Algernon Sidney's *Discourses concerning Government*: Textbook of Revolution', *William and Mary Quarterly* Williamsburg, 1947, pp. 267–96. See pp. 68, 165.

Shelburne—'Malagrida'—who sinks back into the arms of his protégés, Price and Priestley, both disparaged as materialists and pro-Americans. Burke leads Lord Rockingham by the nose, and Fox carries the Prince of Wales on his shoulders; the young man tries to grab the crown (on a sign-board) but North—Boreas—blows it out of his reach and Fox exclaims, 'Here end the hopes of me and the Jews.' Very faintly sketched in the background is a man blowing the 'Horn of Rebellion'. The early recognition of the political association of Fox and the Prince (usually attributed to 1782) is remarkable. Or was it anticipation, based on the usual attitude of Hanoverian heirs apparent?[1]

Nevertheless, in 1780 Charles Fox was at the peak of his popularity, established as the 'Man of the People'. One of the landmarks of this year of landmarks was the founding of the Westminster Committee and the invitation to Fox in February to stand for Westminster (without expense), followed by his return at the general election after a heated contest—an event celebrated by the founding of the Whig Club. It is true he was second to Rodney, elected in his absence. An interesting print of the scene in Covent Garden is one of a long line; Rodney is supported by Neptune, Fox by a band of butchers with marrow-bones and cleavers; the second Court candidate is denigrated for bribery. Another foretaste of the future was *Florizel and Perdita* [5767], a Green Room scene at Drury Lane between the Prince and 'Perdita' Robinson—a prelude to the prolonged obsession with the *amours* of the future George IV.

Faction had raged disastrously in the Navy—mainly owing to hatred of Sandwich; it had exploded over Keppel's court martial for inaction at Ushant (27 July 1778), and on his acquittal he became a popular hero. But he had justified himself by pleading the dangers of a lee shore; this was long remembered against him, especially when (after January 1780) he was brought into rivalry with the more daring and successful Rodney. Already in December 1779 Keppel was satirized in *Who's in Fault?* (*Nobody*). *A View of Ushant* [Pl. 58]. (Since Palliser had also been acquitted nobody was in fault.) Keppel stands on the shore pointing to a naval engagement: his legs are joined to his shoulders to show that he is Nobody—an old folk-print device:[2] '. . . if *it* has a Heart it must lay in its Breeches.' In January 1780 there was national rejoicing, vividly illustrated, at Rodney's victories: two Spanish squadrons defeated, prizes taken,

[1] In the Windsor election, Sept. 1780, George III actively and openly opposed Keppel and secured his defeat: the Prince 'took great part for Keppel'. See *The Stable Voters of Beer Lane Windsor* [5700]; Ian Christie, *The End of North's Ministry*, 1958, pp. 86–87.

[2] Cf. C. Mitchell, *Hogarth's Peregrination*, Oxford, 1952, pp. xxiv–xxviii.

Gibraltar relieved. Popular sentiment was expressed in a rebus, *An Herio-glyphical Epistle from Britannia to Admiral Rodney* [5658]:

> To you my darling Child I deign to write
> Who dared the haughty Spanish Dons to Fight
> The Cause like others you did not betray
> Who faintly Fought and almost Ran away
> Like a Bold Man you us'd Britannia's Power
> And scorned that dreaded Circumstance—LEE SHORE . . .
> Go on Brave Rodney in thy Bold career
> And let thy Vengeance, Burst on False Mounseer
> Then lost America no more shall Roam
> But find with me true Greatness is at Home . . .

Though a Tory, Rodney had the merit of being on bad terms with Sandwich; it was understood that he got a command only through the King's intervention. Hence *The Appointment of the Brave Admiral Rodney and Jemmy Twitcher in the Dumps* [5673] in May 1780. The King says to the kneeling Rodney, 'do all in your power for the honour of my Crown & y$^e$ good of y$^e$ Nation.' Rodney: 'May it please your Majesty I will never fear a Lee Shore but conquer or Die.' His action off St. Vincent had in fact been 'regardless of a blowy night, lee shore and dangerous shoals'. Two years later the politics implied in this rivalry became crucial.

In this war the perennial resentment against Holland reached its climax. It was forcibly expressed in the much-copied *Picturesque View . . .* of 1778, so gratifying to the Dutch. *The European Diligence* [5557] in October 1779 is a wheelbarrow containing Britain's enemies; a boorish Dutchman, charged with 'Ingratitude & Duplicity', trundles it over the prostrate Britannia, saying, 'What's treaties to gelt?' Despite three treaties of alliance between Britain and the United Netherlands, Dutch merchants were carrying on an immense trade with her enemies; Dutch papers were freely given to American privateers; Paul Jones was allowed to refit his ships in Holland and acclaimed as a hero; the Dutch West India island of St. Eustatius was a vast storehouse of munitions of war for America and her allies, without which, it was contended, they must have been defeated. All this can be followed in the prints. As an enemy Holland would be far less dangerous than as an unfriendly neutral, and the King's manifesto of 20 December 1780, a virtual declaration of war, nicely timed to forestall Dutch adherence to the Armed Neutrality, was highly popular though denounced by the Opposition. This was a moment when Horace Walpole could reflect despondingly that the Government were more popular than the Opposition.[1]

---

[1] *Last Journals*, 1910, under date 31 Dec. 1780.

Rodney's capture of St. Eustatius was a blow to the enemy. It was also, as Selwyn wrote to Lady Rodney, 'a thunderbolt to the Opposition'. Reactions are illustrated in Gillray's *The Dutchman in the Dumps* [5837] in April 1781. An English sailor rejoices, the enemy are horror-struck; 'St. Eustatia by gar / Vas de Storehouse of War', says a foppish Frenchman. America, an unimpressive youth, adds, 'America now, / To Old England must Bow.' It was otherwise, and faction raged round Rodney's high-handed disposal of captured stores, satirically depicted in *The Late Auction at St. Eustatia* [5842]. It was found that many British subjects had been using the island for enemy trading. Rodney was violently attacked by Burke in Parliament; charges and counter-charges filled the newspapers, and he was involved in lengthy lawsuits—claims being made that exceeded the whole value of the captured property. The loss of the command of the sea that led to the surrender at Yorktown has been attributed in part to his prolonged stay on the island. But the dismay with which British Patriots (enemy traders) heard the news of the capture was illustrated by Bunbury in October in a realistic coffee-house interior: *The Coffee-House Patriots: or News from St. Eustatia* [Pl. 59].

From 1780 it is possible to trace the beginnings of the revolutionary change of opinion that accompanied and sanctioned Pitt's triumph in 1784. Never were prints more potent, more revealing. They forcibly suggest that behind the change was a basic patriotism and a basic loyalty to the Crown, both offended by the attitude of the Rockingham Whigs to the war and the monarchy. We all know how Fox had 'grieved at the terrible news from New York' and rejoiced at Saratoga and Yorktown. The Duke of Richmond when Lord Lieutenant of Sussex sailed his yacht through the fleet when the King was there, with the American colours at his mast-head.[1] The Opposition, in their blue and buff, called Washington's army 'our army'. 'It is strange that they should never learn', wrote Lord Loughborough after Yorktown, 'that to show rejoicing at a public calamity makes them odious and aids those they are attacking.'[2] This is one of the occasions when the prints throw light on a change in popular opinion—a striking change indeed from the anti-monarchical peak of 1779–80 to enthusiasm for prerogative in 1784. The check given by Yorktown was surprisingly slight.

But bad news from the West Indies had revived the declining hopes of Opposition and after Yorktown Ministers were clearly doomed, though

---

[1] Greville, *Memoirs*, under date 5 Sept. 1834 (information from Lord Holland).
[2] *Hist. MSS. Comm., Carlisle MSS.*, p. 539.

they held on for nearly four months. At last North's long, disastrous Ministry came to an end. He resigned on 20 March 1783; on the 25th Fox took office as Foreign Secretary under Rockingham. *The Royal Hunt, or a Prospect of the Year 1782* [5961], dated 16 February, anticipated the change and yet more disasters, exaggerating those already known. The print is noteworthy for the first appearance of Pitt the Younger: aligned with the Patriots, Fox, Burke, and Richmond (the omission of the nominal First Minister is characteristic), he says to North, 'shake off this indolence'. On 22 March Gillray produced *Changing Places,—alias; Fox Stinking the Badger out of his Nest* [5964]; the badger (North) runs off from his little cave towards 'Tower Hill', snarled at by a fox which excretes a stream of 'Eloquence'. In the distance is the royal hunt; the King leaps a gate and falls on his head, losing his crown; North's attributes are his budget and taxes; Fox's are emblems of gaming—a 'faro bank', discharging guineas. Fox's faro bank at Brooks's had been extremely profitable, and is the scene of Gillray's *Banco to the Knave* [5972] in April, where North and Co. have lost everything to the new Ministers, and Fox (with a fox's head) has acquired a heap of coin and notes. It was his fate to be disparaged both as a ruined and a fortunate gambler.

The *Morning Herald* (30 March) acclaimed the change as 'the end of the Butean system' and prophesied that a popular Ministry would bring ruin to the print-shops. But the new Ministers soon ceased to be popular and the print-shops went on from strength to strength. One of the relatively few pro-ministerial prints is *The War of Posts* [5984] by Colley on 1 May: the Devil drives ex-Ministers into the jaws of Hell; their successors are astride on 'posts' (small columns), and beside them stands Pitt, who had refused a post; he holds a sheaf of thunderbolts with darts inscribed 'Vox Populi', and says, 'The Lightining of my Father.' Though the antagonists are Fox and North, the rivalry of Fox and Pitt is latent. Another print which by exception is ministerial appeared in May, *Anticipation, or, the Contrast to the Royal Hunt* [5988], a complicated condemnation of the old Ministry and eulogy of the new one. Rockingham is an oculist removing a film from the King's eyes; North, an old washerwoman (he had taxed soap), says, 'My Northstrums had almost totally blinded him.'

But increasingly Ministers are attacked for their attitude to the Crown. The caricaturists, Gillray especially, make the most of damaging allegations of Republicanism. 'Every Devil is at work to divide us', wrote Walpole on 2 April, 'and half Styx at work to calumniate our party and represent us as worse levellers than John of Leyden and his Anabaptists.'[1] Fox's indiscreet talk at Brooks's was retailed by Selwyn to Carlisle: 'He talked of the King under the description of Satan . . .' He said, 'That this Revolution which he brought about was the greatest for England that ever was; that excepting in the mere person of a King, it was a complete change in the constitution. . . .'[2]

In *The Captive Prince—or—Liberty run Mad* [Pl. 60] George III exclaims, 'Oh! My misguided People', but stands passively while his new Ministers fit shackles to wrists and ankles—Fox kneels to adjust a fetter, saying, 'I command the Mob'; Lord John Cavendish silently attends to the other ankle. Keppel and Richmond chain his wrists; Rockingham walks off with the crown, saying, 'Dispose of these jewels for the Publick use'; other ministers speak in character; Burke eulogizes the king. One of Gillray's double-edged thrusts is *Guy Vaux* [6007, n.d.]: the King, with an ass's head, sleeps on the throne above a cask of gunpowder, with the crown and sceptre in a sack, ready for departure—presumably to Hanover; Fox, with a fox's head and holding a dark lantern, leads in his band of conspirators. On 10 May Gillray produced *Britania's Assassination—or—The Republican Amusement* [Pl. 61]. Ministers try to break up and pull down a sadly mutilated statue of Britannia seated on a globe, while two judges, Thurlow and Mansfield, try to protect her. A fox (Charles) bites her leg; Wilkes threatens her with the 'North Briton' and 'Libel', Dunning with 'Sydney on Government', Richmond with a musket. Keppel hauls down the flag, quoting 'He that Fights and runs away . . .'. America (an Indian) runs off with Britannia's head, and is pursued by the empty-handed France; Spain has got a leg, Holland the shield. Here is a complete reversal (anticipated in *The Parricide*) of the old attitude to North's Ministry, and an attack on Whig factiousness: 'Sydney on Government' is no longer an emblem of Liberty[3] but of sedition, and approval for Mansfield and Thurlow is unprecedented.

The Ministry were further discredited by Rodney's resounding victory over de Grasse at the battle of The Saints, removing the threat to the West Indies. News reached London on 18 May: in the moment of victory Rodney was recalled to be replaced by the inadequate Pigot; it was freely said that the appointment was made to enable him to pay his notorious gaming debts to Fox. Exultation at the victory was combined with resentment at Pigot's appointment, which was 'loudly and generally expressed in every

[1] *Letters*, ed. Toynbee, Oxford, xii. 216.
[2] *Hist. MSS. Comm., Carlisle MSS.*, pp. 599, 604 (19, 23 Mar. 1782).
[3] See pp. 68, 160 and n.

part of London'.[1] Gillray exploited the situation in a set of four cartoons. The first was a plate already 'worn out' and reprinted by 31 May: *Rodney Triumphant.—or—Admiral Lee Shore in the Dumps* [5992]. Keppel, now a viscount and First Lord, gloomily watches de Grasse's surrender to Rodney and the long procession of prizes: 'This is more than we expected more than we wished.' Fox: 'Dam the French for coming in his way say I.' Rodney's triumph, Pigot's appointment, are the subjects of the second and third. In the third, *Rodney Introducing de Grasse* [5997], Fox and Keppel stand by the King while Rodney kneels to present the captured Admiral; 'This fellow must be recalled,' says Fox, 'he fights too well for us—& I have obligations to Pigot, for he has lost 17000 at my Faro Bank.' Keppel reads a list of prizes: 'Ville' [de Paris]: 'This is the very Ship I ought to have taken on the 27th July.' In the fourth, *St. George and the Dragon* [Pl. 62], Rodney slays the dragon—the naval power of France— while Fox runs towards him, saying, 'Hold my dear Rodney, you have done enough, I will now make a Lord of you, and you shall have the happiness of never being heard of again.' This is an early example of Gillray's penetrating comments: he could not have known that on news of the victory Keppel told the King, 'He thought it absolutely necessary that some ostensible reward should be bestowed . . . the more so that he did not wish this event should stop Admiral Pigot's being sent to relieve him.'[2] Rodney's barony and recall were contrasted with Keppel's viscountcy and appointment as First Lord.

When Rockingham died on 1 July, and the King appointed Shelburne, and Fox resigned five days later, the fatal coalition with North was foreshadowed. The prints spoke with hardly a dissentient voice: 'The man of the people is snouted and foxed in the tap room of every porter house.'[3] Sayers's first cartoon, a famous one, was *Paradise Lost* [6011] in which Fox and Burke stand arm in arm, gazing disconsolately at the gates of Eden—that is—of the Treasury. Milton's poem was also the setting for a classic print by Gillray: *Gloria Mundi—or—The Devil addressing the Sun* [Pl. 63]. Fox, a ruined gambler with empty pockets, stands arrogantly on an E.O. (roulette) table poised on the globe, looking up at the sun which contains the head of Shelburne, looking down in cynical triumph:

> 'To thee I call,
> But with no friendly voice, & add thy name
> Sh—ne! [O Sun] to tell thee how I hate thy beams . . .'

[1] Wraxall, *Memoirs*, 1884, iii. 127.
[2] *Correspondence of George III*, ed. Fortescue, 1928, vi. 33, George III to Shelburne.
[3] *Morning Herald*, 3 Aug. 1782.

(The design was adapted for the vanquished Napoleon *vis-à-vis* the Regent, for George IV *vis-à-vis* his wife, for Queen Caroline *vis-à-vis* her husband.) Six months later, in another Miltonic plate by Gillray, Fox is Satan watching Adam and Eve: 'Aside he turn'd for Envy, yet with jealous leer malign, ey'd them askance' [6044]. In a woodland glade Shelburne sits with Pitt, his Chancellor of the Exchequer, at a table covered with money-bags and coin, the Treasury-Eden they enjoy with sly complacency; Fox stands aloof, scowling towards them. The near unanimity of the condemnation of Fox is remarkable, in view of the extreme unpopularity of Shelburne (Malagrida, the Jesuit). Burke shared the discredit of the resignations and was treated by Gillray as a secret Papist (educated at St. Omer)—a Jesuit, and as a Jesuit (in a biretta) he is depicted for many years. *Cincinnatus in Retirement* [6026], in which Burke is 'driven back to his native Potatoes', is noteworthy as the first of the prints in which he is an Irish Jesuit or a crypto-Papist, and is an example of Gillray's bad manners where emblems of Popery are concerned.

Meantime the peace was the prevailing topic. There is none of the unmixed execration for the peace-makers there had been in 1762–3. An early reaction to the Preliminaries with France, on the eve of the Coalition, was *Peace Porridge all Hot | The Best to be Got* [6172], by Colley, 11 February 1783, the heading to a song: '. . . Yet a Blow or two more might have made them all Stoop . . | Tho things have gone Cross for a long time Confest | Yet now to lament is no more than a Jest | But as well as we can out of Bad, make the best.' As so often in future John Bull and George III agree: 'When I reflect on the Want of Soldiers and Sailors . . .', he wrote in January, 'the more I thank Providence for having through so many difficulties, among which the want of Union and Zeal at home is not to be omitted, enabled so good a peace with France, Spain, and I trust soon the Dutch to be concluded.'[1]

Fox's attack on Shelburne for the Preliminaries revealed unmistakably his 'infamous' coalition with North. A sequel to the *Fox Stinking the Badger out of his Nest* of less than a year before was *Shelb—n Badgered & Foxed* [6176]—on 20 February—the two animals combine to tear at Shelburne and the Preliminaries. Moreover, the chief ground of attack was the treatment of the Loyalists for whom Fox had shown a marked lack of sympathy during the war. It was realized at once that the attack was an excuse for the junction with North. Condemnation was instant, emphatic, and prolonged. 'If satiric prints could despatch them', Walpole wrote before

---

[1] *Correspondence of George III*, vi. 222.

they had been in office a month, 'they would be dead in their cradle.'[1] There is no doubt that satiric prints were potent. Gillray summed up the position in a pair of prints dated 9 March, *War* and *Neither War nor Peace* [6187–8]. The first is a cloud-borne vision of past debates, Fox and Burke make one of their virulent attacks on North—'deserves the ax! disgrace! infamy! . . .', &c., &c. North defends himself, '. . . our Misfortunes entirely owing to Opposition'. In the other, Fox, Burke, and North combine against 'The Preliminary Articles of Peace'. Prints of 1782 had shown Fox and North in conflict for the fruits of office; now they are displayed in a shameless compact to enjoy them. For instance, in Gillray's *The Lord of the Vineyard* [6204] they reach up for an enormous bunch of grapes which Portland, nominal head of the Ministry, hands down to them. According to Lecky, North was more blamed than Fox—but not by the caricaturists: Fox is sly and triumphant, North bewildered and anxious, as in Sayers's famous *A Coalition Medal Struck in Brass* [6183], and in *The Mask* [Pl. 72], also by Sayers. Fox is Catiline (repeatedly), North the Vicar of Bray [6179].

The other lines of attack beside brazen self-interest were the Rockinghams' attitude to America and the Crown. In *The Ass-headed and Cowhearted Ministry making the British Lion Give up the Pull* [6229] on 8 May, the American rattlesnake says, 'The harangues of the British Patriots help me more to Independancy than 40000 Men'; the Ministry is denounced as 'a set of frantic sophistical Patriots'. Only once in 1782–3 is George III blamed for the disasters of the war and the losses of the peace, and that is in one of the very few apologies for the Coalition—an attack on the King for their dismissal when their speedy restoration was expected, *Today Disliked, and Yet Perhaps Tomorrow again in Favour, so Fickle is the Mind of R–y–l–ty!!!* [6291]. In this George II is 'The Father of his People' while George III is 'The Father of his—Children!' This print is the sole exception to unqualified condemnation of the Peace of 1763, which here, by contrast with 1783, becomes 'glorious, honourable & advantageous'. More characteristic is the verdict on Fox and North of Rowlandson's *The Times . . .* [6384] in January 1784: 'The cursed 10 Years American War, fomented by Opposition and misconducted by a timid Minister.'

With reprobation for Fox's attitude to the King went blame for his relations with the Prince—foreshadowed in 1780. On the eve of the Coalition Walpole recorded: 'The Prince of Wales had of late thrown himself into the arms of Charles Fox, and this in the most indecent and undisguised

[1] *Letters*, ed. Toynbee, xii. 436 (25 Apr. 1783).

manner ... Fox's followers were strangely licentious in their conversation about the King. At Brookes's they proposed wagers on the duration of his reign.'[1] This is the context of *Out of the Frying Pan into the Fire* [6237] in which a fox executes a crowned goose, while North and the Prince caper delightedly.

A new phase opens for Cromwell—he no longer stresses a threat to the monarchy—he has become—*quâ* dictator—a reproach to Charles Fox, who is more repeatedly Cromwell than he is Catiline, or Guy Vaux or Milton's Satan, or even Carlo Khan, extravagances to be explained by accumulated resentments and Foxite indiscretions. *Falstaff & his Prince* [Pl. 64] by John Boyne, in May, with Fox as the misleader of youth, is the first of a number of prints over many years in which the pair are Falstaff and Prince Hal; eventually the Prince succeeds to the Falstaff role.

These and many other satires prepared the way for Fox's two India Bills and the King's dismissal of the Coalition, when the influence of the prints was all-important, as Fox and North both complained in Parliament. The Bills were brought in on the 20th and 26th of November; on the 25th Sayers struck his first blow, *A Transfer of East India Stock* [Pl. 65]. Fox runs off in triumph with the India House on his shoulders, transferring patronage and sovereignty from the Company and the Crown to himself and the Coalition. It is a brilliant summary of the attacks on the Bill, though less striking than the more famous *Carlo Khan's Triumphal Entry into Leadenhall Street* [Pl. 66] on 5 December: Fox, as an oriental prince, rides an elephant with the face of North. Burke—inspirer of Fox's Indian policy—leads the animal towards the India House. Fox has a triumphant smile, North registers pained anxiety; a raven croaks a prophetic warning. The effect of the print was multiplied by sequels, piracies, and imitations, and the name 'Carlo Khan' stuck. 'It is difficult to conceive the moral operation and wide diffusion of these caricatures through every part of the country,' wrote Wraxall.[2] And Lord Eldon records that, 'Fox said that *Sayers's caricatures* had done him more mischief than the debates in Parliament or the works of the press. ... These and many other of these publications, had certainly a vast effect upon the public mind.'[3] An almost equally impressive testimony to their effect is that Pitt rewarded Sayers with the sinecure office of Marshal of the Court of Exchequer; this must have been a return for his services, not the hire of his pencil: Sayers turned more and more to social subjects, though he did some effective political prints. The

---

[1] *Last Journals*, 1910, ii. 496 ff. (Mar. 1783).     [2] *Memoirs*, 1884, iii. 254.
[3] Twiss, *Life of Lord Eldon*, 1844, i. 162.

political impact of caricature is spotlighted by the extraordinary conduct of Lord Abingdon: in the course of a violent speech on 2 December, he laid on the Table of the Lords one of the most savage (and unpleasant) attacks on the Coalition. This was Dent's *The Coalition Dissected* [6257], published in August; a composite figure of Fox and North, each bisected, and with their organs laid bare and covered with insults. The plate was thereupon reprinted, with more insults, and the whole text of Abingdon's speech.

The defeat of the India Bill in the Lords on 17 December by the King's intervention, followed by his dismissal of the Ministry and the appointment of Pitt, was acclaimed in two sequels to *Carlo Khan* (not by Sayers), both published on the 24th. In *The Retreat of Carlo Khan from Leadenhall Street* [6285] by Boyne, Fox sits on an ass with North's face, facing its tail, and vomiting into his feathered turban; the City, a woman wearing a mural crown and a brooch with the City arms, leads the ass, and scourges it with the whip of 'Public Resentment'; Burke, dressed as a Jesuit, follows in deep dejection. George III leans from a window of the India House, which is inscribed 'Business done as usual,' flourishing a cap of Liberty. In *The Fall of Carlo Khan* [6286] Fox, crying 'Secret Influence', falls head-first from his elephant which is being chased by peers among whom the King is active and aggressive; Burke runs away, having dropped his 'Plans of Œconomy'; Pitt shores up the India House with large beams.

Soon after the experiments of the Montgolfier brothers in 1783, a new symbol appeared, the balloon.[1] In a double-edged satire, *The Political Balloon or, the Fall of East India Stock* [6275], on 4 December Fox ascends on a terrestrial globe, from which he has hurled three men, whose pockets empty as they fall; his aims are 'the gold and silver mines' of India; one of the falling Directors says, 'If the Nation knew his treacherous heart as well as me, the directors wou'd be prefer'd.' It was soon clear that they were preferred. The balloon is used as a symbol for sudden rise and sudden fall in Rowlandson's sequence of ten little designs on the Coalition on 29 December, *Two New Sliders for the State Magic Lantern* [6287]: in 'Political Montgolfier' a balloon ascends with a fox's head projecting from its summit; in the next, 'His Fall into a Pitt', Fox falls from the balloon into a round hole (like his father in a print of 1757).

[1] The earliest satirical balloon print in the national collection is *The Montgolsier* [sic] *A First Rate of the French Aerial Navy* [6333], 25 Oct. 1783, a burlesque, with emblems of folly.

# X

# THE CLASSIC AGE OF ENGLISH CARICATURE

THE Christmas holidays were a breathing space before the issue between Fox and Pitt could be joined in Parliament. Something must
be said of the changes which were transforming caricature under
the impact of Gillray's early work and the political tensions of the early
1780's. Gillray, who had pursued Fox so unrelentingly, contributed almost
nothing to the post-India Bill phases of the war against the Coalition. The
field was left to Sayers and a number of new caricaturists and of artists and
amateurs who, under the stress of politics, became caricaturists. The classic
age of English caricature which was beginning depended also on Rowlandson, whose political satires begin effectively with attacks on the Coalition
and the India Bill, and though he was primarily a water-colour artist, and
his most characteristic prints are social comedy, his cartoons are an important contribution to graphic satire. These two had many followers, and
at first both owed much to J. H. Mortimer, with his burlesques of the grand
manner. The new look was a product both of changing techniques and of
a more realistic approach to politics. The old school had been based on the
technique of the engraver, modified by the use of etching. The new school
was influenced by the water-colour and the pen drawing as well as the
etching needle.

By the old school people had been depicted conventionally—often
identified only by attributes or inscriptions. Gillray's people were human
beings, with personalities and passions—studies in character. His portraiture was based on sketches from life, drawn on little pieces of card, sometimes from the gallery of the House of Commons. At first, it is true, North
may be a badger, and Fox is often a fox or has a fox's head (like his father
a generation earlier). But the fox has a sly rapacity and the animals have a
strong individuality that was new (and reappears in the caricatures of
F. C. Gould in the later nineteenth century). Soon Fox's 'gunpowder
jowl', heavy eyebrows, and slovenly dress were to be charged with meaning
and character. Though Hogarth has been styled the father of English caricature, and artists—for instance Paul Sandby and Benjamin Wilson—had
occasionally done political satires, Gillray can perhaps be called the first
professional English caricaturist. Most of the old prints were the work of

professional engravers and book-illustrators, notably George Bickham the younger who specialized in satirical prints; they turned out emblematical designs on conventional lines or worked on ideas suggested to them.

The change of course was gradual. Gillray had forerunners: Hogarth's *John Wilkes Esq[r]* was a classic hard to equal. The old school had been associated with the conventions of 'Corruption' versus 'Opposition'—'Court' against 'Country'. In 1782–3 these conventions died, and 'Patriot' acquired an ironical Johnsonian sense, though the bias against the executive remained and 'Corruption' (with varying implications) was recurrently a main theme of satire. But in the past simple-minded print-gazers had learned that Ministers were nearly always wrong and often wicked. Anything to the contrary could be attributed to hirelings. The new lesson might well be that there is more than one side to most questions. Gillray delighted in irony and in disrespect for the highly placed; his prints were not more savage in intention than those of his predecessors, but they were more effectively cruel, and the savagery was blended with wit and humour. Till late in 1797 (when Canning's influence got him a pension), he was scarcely a political partisan, and he was never a mere hireling. Though it is seldom safe to deduce a cartoonist's politics from his work, it is impossible to study Gillray without concluding that his political penetration went with some strong prejudices. From first to last he was a bigoted anti-Papist and a patriotic John Bullish anti-Gallican. From 1782 he showed consistent hostility to Charles Fox and progressively to Burke and Sheridan. He was fond of mystification; all his early prints are anonymous or pseudonymous; he would occasionally hide his own style under an assumed incompetence —either as part of the joke or to cover his tracks. In 1787 he adopted Sayers' signature and imitated his manner, probably more to tease than to deceive—his own hand is unmistakable.

It is impossible to study Rowlandson without concluding that he was indifferent to politics but excelled at illustrating the ideas of other people. The uprush of political excitement, the stimulus of a developing art, competing print-sellers, brought new caricaturists into the field round about 1783–4. John Boyne, a water-colourist and engraver, and like Darly a drawing-master, did effective Pittite prints. Isaac Cruikshank's caricatures begin tentatively and imitatively in January 1784 when he seems to have left Edinburgh for London, but his work does not become characteristic and assured till about 1789. Other clever artists are concealed by anonymity, particularly the elusive Henry Kingsbury, a painter and engraver and a follower of Rowlandson.

More important than these was Richard Newton, whose work does not begin till 1791 when he was only fourteen. His death at the age of twenty-one may have robbed England of a great caricaturist. He had a rollicking boyish humour and a gift for bold design and the grotesque. He was also a miniaturist, and had an alternative manner, realistic, charming, almost graceful. His short career illustrates the talent for caricature so often remarkable in the young. Newton's prints are youthful—to their advantage —but they also have political bite. James Hook (Dean of Worcester and brother of Theodore) did some striking cartoons as a Westminster school-boy, and a gifted caricaturist may have been lost in a pillar of the Church. William Heath's career belongs to the last phase of the Gillray tradition, and he regarded himself as primarily a 'straight' artist, but he was a prolific and much-admired caricaturist whose published work begins when he was about fourteen. The obvious instance of the youthful caricaturist is George Cruikshank; he began to work on his father's plates at a very early age, adding details and lettering, but his own original cartoons hardly begin before he was seventeen or eighteen when he helped to fill the gap left by Gillray. We know tantalizingly little about such beginnings, but there is an illuminating modern instance in the career of David Low.[1]

The influence of the amateur has been noted. It increased as caricature gained in status and became a modish hobby. At first an Italianate art form practised by virtuosi, it was now an affair of infinite variety. Many well-known people have left examples of their work. But besides fashionable practitioners such as Lady Burlington, Lady Di Beauclerk, Lady Craven, Lord Bolton, and the more important Bunbury (whose work rarely touches politics), there were the semi-amateurs whose work was published by themselves or print-shops and who made a serious contribution to political caricature. The chief of these were James Sayers, John Nixon (of the Bank of England), whose political designs were infrequent but sometimes striking, and William Dent. Sayers, a Yarmouth attorney, was also a writer of political squibs in prose and verse; he contributed a famous song against Coke of Norfolk to the Norfolk election squibs of 1784,[2] and he was occasionally paid by the Treasury for 'writing in the newspapers'.[3] His best-known prints, those of 1783, are the least competent; he afterwards adopted soft-ground etching and aquatint to his great advantage; his work is in black and white, without colour, but otherwise belongs to the

---

[1] *Low's Autobiography*, 1956, pp. 25–36.

[2] Sarah Sophia Banks MSS., Print Room, British Museum. The verses are printed, A. M. W. Stirling, *Coke of Norfolk*.

[3] A. Aspinall, *Politics and the Press, c. 1780–1850*, 1949, p. 165.

new school. Dent's prints begin in 1782 and end in 1793—at first little scratchy etchings without merit, but as he learnt to exploit his own short-comings and adapt his work to colour, they greatly improved. He had a gift for burlesque portraiture, uninhibited personalities, and ribald comment which made his prints very popular.[1] There was also Thomas Colley of whom nothing is known beyond his prints which are found only from 1780 to 1783, admirable burlesques, with a crude attractive *naïveté*. He takes a special pleasure in naval victories and his ships are drawn in a way that suggests he had been in the Navy. His style lent itself to imitation, and there is, I think, a pseudo-Colley using his signature, but with a more skilful touch and in a very different spirit, whom I believe to be Gillray.[2] George Murgatroyd Woodward worked professionally for the print-sellers, but was an amateur in that he was an untrained artist who never etched his own designs, the son of a William Woodward of Stanton Hall, Derby, a large house still standing in 1940. His work does not begin effectively before about 1790 and his political prints belong mainly to the time of the French wars. He was original, prolific, varied, humorous, and good-humoured. His designs were etched by Isaac Cruikshank and Rowlandson (and others), and the Woodward–Rowlandson collaboration was fruitful. He was the inventor of the sailor ashore—typical of Nelson's day—generous, reckless, pugnacious, tough but tender-hearted, simple-minded and shrewd—belonging to a race apart, and to the world of Charles Dibdin's songs. It was a loss to caricature when he died suddenly in 1809.[3]

Among the countless amateurs, usually anonymous, who supplied the print-sellers with occasional sketches to be etched by professionals, two demand attention. One is Colonel Braddyll who designed among other things the two famous plates of George III inspecting a Gulliver-Napoleon through his spy-glass. Water-colour originals of one of these and of other prints show how closely Gillray followed his designs, though improving the drawing and adding touches of his own.The other is Gillray's friend and patron the Rev. John Sneyd who designed, among other things, Gillray's very elaborate *Apotheosis of Hoche* [9156] and the set of plates on the weather, one of which is the familiar *Very Slippy-Weather*, with its view of Humphrey's shop window in St. James's Street.

[1] Angelo, *Reminiscences*, 1904, p. 334.

[2] I believe *Out of the Frying Pan into the Fire* (mentioned above) signed 'Colley' to be one of these crypto-Gillrays; the motive for concealment is obvious; the true Colley prints are without rancour.

[3] After his death many plates were reissued with the 'Woodward del' erased and they have been attributed to Rowlandson: the social comedy of the two men was essentially different.

The newspapers and the print-shops had a great share in the changes which were giving political caricature so much more realism and penetration. Particularly the day-to-day publication of debates, by which for instance Fox's former tirades against North were put into his mouth with devastating effect. The development of the satirical newspaper paragraph, often with quotations from speeches, was a boon to the caricaturist. Sheridan attacked Dundas for a speech which 'might fairly be deemed hints for paragraphs and sketches for prints'.[1] And print-shops multiplied. The old-fashioned window-displays of the two Bowles's, one in Cornhill, the other in St. Paul's Churchyard, were long established. They chiefly exhibited humorous mezzotints into which politics intruded only by exception. Prints were sold by booksellers and in pamphlet-shops as well as in print-shops and many engravers sold prints, as Hogarth did from the Golden Head in Leicester Fields and George Bickham from the Blackmoor's Head in the Strand. For many years Darly's at the Acorn (afterwards 39) in the Strand was the leading caricature shop [Pl. 43]. With his disappearance after 1778 the two Humphreys came to the front, William in the Strand, Hannah in Bond Street, both with early associations with Gillray. Fores was established in Piccadilly by January 1784 and at once took the lead, a rival of Miss Humphrey who surpassed him only when (about 1794) she had monopolized Gillray's output. In 1797 she moved from Bond Street to St. James's Street and her fame was secure. She and Fores were both personalities, and so was Holland whose shop (at first in Drury Lane and then in Oxford Street) was opened by January 1784. He was a caricaturist and a publisher of books as well as of prints, with Radical views which landed him in Newgate in 1793 for a seditious publication, after which Radicalism gradually disappears from his prints. When he died in 1816 he achieved an obituary in the *Gentleman's Magazine* which throws light on the role of a print-seller: '. . . an eminent publisher of caricatures and a patron of Woodward, Rowlandson, Newton, Buck and other artists, was himself a man of genius and wrote many popular songs and a volume of poetry, besides being the author of the pointed and epigrammatic words which accompanied most of his caricatures.'

The print-shops were an institution. The exhibitions—entrance a shilling—belong to the early years of the French Revolution, when French caricatures were an additional attraction. But the fashionable shops always provided what was then called a lounge, and their windows were the picture galleries of the public. Like a visit to Tattersall's, a visit to the cari-

[1] *Parl. Hist.* xxiv. 295 (12 Jan. 1784).

cature shops to see the new caricatures, was an incident in the daily round of a man of fashion according to a German visitor in 1802.[1] Fores, like some other print-sellers, advertised 'Folios of Caricatures lent out for the evening'.[2] The rate was 2s. 6d. a day, with a pound deposit to secure return in good condition. He also lent individual prints by the year or less 'for copying'; he arranged prints for screens and scrapbooks and sold large collections of caricatures bound in many folio volumes, and he advertised 'Prints and Caricatures wholesale and for exportation'.

From late in the century Rudolph Ackermann's 'Repository of Arts' in the Strand was more than a print-shop, and he advertised it as 'the best morning's lounge'. Caricatures were the last of many items in his advertisements, but he published some notable ones, including copies of German prints (1814–15) as part of a campaign against Napoleon. In his way Thomas Tegg was also a man of note, a bookseller in Cheapside who specialized in cheap reprints and abridgements for a wide public. From January 1807 he applied similar methods to print-selling, advertising prints at a shilling coloured—half the usual rates—but the paper was poor, the colouring crude, and with repeated reissues the plates were worn. His first titles were reissues of invasion prints by Roberts, an engraver-publisher who had gone out of business. In 1807 he also began what he called a 'Caricature Magazine'—eventually five volumes of it with a total of 499 plates originally published separately or in pairs. It was not a magazine in the usual sense: Darly had done something similar in his six volumes of 'Characters, Caricatures and Macaronies', and these have more coherence. Tegg's innovation was to apply—so far as was possible—the methods of mass production to the hand-coloured etching, and to cultivate a wider public than that of the fashionable print-shops. Others followed his lead, especially three Radical ones with shops in the City who were active in the post-war period—Marks (a caricaturist), Fairburn, and Johnstone. As a rule print-sellers rather than caricaturists seems to have influenced the political bias of their prints, though a majority were concerned to give the public what it wanted.

Besides the influence of caricaturists and print-sellers, there was inevitably that of events. Not only do prints multiply in times of crisis, but their forcefulness varies with the intensity of convictions and passions. Something was lost, for instance, with the deaths of Pitt and Fox. The evolution

---

[1] C. A. G. Goede, *The Stranger in England*, 1807.
[2] A usual inscription on his prints. The further details are from an advertisement of *c.* 1819 in the Windsor Archives.

of John Bull was conditioned by ideas and situations as well as by artists. In the days of the separately published cartoon there is no standardized Bull, but much variety. Beginning in the 1750's as a symbol for England, he gradually becomes also both the typical Englishman (the bearer of burdens who grumbles and pays) and the mouthpiece of collective opinion. He is perennially the victim of doctors and quacks—official and unofficial —but under the stresses of war and politics he criticizes, admonishes, judges, condemns, even dictates. In fact his development corresponds to the subtle process of democratization which was going on despite appearances of political reaction.[1] In 1803 (both as Britain and Briton) he is the sole obstacle to Boney's 'Stride over the Globe'.[2] Gillray invented, and others imitated, the uncouth yokel, probably because this was a character in which a seeming *naïveté* could be a cover for shrewdness blended with malice. At the opposite extreme, nearly forty years later, was HB.'s dignified and portly gentleman farmer or squire. But John Bull was as often citizen or merchant as countryman; he was also, less often, an artisan, or a sailor, or a soldier—but when a soldier essentially a civilian. Despite his double role and his occasional identity with the King, when a typical Englishman he was outside the governing classes. Something was lost when John Bull became stereotyped—in these prints he is a splendid personification of changing mental climates and shifting currents of opinion. But there is already something of the traditional Bull of the mid-nineteenth century and after, especially *vis-à-vis* France, and this is mixed up with the Roast Beef of Old England mystique (still 'Hogarth's Roast Beef' in 1810), and contempt for frogs and *soupe maigre*.

[1] Cf. Mackintosh on newspapers in his defence of Peltier (Feb. 1803): '. . . it is very certain that the multiplication of these channels of popular information has produced a great change in our domestic and foreign politics. At home, it has, in truth, produced a gradual revolution in our Government. By increasing the number of those who exercise some sort of judgement on public affairs, it has created a substantial democracy infinitely more important than those democratical forms which have been the subject of so much contest.' *Trial* (for criminal libel on Napoleon at the instance of the French Ambassador), 1803, pp. 160-1.

[2] See *E.P.C. 1793–1832*, Pl. 26.

# XI

## FOX VERSUS PITT

THE prints do not reflect the Foxite confidence that Pitt's ministry would not survive the Christmas holiday. For the first five months of 1784 the temperature chart of polemical print production registered an unprecedented peak with over 260 surviving prints in the national collection. The battle raged in the print-shops as well as in the Commons. While Pitt gained rapidly in the country and in the House, the number of Foxite prints—small at first—tended to increase, as (presumably) propaganda came into play.

This supreme crisis began with one of the recurrent waves of popular indignation fomented by the Opposition against the Ministry—Excise in 1733 being a classic example. But the outcry against the Coalition and the India Bill was exceptional—the Crown was ranged against the Ministry. In the second phase of the crisis, after Pitt's appointment, the situation was more exceptional still—the clamour was against the Opposition. Besides the basic constitutional issues involved there was the drama of the contest between Pitt and Fox which was to influence politics to the end of their joint lives. One of the central threads of political caricature for the next twenty-two years—the relations of Pitt, Fox, and the King—was manifest.

In 1783-4 the themes were, on one side, Fox as a would-be dictator, trying to usurp the patronage and prerogatives of the Crown by a corrupt alliance with North which gave him a majority in the Commons against 'the sense of the People'. On the other was 'Master Billy', a presumptuous youth, the creature of 'secret influence', achieving office by the back stairs, and attacking the House of Commons, the palladium of British liberties. This line of attack broke on the popularity of the King's action and belief in Pitt's integrity and public spirit. 'Prerogative' is a parrot cry in Foxite prints while Addresses were pouring in (first, according to precedent from the City) thanking the King for the salutary use of his prerogative in the overthrow of 'a corrupt oligarchy' or 'a desperate faction'. And 'secret influence' had been so much the cry against North that it was doubly ineffective against Pitt.[1] It is significant that in the 'secret influence' prints a sinister but totally irrelevant Bute is nearly always introduced.

[1] At the great Yorkshire meeting on 25 Mar. Spencer Stanhope declared: 'Secret influence

To return to January 1784. In this contest for power in which popularity was a factor the antecedents and reputations of the rivals were important, and the advantages were overwhelmingly with the son of Chatham
against the son of the hated 'public defaulter of unaccounted millions' who
had been depicted repeatedly as a ruined gambler devoured by ambition.
In a print on the first day of the year by Collings (sometimes attributed to
Gillray), *Hudibrass and his Squire* [6361], Fox and Burke sit in the pillory
guarded by Pitt; behind Fox hangs a scourge with two lashes, 'Prerogative'
and 'Vox Populi'.

Even more persistent than the Carlo Khan theme was the comparison
with Cromwell. Fox's truculent tactics in January and February laid him
wide open to this line of attack—his attempts to stop the issue of money
from the Treasury, contending against law and precedent that the King
had not the prerogative of dissolution. This was the context of a famous
print by Sayers, *The Mirror of Patriotism* [Pl. 67], dated 20 January. Fox,
as if rehearsing a speech, looks in a glass and sees himself as Cromwell
scowling back. 'Je sais de bonne part', wrote the French Ambassador, 'que
M. Fox a été sensible a cette caricature.'[1] And in Rowlandson's *His Highness the Protector* [6379] on the 19th, Fox guards the Treasury door, dagger
in hand. In *The Historical Painter* [6408] on 10 February, by Dent, Fox,
as Cromwell, paints a picture of Charles I's execution, putting his brush,
a sceptre, against the King's head; on the wall hangs a picture of a fox
holding a cap of Liberty, and presenting 'Independence' to an Indian
warrior, America.

At a meeting of Westminster electors on 14 February Fox was shouted
down and insulted with cries of 'No Grand Mogul!, No India Tyrant!,
No Usurper!, No Turncoat!, No Traitor!, No Dictator!, No Catiline!'.
This occasion, an important one, was the subject of several prints; in
Sayers' contribution [6426] Fox was charged with (among other things)
'Cromwell's Ambition, Cataline's Abilities, Damiens Loyalty, Machiavels
Politics'. How does Fox resemble Cromwell? asked a Westminster Elec-
tion squib, and answers, 'A Republican who is in his heart so attached to
monarchy as to despise every other form of government—a tyrant, a hypo-
crite, a notorious enemy to the constitution of his Country.'[2]

Fox's relations with the Prince encouraged the Cromwellian allegations.
Even in January, in *An Harangue about the Goose* [6377], when he and Pitt

has been the cry since Lord Bute's time . . . yet all his sons vote with the Coalition, Lord North
too has been called the creature of secret influence.' *Wyvill Papers*, ii. 340.
   [1] Britsch, *La Jeunesse de Philippe Égalité*, 1926, p. 406.
   [2] *History of the Westminster Election*, 1784, p. 355.

compete for the goose that lays the golden eggs, Pitt concludes: 'You say you'll have the Goose again / Not surely Fox in this King's reign, / But be not over much perplext / You have a prospect in the next.' In *Political Sculpters* [6401] Fox kneels to carve a bust of the Prince, complacently using a mallet inscribed 'Distruction' on a chisel inscribed 'Vice'. North sharpens a chisel with an expression of angry distress. The pedestal is inscribed 'extremely docile, easy moddel'd into Vice and exceedingly soft about the head'.

The inevitable hydra allegory was used on both sides. One celebrates the defeat of the India Bill: in *In Memory of Decemb^r the 17th, 1783* [6443] a hydra with the heads of Fox, Portland, and Co. attacks the 'British Constitution', a column topped by a bust of the King which is defended by Pitt supported by Britannia and her Lion. In the other, by Rowlandson, three days later, Fox is *The Champion of the People* [6444] wielding the sword of 'Justice'; eight fanged mouths spit out 'Tyranny, Assumed Prerogative, Despotism, Oppression, Secret Influence, Scotch Politics, Corruption'. Fox's supporters are East Indians (naked and prostrate), Englishmen with the standard of Britannia and 'Universal Liberty', and a band of Irish Volunteers. The Indian and Irish allusions are altogether exceptional.

For the first time—in *George and the Dragon* [6405]—the King is Saint George (highest of praise in these prints); he strikes down a monster with the heads of Fox, North, and Burke which is under the hooves of his rearing horse. He is also Jove holding thunderbolts and hurling the Coalition 'down to their native Hell', in *The British Titans* [6419]; his crown is inscribed Prerogative, and he is surrounded by the other gods— Pitt and his supporters.

A characteristic of the new look was a lighter touch, both in conception and draughtsmanship. Rowlandson's burlesque of Pitt's triumphal progress to receive the Freedom of the City is an example: *Master Billy's Procession to Grocer's Hall* [6642]. So is his second set of lantern slides, in nine little scenes, *The Loves of the Fox and the Badger—or the Coalition Wedding* [Pl. 68]; beginning with the Fox savaging the badger in the Commons—'Ye Bear Garden'—the two come together, each compelled by a menacing dream: the ruined gambler sees himself as a highwayman in jail; the badger sees a vision of impeachment and the scaffold. So, 'from necessity', Satan unites them, and they have a 'mopstick majority' in the House.

Fox's dwindling majority was attributed to the activities of John

Robinson, North's Treasury Secretary, who had put his knowledge of borough patronage, so acquired, at the service of Pitt. Those who changed sides were known as 'Robinson's Rats'. On 10 February the *Morning Post* printed a woodcut of six rats above a list of twenty-three names, given in full and headed 'Jack Robinson'. Three cartoons followed, one a famous print of Rowlandson, *The Apostate Jack R— The Political Rat Catcher— N.B., Rats Taken Alive!* [6431, n.d.]. Robinson kneels to trap rats with human heads—the bait being place or peerage; the rats are identified by the list from the *Morning Post*, the names being ostensibly hidden by the use of initial and final letters only. This was an ancient theme and long survived. Robinson's rats were a trickle which Pitt's popularity out of doors soon turned into a landslide that left the Opposition with a majority of one on 8 March. 'So strong was the tide without doors against Mr Fox and his majority, that they thought proper to pass the Mutiny Bill in compliance with the wish of the public.'[1] No further obstruction was possible, and the long-awaited dissolution followed on 25 March.

Pitt's popularity, shared by the King, was manifested in Addresses and was denounced in Foxite prints as 'Popular Frenzy' [6438] or 'The Breath of Popularity' [6445]. In the first, on 4 March, the title explains itself: *Popular Frenzy; or, the Destruction of St. Stephen's Chapel* (by a rabble of Addressers). In *Solomon in the Clouds!!* [6486] on 1 April the King excretes a 'Proclamation for Dissolution' while he is supported by Pitt and Thurlow, who are themselves held up by 'Air Balloons' inscribed 'Wishes of the People'. The Pittite version of the 'breath of Popularity' was national indignation with the Coalition, repeatedly illustrated, and nowhere better than in Rowlandson's *Brittannia Roused, or the Coalition Monsters Destroyed* [Pl. 69]; the massive giantess with her cap of Liberty beside her has seized two little manikins, Fox and North, and hurls them into space.

There is a set of three prints etched by Rowlandson which demands attention (the feeble drawing for one of them survives in the British Museum). It is difficult not to believe that they were devised in the highest Foxite circles: here, if anywhere, is Fox's answer to the Carlo Khan prints whose effect he so deplored. *A Peep into Friar Bacon's Study* [6436] on 3 March shows George III as the Bacon of chapbook legend, a magician consulting his 'brazen head'. He evokes three visions of the Constitution, each in a circle: in the remote past, unlimited monarchy with bubble appendages to the throne to indicate embryo Houses of Parliament. In

---

[1] *Pol. Memoranda of the Duke of Leeds*, ed. O. Browning, 1884, p. 95.

the recent past, that is, till the dismissal of the Coalition, King, Lords, and Commons are equal. In the present, the King dominates the Lords, the Lords the Commons; but he is far from satisfied and points to the ancient Constitution, saying, 'What is this to this?', showing that he aims at despotism; the new Ministry, led by a demon, hurry down the 'back stairs', expressing contempt for the resolutions of the House, while Fox, saying 'Beware', watches the scene with Burke and North. In *The State Auction* [6469], dated 26 March, the auctioneer—'licensed by Royal Authority'— is Pitt, with Dundas as his porter; raising the hammer of 'Prerogative', he orders 'Harry' to hold up 'Lot 1', a huge pile of books, 'Rights of the People in 558 Volumes' (the 558 M.P.s). There are other lots, with 'Magna Charta' as Lot 2. The members are leaving the House, but Fox confronts Pitt, saying, 'I am determined to bid with Spirit for Lot 1. he shall pay dear for it that outbid's me.' In the third, five days later, *The Hanoverian Horse and British Lion* [Pl. 70], the scene is again the House of Commons, and again the Dissolution. Pitt rides the horse (the King) which snorts 'Pre-ro-ro-ro-ro-ro-ro-ro-tive', kicks at Fox (who rides the British Lion), and drives away the M.P.s with his heels and a blast of 'My faithful Commons'. Its forefeet are planted on 'Magna Charta', 'Bill of Rights', and 'Constitution'. The Lion, which has descended from the Royal Arms above the Speaker's Chair, says, 'If this Horse is not tamed he will soon be absolute King of our Forest.' Fox invites Pitt to dismount and 'let some abler jockey' take his place. More than any of the other prints these three by the same hand embody Foxite doctrine and Fox's obsession with the power of the Crown. The weak point in such protests against the Dissolution was that this was a Parliament returned in 1780 to strengthen North, which had supported four Ministries in turn. And that in 1780 Fox had denounced the House as corrupt, maintaining that 'the sense of the People' was in the Addresses—the exact opposite of his contention in 1784.

With the Dissolution the cartoonists switched their energies to the Westminster Election, the most sensational of all English elections. The momentous contest from 1 April to 17 May is displayed in all its aspects. The aim of one side was to discredit Sir Cecil Wray (Admiral Lord Hood the senior ministerial candidate was unassailable); a chief aim on the other side was to neutralize the canvassing of the Duchess of Devonshire—indeed the grosser prints can be interpreted only as an attempt to stop her canvass. The election was fought on personalities—an attempt to make an issue of Reform failed. For the first twenty days Fox despaired, though on the eleventh day the tide had turned against Wray; on the twenty-third

day Fox passed Wray but the struggle was bitter to the end, with a satur-
nalia of rival mobs (sailors for Hood and Wray, Irish chairmen for Fox),
flags, mottoes, and uproar. The wild scene is the subject of a Pittite print,
*The Humours of Covent Garden or Freedom of Election* [6511]. Throughout
the forty days there was an orgy of squibs, lampoons, songs, bill-posting,
newspaper paragraphs, and caricatures, unprecedented, and unsurpassed
until the greater excitement and 'boundless rage of the Press' during
Queen Caroline's affair in 1820. That the Duchess turned the scale was
agreed: Walpole even says, 'she certainly got the greater part of Mr Fox's
votes for him, though the Court party endeavoured to deter her by the
most illiberal and indecent abuse'.[1]

Wray was vulnerable because he had been brought in by Fox—as a
Reformer—for Westminster in 1782; as a Reformer he now supported
Pitt and could therefore be traduced as Judas. He was even more vulnerable from a reputation for parsimony and addiction to small beer. And he
had made two unlucky financial proposals which were misrepresented
with deadly effect. One was for the abolition of Chelsea Hospital (to have
a greater number of out-pensioners), the other for a tax on maidservants
(actually on their employers). Thus he was called in the prints and squibs
'Sir Judas Iscariot', Lord High Keeper of the Small Beer Cellar', 'Sir
Chelsea Tax Girl', 'Woman Hater', 'Knight of the Back Stairs', 'Knight
of the Key'. In Isaac Cruikshank's *Plumpers for Sir Judas or the Chealsea
Pensioners Revenge* [6502] he is assailed by maids with mops and old soldiers with crutches and peg legs.

The first election print, on 29 March, was probably intended to push
aside the Reform issue. It was Rowlandson's *Drum Major of Sedition*
[6374]: Wray's supporter, Major John Cartwright, advocate of manhood
suffrage and annual Parliaments, speaks from the hustings, inviting
electors to help to pull down the House of Commons and so gain the favour
of Bute and Jenkinson (the so-called King's Friend); in Foxite prints Fox
stands for Liberty, Wray for slavery and wooden shoes.

Prints on the Duchess's canvassing begin on 1 April with *Election Tate
à Tate* [6487] in which she and Sam House (who appears in many prints)
hob-nob over tankards of porter. Sam was a Westminster character, a
publican who canvassed and kept open house for Fox at his own expense,
though 'when political reasons made it necessary for Mr Fox to unite with
Lord North, Sam's confidence in Mr Fox was shook to the centre'.[2] This
and other prints show that the Duchess's canvass began at once, not, as is

---

[1] *Letters*, xiii. 41 n.     [2] *Life and Opinions of Sam House*, 1785, p. 24.

often said, when the tide turned. The gross abuse heaped on her, though 'all the world, young and old, male and female' was 'employed on canvassing on either side',[1] is a measure of her achievement. When she left London, ostensibly for her mother's health, she was urgently recalled by the Duchess of Portland, another canvassing lady: 'I am almost worn out ...', she wrote on 13 April, 'if we should lose it is owing to your absence.' And Georgiana wrote later to her mother who was imploring her to give up canvassing: 'I am unhappy here beyond measure and abus'd for nothing. Yet as it is begun I must go on with it. . . . My sister and Lady (name illegible) were both kiss'd, so it's very hard I who was not should have the reputation of it.'[2]

The *Morning Post* specialized in spiteful paragraphs, but the prints must have been the most offensive part of the campaign, not only on their demerits, but because they were posted up in ginshops, alehouses, and taverns. Since they failed to stop the Duchess they can only (one supposes) have damaged Wray. A Foxite squib gives among the items of a 'Secret Service Ledger', 'To several Print Shops £2000', 'To Mr — for his indecent engravings £500':[3] the blank can safely be filled with Dent's name. One of the advertisements for Hood and Wray began, 'To be hired for the day, several pairs of ruby pouting lips of the first quality . . .', &c., &c. Time has made many of the prints—by no means all—innocuous. Prints of kisses bestowed on butchers have a distinct attraction, and some even convey something of Georgiana's dazzling charm.

The balance of youth, beauty, and fashion was heavily for Fox, who had, among others, Mrs. Crewe, Lady Duncannon, the Ladies Waldegrave. On the other side, Lady Salisbury was praised for her 'correct' canvassing, and Mrs. Hobart was perhaps a liability. She was 45, very fat and very lively, and was to become a target of caricature for her social activities. 'Where ye agents and observers can you find one fitter to be placed in *contrast* to the fair *Duchess*?' asked a newspaper wit. She was derided in prints and newspapers as 'Madam Blubber'. In *The Poll* [Pl. 71] by Rowlandson, a see-saw represents the state of the poll while still favourable to Wray—Mrs. Hobart sits on one end, held down by Hood, and completely outweighing the Duchess, though Fox tries to pull down her end of the plank; the ladies face each other, astride and with bosoms bare; Wray watches with an enigmatical expression. Behind are the hustings.

[1] Malmesbury, *Diaries and Correspondence*, 1844, ii. 65 (letter from Sir Gilbert Elliot, n.d.).
[2] *Georgiana . . .*, ed. Earl of Bessborough, 1955, p. 79.
[3] *History of the Westminster Election*, 1784, p. 352; cf. pp. 194, 324, 327, 376.

Like the Duchess, Mrs. Hobart took voters to the poll in her coach; a ribald drawing attributed to Townshend (now Viscount) was etched by Rowlandson as *Madam Blubber's Last Shift or the Aerostatic Dilly* [6561] with an offensive explanation and a song. Enclosed by a balloon from the waist downwards—her inflated petticoats—she carries voters towards Covent Garden. The print, dated 29 April, had been prepared for by a poster adjuring the friends of Hood and Wray not to despair: 'A much distinguished lady has found a way. . . .' A newspaper afterwards announced that 'Mrs H—t has not ballooned a single vote since she was caricatured by the unmerciful Viscount . . .'. Here, seemingly, was an elaborate device to stop Mrs. Hobart from collecting outlying voters—a counter-thrust to attacks on the Duchess.

Among the allegations of Pittite prints was the polling of unqualified voters—lodgers, or those who had not paid poor rates and so on. This, and wholesale bribery, was associated with the Duchess's canvass in the poorest parts of Westminster. Such was the context of *Wits' Last Stake or the Cobling Voters and Abject Canvassers* [6548] by Rowlandson in which the Duchess, supported on Fox's knee, lavishly pays a cobbler for imaginary repairs to her shoe. The result was the unfortunate demand for a scrutiny which kept Fox out of his Westminster seat till March 1785.

The Prince's electioneering for Fox was the subject of a few savage prints. Gillray, under cover of assumed incompetence, produced *Returning from Brooks's* [6528]. The Prince, wearing the usual election badges of a 'Fox' favour and his own plume of feathers, staggers along very drunk, held up by Fox and Sam House. With one doubtful exception this is Gillray's only political print for 1784.

In this struggle, where personal popularity was all important, two of Pitt's supporters emerge as liabilities—Thurlow and Wilkes (this is seen also in pre-election prints). Thurlow is natural enough with his reactionary views, overbearing ways, and blackbrowed scowl. Wilkes's reconciliation with the King (which followed his wholehearted support of Pitt) was a godsend to the caricaturists, and this 'new coalition' was the subject of prints and newspaper squibs: 'When Piety and Blasphemy agree, / Can there a stranger Coalition be! / O best of Kings! cries W—kes, for ever live, / Subjects like W—kes, says G—, kind of fortune give!'[1] This is the theme of *The New Coalition* [6568] on 1 May, in which the pair, exchanging compliments, stand with arms round each other's shoulders. Sayers' *Coalition Medal Struck in Brass* was parodied in *The Grand Coalition*

---

[1] *Asylum for Fugitive Pieces*, 1785, i. 264.

*Medal, Struck in Base Metal Gilt* [6571] on 3 May. Instead of Fox and
North are busts in relief of the King and Thurlow facing each other, with
Wilkes squeezed between and squinting violently; emblems of slavery
decorate the background. In *A New Coalition Mask* [6584] on 17 May,
Sayers' famous composite of Fox and North [Pl. 72] is imitated by a
mask of George III and Wilkes. The notion had already been applied to
Fox and the Duchess in *Cheek by Joul or the Mask* [Pl. 73] on 3 May.

The Ministry were ill served by caricaturists during the election. Fox's
chief enemy, Gillray, and Pitt's chief supporter, Sayers, left the field to
others (Sayers was using his pen in Norfolk). Rowlandson, active against
both sides, was the chief artist of the election. One of his prints stands out
in cartoon history. *The Covent Garden Night Mare* [Pl. 75] is a parody of
Fuseli's *The Nightmare* exhibited at the Royal Academy in 1782 and
familiar from engravings [Pl. 74]. Fuseli's arrangement is closely followed
but, instead of the elegant female in classical draperies, Fox lies in burly
nudity, dreaming of defeat; dice box and dice replace the toilet bottles on
the little table. As in the picture, a demon sits on his chest and the horse
with starting eyeballs puts its head through the curtain. This is the first
of a long series of burlesques of Fuseli's picture. Like the Laocoon
(parodied first by Titian and many times since then) it has shown itself
peculiarly attractive to travesty. And though Hogarth had burlesqued the
old masters in *Paul before Felix*, this is the first English example of the
travesty of the picture as a political satire—a genre developed by Gillray.

As the end drew near gibes at the female canvassers gave way to praise
for the 'female patriotism' that had turned the scale. On 3 May Fox is
*Wisdom led by Virtue and Prudence to the Temple of Fame* [6573], there to
be welcomed by Britannia. The Duchess, of course, is Virtue; her sister
Lady Duncannon is Prudence. *Vox Populi Vox Dei* [6594] on 23 May is
'Dedicated to the Ladies who so conspicuously exerted themselves in the
Cause of Freedom'. Fox, armed with the staff of Liberty, stands besides
the Duchess who holds a 'Shield of Virtue' which protects her from the
arrows of 'Woman Hater', 'Morning Post', 'Malice', and 'Envy'. Wray
walks off, bending under a massive burden of 'Deceit, Ingratitude, Perjury', and acknowledging his 'Transgressions'. In *The Apotheosis of the
Dutchess* [6597] on 25 May, supported by Truth and Virtue, she tramples
on Scandal and the *Morning Post. Carlo Khan's Entry into St. Stephen's*
[6588, n.d.] by Collings is less respectful: followed by a rabble of butchers
she enters the House of Commons with Fox on her shoulders.

In these surviving election prints there are, at a rough estimate (a few undated ones may fall outside the election), 95 Pittite (for Wray) to 44 for Fox, with four that are double-edged. Yet, in studying them, the impression remains that Fox has the best of it (reversing the pre-election position). The advantage of Fox over Wray, of the Duchess over Madam Blubber, is unmistakable. Scurrilous attacks on the Duchess are an asset to her side. If Fox is Satan—Milton's Satan—Wray is Judas. There is not a single defence of Wray, who, quite unjustly, is depicted as a saturnine conspirator. In a Foxite election print of 1782 [5998] he had been 'a Wray of Honesty'. The Admiral hardly appears, Pitt and North seldom do. The election ended only because polling could not legally last more than forty days. Fox beat Wray by 236 votes,[1] as Pittites believed through the polling of unqualified voters—a scrutiny was demanded. Westminster, in the full flood of Pitt's victory, was a triumph for Fox—and he was henceforth impregnable there. In the words of a Foxite election song,

> Our Westminster, Norwich, and London successes
> Are a glorious comment on your boasted addresses.[2]

In each 'success' the single Coalition candidate just managed to beat the *second* Pittite (in the City Foxites scraped into the third and fourth seats). In general, Foxites were thrown back on close boroughs.[3]

The election over, the temperature at once dropped, the prints become fewer and the trend is strongly anti-Foxite. The bankruptcy of the party and their desperate resolves are the theme of Dent's *The Whig Club, or the State of the Blue and Buff Council* [6671]: Fox revengefully presides under a bust of Cromwell. This is noteworthy as the first of the Whig Club prints. In 1785 Pitt's Irish Propositions, defeated by Fox, are the principal topic. There are prints on both sides—blame for Fox's factious and disingenuous tactics (one voice for England, a contrary one for Ireland), condemnation of the Propositions as damaging to British interests—combined with condemnation of Pitt's taxes—especially the very unpopular Shop Tax.

The weight of taxes on John Bull was a perennial theme, expressed especially in two classic forms that went through many adaptations: the cruelly overburdened man and the even more savagely maltreated bull. Both were introduced by Dent in 1786. The *Free-Born Briton or a Per-*

---

[1] Hood 6,694, Fox 6,234, Wray 5,998. After the Scrutiny was stopped as an expensive and unsavoury nuisance: Hood 6,588, Fox 6,126, Wray 5,895 (High Bailiff's return 4 Mar. 1785).

[2] *History of the Westminster Election*, 1784, p. 501.

[3] M. D. George, 'Fox's Martyrs; the General Election of 1784', *Trans. Royal Hist. Soc.*, 1939, pp. 133–68.

*spective of Taxation* [Pl. 76] is more comprehensive than even Sydney Smith's famous squib in which the schoolboy whips his taxed top; John, who 'Pays shillings fourteen in the pound', stamps with rage at the double yoke of debt and taxes on his shoulders—a good survey of the complications of Pitt's budgets in pre-income-tax days. In *The End of Parliament* [6962] taxes are combined with that other standard grievance—politicians enjoying their loaves and fishes. A snorting bull lies down under a monstrous load of taxes new and old, while Pitt, Dundas, and Pepper Arden (the Attorney General) tug at a long chain of alternate loaves and fishes which they drag from the animal's rump: 'Pensions, Annuities, Gratuities &c., &c.'

In the space between Pitt's installation and the mighty impact of the French Revolution three things gave opportunities on which the art of caricature throve and developed, comedy and fantasy gaining still further upon invective and allegory. There was the marriage of the Prince and Mrs. Fitzherbert—a print-shop obsession in 1786; the affair of Warren Hastings which began in 1786, but belongs chiefly to 1788 when the impeachment opened. After the alarming crisis in Holland with its happy ending in 1787, came the King's illness and the Regency crisis in 1788–9, preceded by a sensational by-election at Westminster with a special interest for students of Gillray.

Mrs. Fitzherbert's marriage (in December 1785) was the talk of the town. 'Oh but the hubbub you are to hear and talk of', wrote Walpole (10 February), 'and except which you are to hear and talk of nothing else, for they tell me the passengers in the streets of all ranks talk of it.' The print-shops embroidered on the rumours with a spate of prints, chiefly from March to May. The prevailing genre of the 'marriage' prints, and an innovation, was the conversation piece charged with innuendo and sometimes with burlesque and ribaldry. Kingsbury seems to have been the anonymous author of the most characteristic of these prints which were published by Fores. The Piccadilly shop-window is the background to a coarse attack on the Prince, *The Cock of the Walk Distributing his Favours* [6961], in which Fores seems to declare himself an enemy of the Opposition: his shop-front is decorated with the heads of Fox, Burke, and North on spikes arranged like a pawnbroker's sign.

The marriage was mixed up with the Prince's debts, with his relations with his parents and the Opposition, and with reports of riot and dissipation at Carlton House. This is the beginning of satires on the Prince's boon companions—especially represented by George Hanger—who like Louis

Weltje (Controller of the kitchens and cellars at Carlton House and a factotum of the Prince), figures repeatedly in prints of the wedding. The Prince is not as a rule personally caricatured, indeed some justice is done to his youthful elegance, and he is occasionally the artless victim of a designing widow as in *An Extravaganza, or Young Solomon Besieging Fitzhubbub* [6949]. Fox and the Opposition often abet the marriage (which Fox tried to prevent). Gillray's contribution was the invention of a runaway match promoted by the Foxites. *Wife & No Wife—or—A Trip to the Continent* [6932], 'Design'd by Carlo Khan', is a characteristic blend of fantasy and realism. The scene is a French or Flemish cathedral; Burke, a Jesuit, marries the pair, Fox gives the bride away, with Hanger and Weltje in attendance. North, the coachman, sits against the altar-wall characteristically fast asleep. Pictures on the wall of Susanna and Eve imply seduction by Mrs. Fitzberbert abetted by Fox (Judas). Conversation piece and theatre—another growing influence on caricature—are effectively combined in *A Scene from the School for Scandal* [Pl. 77], a satire on the Prince's relations with the King and his ostentatious retrenchments at Carlton House (much ridiculed by the caricaturists). The Prince is Charles Surface in the auction scene, ordering the auctioneer, George Hanger, to 'knock down the Farmer', that is, 'Lot 1', *Farmer George & his Wife*, a caricature of the King and Queen [6934] which Sheridan holds up. Portraits of Mrs. Fitz and (?) Perdita Robinson are still on the wall.

A theme often elaborated was the supposed miserliness of the King and (especially) the Queen. This was peculiarly the topic of Peter Pindar (John Wolcot) in his vastly popular verse satires, and he may well be the begetter of the long campaign of detraction and ridicule, carried on when the King was popular. Gillray broached the subject on 21 April in connexion with the Prince's debts, in *A New Way to pay the National Debt* [6945], noteworthy as the first attack on Queen Charlotte (but not her first appearance). Pitt wheels a barrow-load of coin from the Treasury, handing a money-bag to the overladen King, while the Queen takes snuff with a smile of greedy and satisfied cunning, her apron heaped with guineas. The henchmen of the Treasury bench, drawn up in military subservience to Pitt, are also handsomely paid, but a disabled and penniless sailor sits on the ground. The Prince of Wales, in rags, hesitates to take money offered him by the Duc d'Orléans (who had in fact offered a loan). Placards on the wall add to the insults of this large striking cartoon, which is 'Dedicated to Mon$^r$ Necker' (an interesting indication of Necker's inflated reputation as a financial wizard). They include reflections on the King's farming activities in Windsor Great Park. Though the King had been 'Farmer George' in a print of 1771, this topic properly begins in 1786 with *The Constant Couple* [6918] in which the Queen rides pillion on a sorry horse behind her farmer-husband. Other farming scenes followed, notably *The Farm Yard* [6947] in which the King feeds pigs and the Queen feeds chickens. To quote Peter Pindar, 'Let Great George his porkers bilk / And give his maids the sour skim-milk.'

Another facet to the royal greed *cum* miserliness theme belongs to a far more important affair, the impeachment of Warren Hastings. Public opinion on Hastings had been violently at issue since his return to England in June 1785. Sayers made the subject his own by clever attacks on the Opposition campaign, particularly on Burke as its leading spirit. Gillray produced two outstanding prints, a brilliant defence of Hastings in 1786, a bitter attack in 1788 (when the earlier plate was reprinted). In *The Political-Banditti assailing the Saviour of India* [Pl. 78], Hastings, in oriental dress, rides a camel, which like its rider looks down with proud contempt at the antics of Burke, Fox, and North, who wear armour. Burke, like a malignant insect or a burlesqued Don Quixote, carrying a wallet of 'Charges', fires a blunderbuss at the 'Shield of Honour' on Hastings's arm. Fox, frenzied with rage, lifts a conspiratorial dagger. North grabs at one of the money-bags on the camel—'Rupees added to the Revenue'; his damaged (but sheathed) sabre is inscribed 'American Subjugation'.

The early prints (in 1786) were favourable to Hastings. In March both Sayers and Dent contrast Burke's intemperate violence against Hastings with his screening and reinstatement (when Paymaster) of a defaulting cashier. The trend altered through an accident. At an unlucky moment— the day after the debate (on 13 June) that made impeachment inevitable— Hastings presented a large diamond in a packet (bulse) sent from India for the King by the Nizam of the Deccan. Though Hastings was merely handing over a sealed parcel this was 'as any other possible subject would be, taken hold of to insinuate connection between the Court and Mr Hastings by means of corruption'.[1] Presents from Hastings to the King and Queen (an ivory bed) had already been seized upon by the authors of those famous satires, the *Rolliad* and the *Probationary Odes*. 'Newspapers and print shops formed the channels through which the enemies of Hastings generally transmitted their accusations or insinuations throughout the kingdom.'[2] The print-shops opened fire on 11 July with a set of prints

[1] *Hist. MSS. Comm., Rutland Papers*, iii. 323 (14 July 1786).
[2] *Memoirs of Wraxall*, 1884, iv. 342–5.

using the court cards of the suit of diamonds. Hastings (in his own person) is *Knave of Diamonds* [6966] with packages for the King and a book lettered Bribery. George III is *The King of Diamonds* [6969] in a pack of cards. A portrait of the Queen, bejewelled and taking snuff, is *The Queen of Hearts Covered with Diamonds* [6978]; in this the Nizam's diamond figures as a big heart-shaped jewel surmounted by a crown and embedded in diamonds in a box or 'bulse'. In a companion print George III is *Cheyt Sing in his Eastern Dress* [6979] with the diamond in his turban. Hastings's treatment of Chait Sing, Raja of Benares, was the subject of the crucial debate when Pitt and Dundas voted against Hastings and impeachment became certain. Pitt's motives for the vote are still controversial: the prints suggest that if he had not done so the outcry against 'corruption' would have been noisy indeed.

Tension slackened in 1787. A Foxite attack on Pitt's commercial treaty with France, an attempt to repeat their Irish success, miscarried; the terms were too obviously favourable to British trade. The attempt and failure are the subject of a number of prints, notably two by Sayers [7140–1] in which the importance of Josiah Wedgwood as spokesman of the industrialists is illustrated. Violent but futile attempts to storm the massive door of the Treasury by the Prince and his friends are the subject of *A Convention of the Not-Ables* [7158] (the French Assembly of Notables met in February). Fox bites the padlock, Burke's weapon is 'Impeachment'; North, passive as usual, has an axe inscribed 'To subjugate America'. Their programme is on a placard: '. . . attack the Treasury with all proper Weapons, Get into Place, Humble the Pride of Master Billy, Kick out the Treaty of Commerce, Convict Hastings, Remove the Sceptre, Repeal the Shop Tax, Pass Fox's India Bill. Keep their places & do many more things if they are able.' But inside the gate the crown is 'safe', and Pitt's words float out: 'I have Gain'd the affections of my Sovereign, and they must cut keener than a *Diamond* to affect me.'

One cause of slackened tension was a quasi-reconciliation of the Prince and the King after a quasi-repudiation of Mrs. Fitzherbert by Fox's denial in Parliament: 'a miserable calumny . . . a tale only fit to impose on the lowest order of persons in the streets'; he asserted—under pressure—that the marriage 'not only could never have happened legally but never did happen in any way whatsoever'.[1]

[1] Though illegal by the Royal Marriage Act and the Act of Settlement, the ceremony was regular; it salved Mrs. Fitzherbert's conscience and in some degree was accepted by the royal family.

Gillray's *Dido Forsaken, Sic transit gloriae Reginæ* [7165], is a mordant comment on Fox's denial in the context of the arrangements of Pitt and Dundas with the Prince for reconciliation with the King and the payment of his debts. Mrs. Fitzherbert—Dido—is seated on her funeral pyre, surrounded by emblems of Popery; with a tragic gesture she watches the Prince sail away in a small boat—the 'Honour'—towards Windsor Castle. A blast from the mouths of Pitt and Dundas—two winds—inflates the ragged sail and blows away Dido's crown, sceptre, and coronet. The Prince sits between Fox, who steers, and Burke who wears a biretta and says, 'I never saw her in my life, Never': Fox echoes, 'No never in all his life'; North, seemingly asleep, adds, 'No, never.'

The Dutch affair was another factor in the abatement of party rancour. A state of civil war had developed between the Orangists and the Patriots, supported by France. The United Provinces seemed about to become a French dependency when the joint intervention of Prussia and England caused the complete collapse of the anti-British Patriots and the restoration of the Stadtholder. It was a triumph for Pitt and the only occasion when Fox praised a Pittite achievement—this followed from his recent anti-Gallican outburst against the Commercial Treaty. There are some ten prints on the crisis which ended with the surrender of Amsterdam. Gillray then produced *Amsterdam in a Dam'd Predicament—or—the Last Scene of the Republican Pantomime* [7181]. The sovereigns who had been concerned watch from the boxes the antics on the stage of the Stadtholder —William V—and his frog-subjects. These bring emblems of submission and kneel abjectly to the notoriously inert Stadtholder who is burlesqued as a ferocious soldier slashing and decapitating his frogs, some of whom escape by leaping into the orchestra—otherwise Hell, with its demon-musicians who are dominated by the late Frederick of Prussia blowing his flute. Suppliant frogs fawn on the Princess of Orange, who smiles coquettishly—her energy and courage had contrasted with her husband's apathy. In the boxes George III looks belligerently at the horrified Louis XVI; Catherine of Russia and Joseph II (in a fool's cap) threaten the Sultan. A grotesque figure of Fame dominates the stage background. This is the first of some striking cartoons in which a complicated European situation (notably the peace-treaties of 1814–15) is given a theatre setting.

Excitement seethed and bubbled in 1788. First, over the Hastings impeachment which began as a superb spectacle and a social and political sensation, and thereafter dragged out its weary seven years, little regarded

by the public. The prints are predominantly anti-Hastings—it could hardly
be otherwise: 'All the world against poor Mr Hastings,' recorded Fanny
Burney, 'though without knowing what his materials may be for clearing
away these aspersions.'[1] The rhetoric of Burke, Fox, and Sheridan absorbed attention: the evidence was a bore—the barely audible quibbling of
lawyers. The most savage attack was Gillray's *Blood on Thunder Fording
the Red Sea* [Pl. 79], impressive, though less so than the larger *Political
Banditti* which Holland reprinted in 1788. Was one, or both, commissioned? Or is the contradiction Gillray's ironic contempt (which he shows
repeatedly) for the extremes of propaganda? Or had he simply changed his
opinion? Thurlow, scowling, wades waist-deep in a sea of blood in which
float the mutilated corpses of Indian victims. On his shoulders sits
Hastings, serenely content, with a huge money-bag marked £4,000,000
crooked in each arm. Thurlow, who as Chancellor presided, was openly
opposed to the impeachment, but, to quote the *D.N.B.*, 'by the consent
of all contemporaries he nobly sustained the dignity of British justice'.
This is one of the comparatively few prints to reflect the main contentions
of the orators—the rapine alleged against Hastings. The cartoonists'
favourite theme was bribery and the venal protection of Hastings by Thurlow and George III. A mild example—said to have amused the King—is
*H-st-gs Ho, Rare H-st—ngs!* [7267]; Hastings, as always in oriental dress,
wheels King and Chancellor in a barrow with the motto 'what a man buys
he may sell. Blackstone's Commentaries . . .'. ('Hastings', early green peas,
was a London street cry.)

In Dent's *The Raree Show* [7273] the splendid spectacle in Westminster
Hall is burlesqued as a display of booths at a fair, with their big pictorial
placards advertising the show within (an early example of a cartoonist's
device which may owe something to Hogarth's *Southwark Fair* but more
probably illustrates the familiar fair ground display). Among the placards
are 'Alexander the Great' (Hastings); 'Alexander the Little' (the King);
'A Tragi-comi-Exhibition called the Nabob in Purgatory'; 'The Prodi-
gious Monster arrived from the East' (Hastings devouring an Indian
woman). Spectators fight for access to the fair (as they did to get into Westminster Hall—when fifty guineas was paid for a seat) and in the foreground the King, with a big 'Bulse' hanging from his ribbon, carries
Thurlow on his shoulders; the Chancellor has a demon's body with a
barbed tail inscribed 'Defence'. Burke, Sheridan, and Fox are the clown
and zanies who proclaim the attractions of their booths. Burke, standing

[1] *Diary of Mme d'Arblay*, 1854, iv. 87.

in water, harangues seven ladies and a man, who are all spouting tears and
are submerged to the neck. 'Burke exceeded all his former excesses . . .',
wrote Sir Gilbert Elliot, 'and in one of his excesses he did not, I believe,
leave a dry eye in the whole assembly.'[1]

The defender of Hastings was pre-eminently Sayers; the others were
Ramberg the Hanoverian artist, a protégé of George III, and James Hook
(brother of Theodore), a Westminster schoolboy. Their themes are the
rhetorical exaggerations and the vindictive animosity of the orators, the
conspiratorial spite of Francis, the unworthy insults to a great man. *The
Trial* [7321] (from *The Merchant of Venice*) is a remarkable achievement
for a boy. Fox is Shylock; Hastings, Antonio; Law, his leading Counsel,
is Portia; Thurlow presides and the Managers are in their box. Fox, looking
extremely Jewish, theatrically clasps a knife. The plate is inscribed:

> *Shylock.* My deeds upon my head, I crave the Law.
> *Anthonio.* He seeks my Life, his reason well I know.

This represents Fox's anger at Thurlow's opinion (accepted by the peers)
that the rules of evidence in courts of law should be followed, and not the
*Lex Parliamenti* used at Strafford's impeachment. Sayers did two prints
on the same subject [7276, 7289]. Francis is the instigator in *The Princess's
Bow alias the Bow Begum* [7309] by Sayers; he emerges from the ground
with a conspiratorial stare to say (correctly), 'I am at the bottom of it.'

Rhetorical extravagance is the subject of several prints by Sayers; one
attracted a counter-print by Gillray in an imitation of Sayers' manner.
*Galante Show* [Pl. 80] is a small design; Burke is a showman with a magic
lantern; he has thrown on a sheet four objects, grossly distorted and en-
larged as their titles show: 'A Benares Flea' becomes an elephant; 'A
Begum Wart' appears as three piled-up mountains, Ossa, Pelion, and
Olympus; four large eyes floating half submerged in their own tears are
'Begum's Tears'; 'An Ouzle' (weasel) becomes a spouting whale.
The Managers applaud: 'Finely imagined'; 'Poor Ladies they have cried
their eyes out.' Polonius's words when fooling Hamlet to the top of his bent
are quoted: 'Very like an Ouzle.' Three days later Gillray produced
*Camera-Obscura* [Pl. 81], using Sayers' signature. Hastings displays
objects in the diminishing rays of his camera obscura to Thurlow, the
King and the Queen. An elephant devouring Indians is reduced to 'a Flea';
Mount Ossa becomes 'a Wart'; a British officer murdering women and an
infant while a waggon-load of 'plunder' is driven off is called 'skin'd
mice'; a spouting whale is 'An Ouzle'.

[1] *Life and Letters*, i. 195.

The impeachment was in the hands of the Opposition, represented by the Managers, and it was supposed that they were anxious 'to work it up into a flame against Government'. They failed, and only one print credits them (perhaps) with public spirit. This is Gillray's *Opposition—Coaches* [7323-4], two plates making one design. The 'Opposition', 'Licensed by Act of Parliament' and driven by Burke, is plunging into the 'Slough of Despond'; in the boot are Magna Charta and the Bill of Rights; the crest is a bull (John Bull) with the motto (commonly used ironically by Gillray) 'Pro Bono Publico'. Thurlow drives the other in the opposite direction, uphill towards 'the Temple of Honour'. The passengers are Hastings and his bejewelled wife, the guard is George III with a blunderbuss, and on the roof sits an old market woman—the Queen—with a basket of 'Golden Eggs'. A quotation about 'very gorgeous harlotry' implies a censure on her favour to a divorcée.

Here chronology must be dropped as the impeachment disappears from the political foreground. In 1789 and 1790 there are still one or two allusions to Hastings, chiefly by some reference to a diamond, and after that a silence reflecting public unconcern. Only Sayers produced a print on the final (majority) verdict in 1795—a tribute to Hastings. *The Last Scene of the Managers Farce* [8647] takes place in 'an old Hall (formerly a Court of Justice)'. On the stage a big cauldron filled with the different 'Charges', and inscribed 'Exit in Fumo', sinks through an aperture in the boards sending up a dense mass of smoke which fails to dim a brightly irradiated bust of Hastings. The contents are 'Ingredients mixed up by the Managers to blacken a character out of their reach'. About to sink through another hole in the floor stands Burke, gesticulating furiously with a paintbrush and with a document inscribed 'More Arguments'. He is 'one of the Managers & a principal Performer, who having "Out-heroded Herod" retires from the Stage in a passion at seeing the farce likely to be Dam'd'.[1] Other Managers are in their box, the outside of which is patterned by the meandering slime of a snail, which, starting from '1787', has passed every intermediate year till its head touches '1795'. Just outside the box appears the head of Francis, his eyes fixed balefully on the Hastings bust.

To return to 1788 and the Westminster by-election. When Hood was made First Lord his re-election was not expected to be opposed. Suddenly

---

[1] Burke's closing speech (reprinted as a pamphlet) lasted for nine days between 28 May and 16 June 1794 and was censured in the debate on the vote of thanks to the Managers. Between 13 Feb. 1788 and 23 Apr. 1795 there had been 148 sittings; only 29 peers voted. Thurlow had been succeeded by Loughborough who voted against Hastings on all the charges except the two on which the Not Guilty verdict was unanimous.

the Foxites challenged the Government by putting up Lord John Cavendish—a far-from-strong candidate. The Treasury financed Hood[1] and the
Opposition are said to have raised £50,000 for the disorderly contest which
lasted the full fifteen days to which elections had been limited after the
experience of forty days of riot in 1784. It is the only election in which the
Ministry is known to have paid for caricatures. Charles Stuart, a journalist,
organized propaganda for Hood and his account to the Treasury of disburse-
ments contains (besides payments for newspapers, bill-stickers, hand-bill
distributors, and cockades) the items of £15 each 'for paper' to an engraver
(probably Gillray) and a printer. A few days later there was a further sum
of £20 to 'Mr Gilwray engraver'.[2] During July Gillray produced seven of
the twenty-seven extant election prints (nine of which are Foxite), all anti-
Cavendish, ineffective as propaganda and with claims to be his worst
political plates. The interesting thing is that in August he published his
first signed caricature ('J$^s$ Gillray inv$^t$ and fec$^t$') and that this was a violent
attack on the recent official electioneering. In *Election-Troops, Bringing in
their Accounts, To the Pay-Table* [7369] Pitt stands at the Treasury Gate
dismissing ministerial hacks and hirelings: 'I know nothing of you my
Friends, Lord H—d pays all the expences himself—Hush! Hush! go to
the back door in Great George Street under the Rose!' (apply to George
Rose, the Treasury Secretary). The leading applicant is Topham, editor
of the *World*, who proffers an account 'For Puffs, & Squibs and for abusing
Opposition', and has a claim also 'For changing Sides; for hiring of
Ballad Singers & Grub Street Writers'. Gillray followed up this onslaught
by another (with an obliterated signature), *Charons Boat; or—Topham's
Trip with Hood to Hell* [7371], a savage attack on Hood's electioneering.
The terrified Hood, approaching Hades in a boat propelled by Topham,
is gnawed by a serpent, 'Worm of Conscience'. Here, seemingly, is an
explosion of resentment at having been one of Hood's election troopers.

   The election was so closely fought and so ruinously expensive that both
sides agreed to support one candidate only at the next election; this very
usual compromise was to have important consequences. Meanwhile the
sensation of Cavendish's victory (by 6,382 against 5,569) was followed by
Fox's departure for Switzerland with Mrs. Armistead (afterwards Mrs.
Fox) and soon gave way to the far greater sensation of the King's illness.

   From November to May the illness, the Regency crisis, and its after-

---

[1] By a levy on the great offices of State and leading ministerial peers; the balance was paid
by the Treasury: *Proceedings in an Action for Debt by C. J. Fox against J. Horne Tooke*, 1792;
Buckingham, *Courts and Cabinets of George III*, ii. 16.
[2] Aspinall, *Politics and the Press, c. 1780–1850*, 1949, pp. 420–1.

math monopolized the caricaturists. In the national collection there is not a single political print unconnected with the absorbing drama till mid-May. Some eighty caricatures reflect more of propaganda than of opinion, which, outside Carlton House and Foxite circles, was overwhelmingly for the King and Pitt against the Prince and Fox—for those who wished to keep the crown on the King's head against those who wished to remove it for ever—that being the issue at its simplest. Starting from 5 November the first six prints are anti-Foxite; on 12 December the tide turned and till the King's recovery they are mainly anti-Pitt. Though over the whole period there are 36 Foxite prints against 35 that can be classed as Pittite, with nine neutral or doubtful, during the crucial weeks from 12 December to 17 February the score is Fox 33, Pitt 15, and the Foxite ones are more violently explicit.

The Regency prints illustrate a propaganda campaign of passionate ferocity. Some papers were 'veering towards the rising sun'. Newspapers— 'such as had not virtue to resist temptation'—were bought up; some control of others was acquired by the purchase of shares—this *The Times* (in June) denounced as a conspiracy against the Liberty of the Press.[1] William Combe described a Foxite committee which sat daily, perhaps nightly, in a well-known tavern in Covent Garden, 'to shape paragraphs, frame handbills, and propagate falsehoods: in short to do their utmost, by any and every means, to inflame the people against the *King's* friends, and to influence the public mind in favour of their own masters. . . . Inflammatory handbills seem to have been blown through the air to our market towns, in order (as one of my farmers expressed himself) to make people as glad as the writers of them that the *king* was out of his mind.'[2] Pitt was urged by a pamphleteer 'to be cautious and in manly contempt of Print Shops, Pamphlets, and Prostitute Publications to keep the reins till the King and People are secure'.[3] Owing to the King's timely recovery and the mistaken tactics of the Whigs in obstructing the Regency Bill, he succeeded.

On 29 December the *Morning Post* revealed that a parcel of papers entitled 'Prince Pitt or the Patriot Minister' was dispatched on 27 December to a Bristol stationer (and doubtless elsewhere) by 'C. W.' (? Charles Weltje) with promises to refund the expenses of distribution. On 2 January the *Post* was bought up by Carlton House at an inflated price, Louis Weltje being the negotiator.[4] 'Prince Pitt' is the main theme

---

[1] Aspinall, *Politics and the Press, c. 1780–1850*, 1949, pp. 271–2.     [2] Ibid., p. 283.
[3] *Alfred* [B.M., T. 1120/5].                    [4] Aspinall, op. cit., p. 274.

of a set of caricatures (perhaps crypto-Gillrays) violently attacking him between 29 December and 19 January. The Opposition saw power within their grasp, and refused to believe in the possibility of the King's recovery. As early as 16 November Thurlow turns his coat in *Dead. Positively Dead* [7377] in which the Prince feigns grief and Mrs. Fitzherbert is crowned queen. And in *Filial Piety!* [Pl. 82] by Rowlandson on 16 November the Prince enters the King's room in a drunken frolic, followed by Hanger and Sheridan. 'Damme, come along,' he says, 'I'll see if the Old Fellow's — or not —'; on the wall is a picture of the Prodigal Son, and a bishop is interrupted in a prayer for the King's recovery. Such disrespect to the Prince is exceptional: was he not the rising sun?

Fox's return post-haste from Bologna is satirized in Gillray's *King Henry IVth The last Scene* [7380] on 29 November; Fox is Falstaff, Sheridan is Bardolph (with a fiery face), and Hanger is Pistol, telling Fox 'thy tender lambkin now is King'. Falstaff's words, quoted on the print, are remarkably apt to Fox's nine days of exhausting travel: '. . . to ride day and night . . . to stand stained with travel and sweating with desire to see him. . . .' The terms on which the Prince should be Regent were the subject of the famous debate on 10 December, when Fox laid down that 'the Prince of Wales had as clear a right to exercise the power of sovereignty as if the King were actually dead', and Pitt maintained that, 'except by decision of Parliament the Prince had no more right—speaking of strict right—to assume the Government than any other individual subject', and that 'to assert a right in the Prince to the Regency independent of . . . Parliament was little less than treason to the Constitution . . .'. Fox retaliated with charging Parliament with treason if they 'arrogated a power to which they had no right'. This is the famous occasion when Pitt said he would 'Unwhig' Fox, and Burke called Pitt 'one of the Prince's competitors'. Two days later Dent produced *The Competitors* [7382] in which they fight for the crown, and the Prince treads on a bag, displacing a squalling cat labelled 'King William fourth'. (In the Prince's circle Pitt was called 'Prince William, William IV, and William the Conqueror'.[1])

In some form or other the thesis that Pitt was arrogating to himself the powers of the Crown by a Regency Bill imposing restrictions on the Regent's powers (although he was known to be preparing to return to the bar when the Bill came into force) appears in all the Foxite prints. *Prince Pitt* [7389], with another version of the same design called *King Pitt* [7388], on 29 December, is a key print; it embodies the main contentions of the

[1] *Auckland Correspondence*, ii. 280.

Foxites, except the attacks on the Queen which came later, and has the rather laboured character of concerted propaganda. Hamlet's words on Claudius are quoted, 'A cut purse of the empire and the rule that from a shelf the precious diadem stole, and put it in his pocket.' The Prince lies prostrate, trampled on by the Dukes of Grafton and Richmond; Pitt stands on their shoulders to reach the crown on its shelf. Insults and accusations are heaped on all three. The Prince says, 'I appeal to the People of England to defend their own rights and those of the House of Brunswick against this Banditti of Plunderers.' Verses elaborate the attack:

> See here Prince George! our Sovereign's darling Son,
> Old England's Hope, & Heir to Britain's Throne:
> Trod under Foot the Royal Victim lies:
> The while Prince Pitt above him dares to rise. . . .
> Two base-born Dukes of the curs'd Stuart Breed
> Bend their vile necks to help him to the deed . . .
> Rouse Britons, rouse!—hands hearts in chorus join
> To guard your laws and save the Brunswick line . . .

In his own unmistakable manner, Gillray expressed a similar idea much more graphically in *The Vulture of the Constitution* [Pl. 83] on 3 January. Gorged with 'Treasury' gold, the monstrous bird with Pitt's head crushes crown, sceptre, Magna Charta and the Prince's coronet, from which he tears the feathers.

Attacks on the Queen multiplied after the debate on the fifth restriction (carried 19 January). This gave her the care of the King's person and his household with the assistance of a council, and was attacked as a plot to obtain patronage and money. She was thereupon accused of secretly sending money to Germany (by Mrs. Schwellenberg, Fanny Burney's enemy and a butt of the caricaturists), and charged with concealing the state of the King's health and compelling the doctors to alter their bulletins. In *The Q.A.* [Queen's Ass] *Loaded with the Spoils of India and Britain* [7384] she is a zebra (her own zebra) with a large jewel—'Bulse'—hanging from its neck: 'What are Children's rights to Ambition,' it asks, 'I will rule in spite of them if I can conceal things at Q' (Kew). Pitt rides the animal, which is laden with paniers of jewels, and says, 'I have thrown off the Mask. I can blind the People no longer and must now carry every thing by my bought Majority.' In Dent's *Point-Blank at the Constitution* [7488] on 20 January Pitt fires a blunderbuss at a bull (John Bull), using the zebra as a stalking horse—the saddle cloth with a big crown and the word 'Avarice' proclaims its identity. His bullets are 'Council, Household', and so on, and he tramples on 'Parental Affection'. This is evidently a counter-thrust to Sayers' *A Mis-Fire at the Constitution* [7483] on 12 January; Fox fires at the British Lion, which holds a scroll, 'The Rights of the People'; he takes deliberate aim, resting his gun on a blinkered pony with the Prince's feathers in the *Ich Dien* headband. Sheridan holds the animal's head (to signify his favour at Carlton House) and papers flutter from his pockets: 'Paragraph against the Minister', 'Puffs direct for the P—e'; 'Puffs oblique for the P—e'; 'Abuse of the Minister'. He tramples on 'The Oath of Allegiance' and the pony treads on 'Addresses' and 'Vote of thanks to Pitt'. The management of the Press campaign was attributed to Sheridan and in *Joseph Surface Posted* [7510, n.d.] by Dent he is castigated for the newspaper attacks on the Queen; he writes lies for the *Morning Post* and the *Morning Herald* and gives them to winged demons who fly off with them: 'Vienna Bank Millions' (the Queen's) and 'Settled Melancholy'. His paper rests on the back of a demon who leans against a turn-about pivoting on a post and inscribed 'Wits last Stake' and 'Literary Corruption'. For the *Morning Post* he writes, 'her political interference', but another demon flies towards him to say, 'Recovery complete'. This print is 'Designed by Misrepresentation Executed by Purchase'—the purchase of the *Morning Post*. The *Morning Herald* was to be publicly burnt with 'universal execration' in March[1] and to incur a libel action for a savage attack on the Queen.

The confident Whigs had been cabinet-making when their hopes were suddenly dashed. How suddenly appears vividly in two prints by Sayers, dated 18 and 19 February. In the first, *The Comet* [Pl. 84], the Prince's friends (their heads) fill the tail of the downward slanting star in which the Prince's head is enclosed. They include two of the 'rats' and Sheridan has first place, Fox second with Portland next to him. Burke's angry spectacled face is near the end of the tail. The Prince's comet is expected to be 'within our horizon from Oct^r 1788 to Augt 1789 but is expected to be most visible (if it forces itself upon our Notice) in . . . February and March'. In the second, *The Regency Cake not cut up* [7509], the final distribution of the portions of a Twelfth Cake decorated by the Prince's coronet and feathers and already allotted to the new Ministers, is interrupted by a broad ray of light and the words 'The King shall enjoy his own again'. Weltje drops his knife and the others register varying shades of anger and disappointment. The motto is, 'And all the People rejoiced and said Long Live the King.'

---

[1] For saying (7 Mar.) that the King was incapable of reigning: Aspinall, op. cit., pp. 271, 283.

They did. On news of the King's recovery London was immediately and spontaneously illuminated. Propaganda can seldom have boomeranged more completely.

In the Pittite prints there is no corresponding evidence of a concerted campaign, but presumably Pitt had his propagandists. After the December debate Piccadilly was placarded 'Fox for the Prince's Prerogative, Pitt for Privileges of Parliament and the Liberties of the Nation'.[1] Pitt's chief support was that the popularity which the King had acquired by dismissing the Coalition had deepened into affection which was outraged by Foxite fears of recovery. This is the background of several prints. In Rowlandson's *Blue and Buf Loyalty* [7394, 31 December] Sheridan and Dr. Willis face each other in two pairs of half-length portraits, one inscribed 'Saturday' the other 'Sunday'. Twice the doctor answers an unseen inquirer: 'Doctor how is your Patient to Day.' On Saturday, registering melancholy, he answers, 'Rather Worse—Sir'; Sheridan exclaims with a cunning and satisfied smile, 'Ha-ha—rare news.' On Sunday the contented answer is 'Better thank God', and Sheridan angrily shouts 'Damnation'. Having convinced themselves that recovery was impossible the Opposition cross-questioned and browbeat the doctors and attacked the Queen on reports of improvement. In *A Peep behind the Curtain at Drury Lane* [7484] by Sayers on 14 January the pit are shouting 'Play God Save the King' (not then generally played in the theatre); Sheridan, with a conspiratorial scowl, speaks to the orchestra through a small gap in the curtain: 'Damn'em dont play God Save the King.' On 26 December the Drury Lane audience had called loudly for 'God save the King, when the huzzaing at ". . . Scatter his enemies" exceeded all imagination',[2] an anti-Foxite demonstration that must have galled Sheridan.

The extravagance and unseemliness of Burke's Regency speeches are illustrated. On one occasion he blamed Pitt for not having sent his letter to the Prince in a black box, protested against the decision that the House should not sit on 30 January—'of all days most fit for taking that step which was to annihilate the constitution . . .', went on to attack the Lords of the Household for 'sticking to the King's loaf', while protesting (he said) that 'they did not value the money three skips of a louse'. Rowlandson ridiculed this in *Neddy's Black Box* [7499]: urgently abetted by Sheridan, Burke kneels before the throne, presenting to the Prince the head of Charles I in a 'Treasury Box'; 'My Liege I told them in the House no day

---

[1] Feiling, *The Second Tory Party*, p. 180.
[2] *Harcourt Papers*, ed. E. W. Harcourt, iv. 97.

so proper to settle the Regency as Charles's Martyrdom' (with a quotation from his speech on the plate). These speeches were long remembered against him, especially one on 5 February, when he said that the King had been 'hurled by Providence from the throne'. A handbill on Burke was stuck up in Whitehall imitating the bulletins on the King, 'calmer this morning but tending towards unquietness'.[1] His wild words became a recurrent theme in connexion both with Hastings and the French Revolution, with flames or smoke rising from his over-heated brain. In May Gillray depicted him [7529] as a lunatic in a cell, screaming accusations against Hastings as he sees a vision of his *bête noire* being welcomed into St. James's.

The crisis ended in laughter with the arrival 'a day after the Fair!' [7511] of a deputation from Ireland headed by the Duke of Leinster to offer the unrestricted Regency to the Prince. The expected mission had been the subject of *Irish Wolf Hounds putting English Blood Hounds to Flight!* [7512]. Their arrival, 'just soon enough to be too late', on 27 February, the day the King was declared 'free from complaint', was ridiculed in six prints. 'It is impossible to describe how much and how universally their Excellencies are laughed at', wrote Grenville.[2]

Rejoicing at the King's recovery was unbounded. His thanksgiving procession to St. Paul's could hardly be directly attacked (though the Prince and the Duke of York did their best to mar the occasion). Opposition rancour found an outlet in representing that seats on the route were too dear and were unsaleable, and ridiculing the clumsy horsemanship and unsoldierly appearance of the 'cits'. Such was the theme of two striking prints, one by Dent [7524]. The other, *The Grand Procession to St. Paul's on St. George's Day 1789* [7525], is a large strip design, starting at Temple Bar with the King's coach (burlesqued and with Pitt as sole postilion). On placards in windows 'Seats two guineas' are scored through and replaced by 'Seats 5 Shill[gs]'. There are 'Seats in the Gutter one shilling'. This is probably by Wigstead, an imitator of Rowlandson who was Pitt's most persistent (pictorial) enemy during the Regency crisis.[3]

Gillray produced an epilogue to the Regency in one of the recurrent funerals of Whig expectations, *The Funeral Procession of Miss Regency*

---

[1] *Harcourt Papers*, ed. E. W. Harcourt, iv. 195.

[2] Buckingham, *Courts and Cabinets of George III*, ii. 124.

[3] Twelve drawings by Wigstead in pen and wash were exhibited at the Léger Galleries, New Bond Street, in Nov.–Dec. 1951, one of them endorsed, 'Mr Weltje with Mr Wigstead's compliments.' Seven are not known to have been engraved—they were probably overtaken by the King's recovery. The other five have been attributed to Rowlandson, whose authentic Regency prints are Pittite.

[7526], an important processional design. The coffin is carried by the six
'Irish Ambassadors' with bulls' heads, hooves, and tails; on it are dice and
an empty purse. Burke is a Jesuit, 'Ignatius Loyola'—Mrs. Fitzherbert
chief mourner, followed by Sheridan and Fox as 'second mourners' exchanging reproaches (many rancours were left behind by the crisis,
notably as between Fox, Sheridan, and Burke). Of course Weltje is there,
so, among others, is Loughborough—Chancellor-elect to the Regent. It is
remarkable that, apart from one or two allusions to Sheridan's impecunious-
ness, this is the only reference in the prints to the fact that the Prince, Fox,
Sheridan, and Burke were in financial straits that a Regency would have
removed.

The King's restoration probably marks the peak of Pitt's popularity
though there is no obvious sign of this in the prints. Startling events in
France could now demand attention, but Cowper's *Annus Mirabilis 1789*
celebrates, not the opening of the Revolution, but 'His Majesty's happy
recovery': 'A theme for poetry divine/A theme to ennoble even mine/In
memorable eighty-nine.' In this time of calm after storm the most vocal
grievance was Pitt's transference of the tobacco duties from customs to
excise, and there was an attempt to revive the clamour that had been so
effective against Walpole and Bute. It failed, but in 1789 and 1790 it
inspired some nine surviving prints. One is to be noted as the first print on
the French Revolution: on 28 July Gillray produced two designs on one
plate with the captions *France/Freedom* and *Britain/Slavery* [7546]. One
is the triumph of Necker in a land of freedom (restored to office after the
attack on the Bastille), the other that of Pitt in a land of slavery. Necker,
stout, bland, beneficent, sits in a chair carried by Orléans and Lafayette.
He holds a royal crown and the staff and cap of Liberty; an irradiated
laurel-wreath floats halo-wise above his head, giving a touch of absurdity;
behind are the ruins of the Bastille. Pitt, lean and arrogant, stands on a
crown, holding implements of death and torture and also chains attached
to the King and others who kneel at his feet. Behind are gibbets and an
executioner standing on a scaffold. The application is shown by a big
tobacco pipe marked 'Excise' in his pocket. Is this ironical? One supposes
so—a satire on both the excise agitation and the 'Prince Pitt' propaganda
(and characteristic of Gillray that he should satirize what he had himself
taken part in). However that may be, the print was copied in France with
deadly seriousness, without acknowledgement, and as two separate prints.
The print of Pitt, 'foulant au pied la couronne d'Angleterre', was again
copied, probably during the war, with an addition to the title: 'D'une main

il tient une hache et les chaines dont il a su charger la Nation et le Roi, de l'autre il porte le Drapeau de l'Esclavage, les impôts et les Echafauds sont les moyens qu'il employe pour soutenir son pouvoir chancelant' [8364]. An excellent example of the way in which English irony or faction could be used by the enemy.

# XII

## THE FRENCH REVOLUTION

ENGLISH impressions of the French Revolution must have been largely coloured by the print-shops. The caricatures—French as well as English—were almost the only rapid pictorial reactions to events in France. This was the time when more or less permanent exhibitions were being advertised by Holland and Fores. Holland's exhibition began in 1788 and may have lapsed after 1794. Fores's lasted from 1789 to 1794 at least; both charged a shilling entrance. By September 1789 Holland was advertising, besides 'all the French caricatures', 'the largest collection in Europe of Humourous Prints' [7554]. From February 1790 the formula was 'In Holland's Caricature Exhibition Rooms may be seen the largest Collection in Europe of Political and other Humorous Prints with those published in Paris on the French Revolution' (an early use of the new phrase).[1] Fores began with 'Fores's Museum is now Opened . . . the largest Collection in the Kingdom', but in 1793 this became 'The largest Collection of Caratures [sic] in the World . . .' [8332]. He expanded his advertisements in his own *New Guide for Foreigners* (c. 1790): 'To the works of Hogarth, Bunbury, Sayre, and Rowlandson, is added every other Caricature Print executed by other hands that has been published during many years, the whole forming an entire Caricature History, political and domestic of past and present Times. . . .' In 1790 Fores added the attraction of 'the head and hand of Count Struenzee'[2] and in March 1793 'a correct model of the Guillotine, 6 feet high'. For many years—even into the 1830's—the guillotine continued to be the emblem of horrific revolutionary ruthlessness.

The two events in France that attracted the cartoonists in 1789 were—naturally—the fall of the Bastille in July and the march of the women to Versailles in October. Isaac Cruickshank, who was specializing in French subjects—probably commissioned in France—produced *Les Sacrefices*

---

[1] Holland's exhibition (c. 1794) is the subject of a water-colour by Richard Newton [Pl. 85]; many exhibits are recognizable versions of his own caricatures (seemingly original drawings) and there is a self portrait of the artist—a boy in fashionable riding dress.

[2] From casts taken after the execution (1772) of the lover of the Queen of Denmark (George III's sister) by order of Christian VII.

*forces* [7553] on the surrender of feudal privileges on 4 August. It is hostile to the King and Queen and to the first *émigrés*. Gillray followed up his Necker-Pitt plate with *The Offering to Liberty* [7548] on 3 August, a processional design. Liberty, irradiated, and enthroned on the ruins of the Bastille, receives the acclamations of the French people, headed by Louis XVI, 'a repentant Monarch'; he proffers his crown to her, she returns it graciously. Orléans and Necker, as 'Honor & Virtue', walk behind the King, Orléans proffers his sword and a chain of five prisoners, the first is 'Messalina', a hideous travesty of Marie Antoinette.[1] Lafayette as 'General of a Free People' heads the National Guard who are followed by a cheering crowd. *La Chute du Despotisme* [7550] on 14 August, a large elaborate design with inscriptions in (incorrect) French and English, shows the fall of the Bastille as a symbol of the iniquities of the *ancien régime* and the aspirations of the Revolution. D'Artois and Marie Antoinette are enclosed in a setting sun of tyranny which is encircled with instruments of torture. On 31 October Isaac Cruikshank produced *Le Roi Esclave ou les Sujets Rois* [7560], a long processional design with all the inscriptions in French except for a sub-title, 'Female Patriotism'. The women are driving the King, Queen, and Dauphin from Versailles to Paris; a woman carrying a head on a pike threatens Lafayette: 'si vous êtes traitre on vous traitera ainsi'; five bodies hang from a lamp-post and in the foreground a little demon blows a trumpet: 'chacun y trouve son avantage'. The royal family are depicted without sympathy.

In the next few years there is a rapid change from sympathy or tolerance for the Revolution to horror. The chief factor in this is the revolutionary enthusiasm of the dissenters, especially the Unitarians. Here was the irreligion which had had such dire results in France; here was the old antagonism to Church and King. Anti-dissent is the dominating emotion, with Priestley and Price as arch-villains. The attitude to the Church is usually symptomatic of opinion. The motions for relief of dissenters by the repeal of the Test Act in 1787 and 1789 had been ignored by the caricaturists. In 1790 relief became a party question and an organized agitation by dissenters for a pressure campaign at the general election (they agreed to support 'those well affected to civil and religious liberty') roused a storm of protest and a pamphlet war which recalls the days of Hoadley and Sacheverell. Indeed they were recalled in a popular ballad satirizing

---

[1] It is to be suspected that the harsh treatment of Marie Antoinette derives from cruel French caricatures of *l'Autrichienne*.

the Church and the Universities, *Now or Never; or, a Reveillée to the Church:*

> Oh who shall blow the brazen trump
> By famed Sacheverell sounded,
> That spread confusion to the Rump,
> And silenced every Roundhead.
>
> The Sects they prate of rights and stuff
> And brawl in fierce Committees
> And soon will put on blue and buff
> While Price sings *Nunc Dimittis.*[1]

In the prints the dissenters are compared with the Republican sectaries of the seventeenth century. A sudden upsurge of 'the Church in danger' cry was inflamed by events in France and by Price's famous sermon (*Nunc Dimittis*) to the Revolution Society (which was celebrating the centenary of the Glorious Revolution) and by a pamphlet[2] by Priestley in which he anticipated grains of gunpowder which would blow up orthodoxy and hierarchy 'perhaps as suddenly, as unexpectedly, as completely, as the overthrow of the late arbitrary government in France'. Hence Priestley's firebrands and the explosion which blows up St. Paul's in *Puritanical Amusements Revived!* [7632], 'Designed by Oliver Cromwell, etch'd by William Holland'; in a composition crowded with separate incidents, dissenters renew the reputed excesses of Puritans in England and New England—savage punishments are inflicted for such offences as 'being detected in the abominable Sin of Kissing his Wife on the Sabbath Day'. This burlesque may not be wholly serious. But an elaborate print by Sayers is in deadly earnest; 'the most forcible stroke of satire', said the *St. James's Chronicle*, 'that, since the time of Hudibras, has been aimed at the cause of fanaticism.' This is a key print, the first general indictment of the French Revolution, and in its crude way an anticipation of Burke's attack on Price in his *Reflections*. In the *Repeal of the Test Act A Vision* [7628], 16 February 1790, the point of departure is Price's sermon on 4 November (widely circulated as a pamphlet) and the Address he then moved to the National Assembly (signed by Stanhope as chairman), congratulating them on the Revolution. The scene is a church; Price stands in the pulpit between Priestley and Dr. Lindsey (who is tearing up the 39 Articles). The clerk has passed up a paper to Price: 'The Prayers of this Congregation are desired for the Patriot Members of the National Assembly now sitting in France.'

---

[1] Quoted, Wright, *Caricature History of the Georges*, n.d., p. 449.
[2] *Letters to the Rev. Edward Burn.*

With a sanctimonious gesture Price responds, 'And now let us fervently pray for the Abolition of all unlimited and limited Monarchy, for the Annihilation of all ecclesiastical Revenues and Endowments, for the Extinction of all Orders of Nobility and all rank and Subordination in civil Society and that Anarchy and Disorder may by our pious endeavours prevail through the Universe—See my Sermon on the Revolution.' Flames from his mouth expand into four columns of smoke, 'Atheism, Deism, Socinianism, Arianism', which drive a cross-bearing angel out of a window. The details are too complicated for description here. Fox sits in the front pew; his 'Hear hear hear' ascends in smoke. The American flag hangs from the roof and on the sounding board over the pulpit are two books: 'Priestley on civil Government' and 'Price on civil Liberty' (his propaganda for American independence in 1776). Among the many characters are Lord Stanhope and Tom Paine (a first appearance); as an excise man he is gauging a Communion cup. Through a doorway leading to the 'Sanctum Sanctorum' is seen a portrait of Cromwell. Lines are quoted from Samuel Butler: '. . . Fanatics, Hypocrites, Dissenters/Cruel in power and restless out/And when most factious most devout/. . . .'

Other preoccupations of the caricaturists in 1790 were the Nootka Sound crisis and a Westminster election which though uneventful was important. The first began in the usual way with Spanish attacks on British ships and on a trading station on what is now Vancouver Island. The interesting thing about this is that the cartoonists saw it in terms of past slogans (against Walpole and North) and accused Pitt of truckling to Spain [7662]; Admiral Howe is reluctant to fight [7769]; the Navy is not intended to fight [7674]. Fox on the contrary attacked him for bullying Spain, and despite these twofold attacks the outcome was deservedly popular and a triumph for Pitt. But one print (probably by young James Hook) was startlingly new, the first pacifist print in the national collection. It reflects Opposition complaints of the financial burden of the armament. In *Arming John Bull to Fight the Bugaboos!!!* [7666] John is a stout, heavily armed, very unmilitary soldier, looking up in angry dismay at the irradiated helmet of 'Glory' which Pitt is about to place on his head. A paper hangs from his pocket: 'List of Ships £5000000.' 'O D—n the Glory,' he says, 'I shall never be able to bear it all!' The Convention in October was a victory for skilled diplomacy and the armament: the demands for reparation were accepted, Spain abandoned her claim to monopoly in the Pacific (with vast but not yet apparent opportunities for Canada). Yet the Opposition denounced it as the unmeaning conclusion to unprovoked bullying—Fox called it loss rather than gain. Cartoonists on the other hand embroidered the Walpolean tradition that a Convention with Spain was a face-saving humbug.

The Westminster election was a foregone conclusion through the agreement that each side would support one candidate. The very usual arrangement was denounced as a coalition. An election on strictly economical lines, without mobs, free beer or favours, was bound to be unpopular. For instance, Fox is *The Man of the People attempting another Coalition to creep in for Westminster*, with Hood as *The Modern Judas* [7641]. Horne Tooke intervened, demanded a poll and stood as an independent Reformer. Seeing that he was unsupported against the candidates of the Treasury and of the Westminster Committee and the Whig Club the results were surprising, a portent of reviving Radicalism and of events that made Westminster the pre-Reform Radical stronghold.[1]

Home politics gave way in November to the sensation of Burke's *Reflections on the Revolution in France* which is vividly illustrated. Prints emphatically do not support the French Ambassador's opinion that the book had united the whole nation against changes in France. The reaction was instant: the book was a favourite subject from November to May, when it merged with the equally attractive topic of the quarrel between Burke and Fox. All but three of the prints are hostile, and range from raillery through derision to reprobation. The caricaturists anticipated Tom Paine by depicting Burke as Don Quixote (for whom the age of chivalry was dead) and by seizing on the famous passage about Marie Antoinette. But one phrase in the book which became a democratic watchword went unnoticed (in the prints) till 1793—this was 'swinish multitude'. Immediately on publication there was a burlesque *Frontispiece to Reflections . . .* [7675], dated 2 November (publication date was 1 November). This was one of a set published, perhaps designed and etched, by Holland. Burke kneels, gazing ecstatically on a crowned and irradiated vision of Marie Antoinette standing upon clouds, and the famous passage is quoted, beginning, 'It is now sixteen or seventeen years since I saw the Queen of France.' A cherub holds a firebrand to Burke's head, drawing sparks from his heated brain. Next came the same artist's *The Knight of the woeful Countenance going to extirpate the National Assembly* [Pl. 86]. Burke as a Jesuit-Don Quixote, wearing armour, a miniature of Marie Antoinette, and a biretta expanded into the hat of a Death's-head hussar, rides out of his publisher's shop on an ass (the Pope). On his 'Shield of Aristocracy and Despotism' are scenes

---

[1] Fox 3,561, Hood 3,217, Horne Tooke 1,779.

of imprisonment and torture. In a third print Burke is *Don Dismallo,
after an absence of sixteen years embracing his beautiful Vision* [7679].
Watched by the weeping Mrs. Burke, who is dressed like a farmer's wife,
he embraces the Queen who pays him extravagant compliments.

The first pamphlet attacks on the book—there were at least thirty-nine—
are the subject of *Don Dismallo running the Literary Gantlet* [7685] dated
1 December. Burke, in a fool's cap and stripped to the waist, is scourged by
his active enemies: Mrs. Barbauld, Sheridan (with whom he had quarrelled),
Mrs. Macaulay (the Republican historian), and Horne Tooke. These are
urged on by Dr. Price and Helen Maria Williams. Liberty walks off arm
in arm with the aged prisoner from the Bastille (actually transferred to a
lunatic asylum) who carries a banner quartered with scenes relating to the
fall of the fortress, including heads on pikes and the anniversary fête. Burke's
'foes show how deeply they are wounded by their abusive pamphlets',
wrote Walpole on 20 December. 'Their amazonian allies headed by Kate
Macaulay and the virago Barbauld spit poison at eighteen pence a head....'[1]

Dent attacks Burke for exaggerations and inconsistencies in *Sublime and
Beautiful Reflections . . . or the Man in the Moon at large* [7689] with the
motto 'Reason to Madness is near allied'. The passionate defence of monarchy
in France is contrasted with his pronouncements (in 1780) on the influence
of the crown, and with quotations from Regency speeches, including
'hurled by Providence from the Throne'. The Radical viewpoint appears
more emphatically in *The Aristocratic Crusade or Chivalry revived by Don
Quixote de St. Omer . . .* [7824], 31 January 1791, an elaborate design by
Isaac Cruikshank in which labels from Burke's mouth contrast his attitudes
to the French monarchy and to the *Tiers État* ('low bred illiterate Traders,
Lawyers & Country Clowns'). Bishops and peers are denounced and so
are members for close boroughs—Old Sarum makes a first appearance.
This is very different from the old Wilkite prints, or the usual tributes to
Liberty. Here, perhaps for the first time, is class consciousness (to which
'swinish multitude' made a contribution). Burke stands on the back of a
monster with five heads (four wearing coronets) which tramples on the
backs of 'base born plebeans'.

The exceptions to the chorus of disprovise are three attacks on Price for
the sermon in the Old Jewry to the Revolution Society. In *The Doctor
indulged with his favourite Scene* [7690] by Cruikshank, Price, kneeling
on a royal crown, looks through a peep-hole into the Queen's bedroom at
Versailles, where murderous ruffians are searching for her. A devil clutches

---

[1] *Letters*, ed. Toynbee, Oxford, xiv. 345.

him round the waist as he utters his *nunc dimittis*: 'Lord now lettest thou
thy Servant depart in peace for mine Eyes have Seen...'. Below is Burke's
passage on the sermon, ending, 'These Theban & Thracian Orgies, acted
in France, and applauded only in the Old Jewry....' Another pro-Burke
print is less serious and tinged with irony, Gillray's *Smelling out a Rat;
—or—the Atheistical—Revolutionist disturbed in his Midnight "Calcula-
tions" owing to a Troubled—Conscience* [7686]. Dropping his pen, Price
turns from his table in horror at a cloud-supported vision of his enemy's
enormous and spectacled nose resting on the back of his chair and framed
by two great hands holding up an irradiated crown and cross, with his open
book poised above his spectacles. Beside Price are his 'Sermon...' and
two imaginary works with revolutionary titles. On the wall is a picture,
'...the Glory of Great Britain'—the execution of Charles I.

The third, by Sayers, on 6 May 1791, is one of many prints on the
famous quarrel between Fox and Burke in the debate on the constitution
for French Canada. It is the first in which the Foxites are Jacobins and it
foreshadows the split in the party. In *Mr Burke's Pair of Spectacles for short
sighted Politicians* [7858] a hand from the margin holds out spectacles en-
closing bust portraits of Fox and Sheridan. The vision displayed to them
is of a Cromwellian Fox cutting down a tree on which are symbols of
monarchy, religion, and aristocracy, with an axe: 'Rights of Man'. He is
aided by Sheridan and Priestley, and in the foreground the skeleton of
Price (who had recently died) rises from the tomb to utter his *nunc dimittis*.
A demon holds out to the horrified Portland 'A Plan of the new Constitution
of France, the Perfection of human Wisdom recommended as a Model for
Canada by the Rt. [Hon. C. J. Fox]'; the plan is a picture of a tree in a pot
of 'Republicanism' whose leaves are 'Atheists', 'Demagogues', and 'The
Mob'.

After the quarrel with Fox attacks on Burke's book were combined with
charges of self-seeking apostasy. Fox's tears were derided, but Burke was
more savagely treated. His wild eloquence and quotations from his book or
his speeches were treated as the ravings of a madman as in *The Volcano of
Opposition* [7863]. This recalls Fanny Burney's comment in her diary
(18 June 1791) on Burke's otherwise delightful conversation: 'politics,
even on his own side, must always be excluded; his irritability is so terrible
on that theme, that it gives immediately to his face the expression of a man
who is going to defend himself from murderers.' In *The Wrangling Friends
or Opposition in Disorder* [7855] Fox's tears are baled up in a bucket, and
a demon applies bellows to Burke's steaming head.

Burke was attacked by both sides—in the Opposition papers for caballing against Fox: 'the Ministerial papers held up Mr Burke . . . in the character of a king's evidence who had impeached his accomplices. The pencil was called in to the aid of the pen, and paragraphs were embodied in caricatures.'[1] The leading print on this theme was Gillray's *The Impeachment,—or—" The Father of the Gang, turnd Kings Evidence* [7861]. Fox and Sheridan (Joseph Surface) are two jail-birds, prisoners at the bar; Burke towers over them with a stern frown, seizing them by the hair. Sheridan curses, Fox weeps, grieving that his 'Chum in all infamy, for Twenty five years, should now turn Snitch at last! . . .' Despite their persistent hostility to Burke the prints are increasingly anti-Jacobin and reflect the emotions that produced the deplorable riots in Birmingham on 14 July. Disparaging allusions to Paine's *Rights of Man* (the principal attack on Burke's *Reflections*) recur, and Gillray gave the book a print to itself: "*The Rights of Man—or—Tommy Paine the little American Taylor, taking the Measure of the Crown, for a new pair of Revolution-Breeches* [7867]. He is a ragged fellow wearing a French cocked hat with a 'Vive la Liberte' cockade, using his inadequate tape-measure on a gigantic crown, and delivering one of those satirical monologues in which Gillray specialized.

His *Alecto and her Train, at the Gate of Pandæmonium,—or—The Recruiting Sarjeant enlisting John-Bull, into the Revolution Service* [7889] on 4 July is a satire on the coming dinner of the Revolution Society on the second anniversary of the fall of the Bastille, and in it Gillray's John Bull as an uncouth countryman in a smock makes a first appearance. The serjeant is Alecto, a ragged fantastic hag with snaky locks, wearing a French cocked hat and tricolour cockade, and holding a pike with the cap of Liberty. Her fifer and drummer are Sheridan and Fox, offering John Bull *assignats* as 'bounty money', and making specious promises: '. . . the glorious 14th of July is approaching when Monarchs are to be crushed like maggots, and brave men like yourself are to be put in their places . . .'. John hesitates between the lure of the drum and the fine prospects, and reluctance to leave 'the Varmer': '. . . Ah Varmer George has been a rare good Measter to I. . . .' Sheridan, small and deprecating, pipes, 'Though I am but a very silly Lad. . . .' Fox is burly and persuasive: 'Then come my Lad, our Glory share. . . .' They stand outside the Crown and Anchor in the Strand (where the dinner was to be held). Stanhope runs off, holding a warning letter from Pitt. He resigned from the Society on 12 August. None of the three attended the dinner.

[1] *Annual Register*, 1791, p. 119.

The passions and fears that raged round the Revolution Society and its anniversary celebrations are illustrated also in two prints by Gillray published on 19 and 23 July—after the Birmingham riots. In *The Hopes of the Party prior to July 14th*—"*From such wicked Crown & Anchor-Dreams Good Lord deliver us*" [7892] Fox—masked—is about to strike off George III's head, while Pitt and Queen Charlotte (cruelly caricatured) swing from the same lamp-post. Sheridan and Horne Tooke hold the King down, while Priestley proffers consolation: '. . . a man ought to be glad of the opportunity of dying, if by that means he can serve his Country, and bring about a glorious Revolution—& as for your Soul, or anything after death don't trouble yourself about that. . . .' Sir Cecil Wray, a steward at the recent dinner, is introduced to be again derided as a small-beer addict. The other print is directed mainly against the Unitarians: in *A Birmingham Toast, as given on the 14th of July by the —— Revolution Society* [7894] the same revolutionaries and Dr. Lindsey drink the toast which Priestley gives, holding up an empty Communion dish and a brimming chalice: 'The —— Head, here!' The other guests applaud and a group of subordinate lankhaired zealots add their prayers: 'Preserve us from Kings & Whores of Babylon!!! . . .' Their sanctimoniousness contrasts with the stern fanaticism of the principals. On the wall is a picture of St. Paul's: 'A Pig's Sty. . . .' The Unitarians were chiefly suspect, but the Birmingham mob which burnt dissenters' houses and chapels and destroyed Priestley's valuable scientific collections shouted, 'damned Presbyterians, Long live the King, No Olivers, down with the Rump, Church and State, No false Rights of Man.' In fact they harked back to the days of Sacheverell at least. In *Self Murder* . . . [7899], a print by Cruikshank, in which Priestley is a wolf in sheep's clothing, a parson answers a bishop: 'Yes Sir, Under the Denomination of Dissenters they P—y, P—e and L—y have brought a stigma on all Dissenters in General. . . .'

In English politics the outstanding event of 1791 was the Russian Armament in which Pitt hoped to repeat the success of his Spanish Armament (still under attack from the Opposition). Pitt's plan was to compel Russia to make peace with Turkey on the basis of the *status quo ante*—that is, to return Oczakof (where Odessa now stands) to the Porte. This was to be done by sending a fleet to the Baltic with support from Prussia and Holland. The stakes were the balance of power, the Russian stride southwards, and the protection of Poland from the pending absorption by Russia. The affair was and remains controversial, involving a whole sequence of might-have-beens. It was one of the occasions when the

Opposition, mobilizing public opinion, forced the Government to abandon its policy—a crisis in the Fox versus Pitt drama in which Fox avenged his failure over the Spanish Armament—not to speak of the Regency fiasco. The prints are almost all Oppositionist with one or two that are merely ribald—Catherine's morals were irresistible. The dominant motives are fear of taxation and the loss of Russian trade. J. H. Rose calls Pitt's policy 'playing the part of Petruchio to Catherine', and that had been Gillray's idea in *Taming of the Shrew:—Katharine & Petruchio:—The Modern Quixotte, or what you will* [7845]. Pitt, an arrogant Petruchio dressed as the Don, rides a Rosinante, the White Horse of Hanover—George III; seated behind him are Prussia and Holland (Sancho) with the Sultan crouching obsequiously behind the horse. He orders the kneeling Katharine to remove her cap—a Turkish crescent—but his words are altered to show that he has usurped sovereign power: "off with that bauble 'tis my royal will. The moribund animal weeps: 'Heigho! to have myself thus rid to death by a Boy and his playmates, merely to frighten an Old woman. . . .'

The affair dragged on with an epilogue: the Empress ordered a bust of Fox, to be placed between those of Cicero and Demosthenes, in gratitude for his opposition to the Armament. The inscription: 'il a délivré, par son éloquence, sa patrie et la Russie, d'une guerre, a laquelle il n'y avoit ni justice ni raison.' Pitt's aim had been, not war, but irresistible pressure. The Opposition taunted him with having been publicly flouted by Catherine (whom they had encouraged); resentments were bitter indeed. Pitt referred to the bust in answering an attack by Fox: he did not reveal what he knew of Opposition relations with the Russian ambassador in London and their intrigues in Moscow against the British Embassy: 'to do so would have covered the Opposition with obloquy but the Cabinet with ridicule.'[1] But there is reason to believe that his answer to Fox was in verses engraved below a print by Gillray which he probably 'invented'. His nephew ascribes the verses to him.[2] *Design for the new Gallery of Busts and Pictures* [Pl. 87], 17 March 1792, shows the three busts on their pedestals, with Fox between 'Demosthenes against Æschines' and 'Cicero against Cataline'. The two pictures—attacks on Catherine—are typical of Gillray—

[1] J. H. Rose, *Pitt and National Revival*, 1912, p. 624.
[2] James Boswell junior said on the authority of Pitt's nephew that the verses were written by Pitt (*Poetry of the Anti-Jacobin*, ed. C. Edmonds, 1890, p. xxxi). They were reprinted in Canning's *Anti-Jacobin* as 'written by a Traveller at Czarco-zelo under the bust of a certain Orator, once placed between those of Demosthenes and Cicero', with slight alterations to adapt them to 1798: the 'tool confessed . . .' becomes 'the advocate of foreign power'.

not so the busts. The first three verses are praise for Demosthenes and Cicero, the last two dispraise for Fox:

Who then in this presumptuous hour
Aspires to share th' Athenian's praise?
The tool confessed of foreign pow'r
The Æschines of modern days,

What chosen names to Tully's join'd
Is now announced to distant climes?
Behold to lasting shame consign'd
The Cataline of later times.

Here, probably, is one of the rare prints 'invented' at the very highest levels.

Seldom did the prints reflect ideas in greater conflict than in 1791–2. The prevailing Church and King climate is seen in violent attacks on dissenters and on the Republican Tom Paine, and in a vogue for militant adaptations of 'God save great George our King'. The democrats were to retaliate with parodies to the treasonous tune of 'Bob shave a King'. Prints on the royal family were never more cruel, though there can be no doubt of the King's popularity. Pitt is an arrogant upstart, usurping the powers of the Crown or presuming on royal favour. Events in France increasingly darkened the scene in 1792. In 1791 the most startling news was the escape and capture of the royal family; this is said to have roused universal sympathy in England, but the caricaturists are far from sympathetic; their prints are rapid reactions to the first reports before details were known, and the flight and capture are treated as comic. One print goes farther; it is the earliest print by Richard Newton in the national collection, remarkable for a boy of fourteen or fifteen—broad burlesque with a serious core. In *An Escape a la Francois!* [7886] the fugitives are escorted by Pope and Devil, 'Ma chere amie, le Diable', asks the King (of the Queen and the Devil), 'what will become of My Oath?' (to the Constitution). But both look complacent and the Devil points to the Pope, 'O never fear that—here is Absolution.' Below the design are two couplets:

Lo here is the King of France, a
Going to lead a War Dance a . . . .

The leading motif in satires on the royal family was parsimony at Windsor. *From the Originals* [altered to 'Original'] *at Windsor* [Pl. 92] is a close parody of 'The Misers' by Quintin Matsys in the royal collection.

George III counts his coins and writes in his ledger, the Queen leans on his shoulder. Gillray's pair of prints are maliciously amusing: *Frying Sprats* [7922] for the 'Royal Supper' and *Toasting Muffins* [7923] for 'the Royal Breakfast'; the Queen with her gridiron, then called a save-all, is much caricatured, her pocket bulging with guineas, but patched. The King is homely and eccentric. In a famous pair of plates by Gillray in July 1792 insults are carried farther. In *A Voluptuary under the Horrors of Digestion* [8112] the Prince, languid with repletion and dissipation, leans back from a table covered with the remains of a meal. The room is crowded with objects reflecting, it would seem, the artist's hatred and contempt for his subject. Books and papers imply (among other things) that the Prince was a gambler (which he was not) with a share in the profits of the faro tables which women of fashion kept as a source of income. In *Temperance enjoying a frugal Meal* [8117] the King eats a boiled egg, the Queen stuffs sauerkraut into her mouth. Everything in the room denotes miserliness; there is no fire, though holly and mistletoe in the grate show that it is winter. Behind the Queen is the heavily bolted door of a strong room, with a 'Table of Interest' from her vast (and mythical) hoard of savings. These are only indirectly political, but in May Gillray related his imputations to politics in a print which is more cruel because less fantastic: *Vices over-look'd in the new Proclamation* [8095] on 24 May satirizes the Royal Procla-mation of 21 May, 'for the preventing of tumultuous meetings and seditious writings' (aimed chiefly at Paine's works) which the Prince approved in his maiden speech in the Lords. Scenes of 'Avarice', 'Drunkenness', 'Gambling', and 'Debauchery' are four designs on one plate. In the first the King and Queen face each other across a table, hugging huge money-bags. Next, the Prince, very drunk, is supported by two watchmen from the door of a brothel. In the third the Duke of York throws dice in a gam-bling hell, and in the last the Duke of Clarence and Mrs. Jordan embrace.

In 1791-2 it was a Foxite–Carlton House tenet that the King and Queen had separate interests, the Queen's preponderating and more favourable to Pitt. That is the context of a brilliant parody by Gillray of Fuseli's picture of Macbeth's witches. In *Wierd-Sisters; Ministers of Darkness; Minions of the Moon* [Pl. 89] on 31 December 1791, Dundas, Pitt, and Thurlow gaze with apprehensive intensity at Queen Charlotte's smiling profile which encloses the old moon, the darkened head of George III. Instead of the outstretched arms and pointing fingers of Fuseli's picture [Pl. 88], each presses his fingers on his lips, intent on seeking knowledge, not foretelling it. Pitt had been shaken by the Oczakov affair and there were rumours that the King wanted to get rid of him. But the strength of his position was shown by the way in which he got rid of Thurlow—who had flouted him in the Lords, counting on the King's favour. He wrote to the King asking him to choose between himself and the Chancellor. Cartoonists treated the affair as a fight between them, one supported by the Queen, the other by the King as in *The Fall of the Wolsey of the Wool Sack* [8096] on 24 May 1792, by Gillray. Out of some six prints the outstanding one is Gillray's *Sin, Death, and the Devil* [Pl. 91] on 9 June, with quotations from Milton, in which disrespect to the Queen reached a climax. I do not think it has been noticed that this is a travesty of an engraved version [Pl. 90] of Hogarth's picture, 'Satan, Sin and Death', now lost. Pitt is Death, emaciated and corpse-like, wearing a crown and with an ermine-bordered mantle hanging from his shoulders. He uses a sceptre as his weapon against the more formidable Thurlow, Satan, whose (broken) weapon is the mace, and whose shield is emblazoned with a tiny Woolsack and the Purse of the Great Seal. The Queen as Sin intervenes with outstretched arms to protect Pitt (thus reversing Milton). She is a hideous hag, with pendent breasts (Milton's Sin is 'woman to the waste and fair'), two massive serpents for legs, and writhing serpents for hair. The large key at her waist, 'The Instrument of all our Woe', is clearly not only the key of Hell Gate but of the back stairs, that is, of secret influence. Cerberus has the heads of Dundas, Grenville, and Richmond, Pitt's chief supporters. The artist recommends 'these portraits of the Devil & his Relations, drawn from the Life . . .' to Messrs. Boydell and Fuzelli, showing that this is not only a political satire but a jibe at the Shakespeare Gallery of Boydell (a *bête noire* of Gillray's) and at Fuseli's projected Milton Gallery. Behind these rancours one guesses personal frustrations—that Gillray would have liked to practise 'high art' as well as burlesque it.[1]

French topics in 1792 begin with *émigrés*—as usual they are ridiculed. In *A German Howl or the Emigrant Princes mourning the loss of their dearest Friend* [8068] by Isaac Cruikshank on 15 March, d'Artois and others surround the coffin of Leopold II, ankle deep in their own tears (but though the Emperor's death was a blow to the cause of monarchy in France, the *émigrés* at Coblentz rejoiced). The French declaration of war

[1] Cf. his large engravings, e.g. *The Wreck of the Nancy Packet*. This is signed 'Drawn & Engraved by James Gillray 1784', when all his satirical work was anonymous or pseudonymous. The art criticism expressed and implied in *Shakespeare Sacrificed;—or—The Offering to Avarice* [7584], 1789, on the Boydell Gallery, and in *Titianus Redivivus . . .* [9085], 1797, is highly significant. The former also expresses resentment at the exclusion of engravers from the Royal Academy.

on Austria was followed by the panic flight from Tournai, when the French murdered their officer, General Dillon: this occasioned two contemptuous anti-Gallican, anti-revolutionary prints [8085–6], one by Isaac Cruikshank, one by Gillray. The invasion of the Tuileries on 20 June and the 'baiser Lamourette' on 7 July, when Republicans and monarchists embraced, swearing 'immortal union' in the face of the enemy, were satirized by Dent in companion designs on one plate: *Limited Monarchy: Unlimited Democracy*[1] on 23 July. Louis XVI in a *bonnet rouge* is assailed by frantic men and women with pikes, who shout, '. . . No Veto.' This is 'The negative Power of France surrounded by the Patriotic Furies . . .'. In the other, 'the Active power of France Reconciling contending Parties by a General Hug . . .', the Devil puts his arms round fourteen Frenchmen.

Then came the September massacres. Gillray produced the most unrestrained and macabre of all his caricatures of French Jacobins: *Petit Souper a la Parisienne;—or—A Family of Sans-culotts refreshing, after the fatigues of the Day* [8122]. A heraldic print, *Democratic Arms, or Emblems of Gallic Liberty*, attacks 'The horrid Massacres that lately happened at Paris'. The supporters are a Jacobin executioner and a sansculotte street-murderer.[2]

Brunswick's manifesto, his defeat at Valmy, and disease-stricken retreat to the frontier are the subjects of six prints. All but one (a disorderly procession of savage unsoldierly sansculottes marching 'to the Frontiers' [8123] by Newton) are anti-Brunswick: he is a braggart, his misfortunes are derided, his soldiers are *Prussian Bobadils, returning to Berlin!!!!!!!!* [8126], another print by Newton. But always the French pursuers are unsoldierly ragamuffins (actually they were a remnant of the old royal army).

French military successes, and the famous decree of the Convention on 16 November, offering 'fraternity and assistance to all peoples who wish to recover their liberty', are the subject of a Cruikshank print favourable to the French Republic on 21 December: *The Genius of France Extirpating Despotism Tyranny & Oppression from the Face of the Earth or the Royal Warriors defeated* [8143]. In English prints the genius of Republican France is commonly a monstrosity. Here—uniquely—she is a comely young woman, wearing a Phrygian cap. She threatens the sovereigns of Europe, who are riding an ass, saying, 'I am determin'd to inflict Death on all Despots and Oppressors'; she plies a scourge with lashes for 'Religious

---

[1] Not in the British Museum: *Collection de Vinck*, no. 4880.
[2] Not in the British Museum; see Broadley, *Napoleon in Caricature*, ii. 232–3.

Bigots, Aristocrats, Monopolizers of Provisions to distress the Poor', &c., &c. This, published by Fores at such a moment, might have seemed ominous.[1] Dent took a different view in *French Liberality, or an Attempt to conquer the World by being too civil by half* [8136] on 8 December. General Dumouriez, holding an order from the Convention to 'Give Freedom to all the World', proffers this to three men, 'having more Liberty den we vos know vat to do wid . . .', but asks them for 'von little bit of a Contribution'. All reject his gift: the German is content with 'the Liberty of being governed by Religion and Law', the Dutchman wants only 'the right of making money where we can and a fig for your Ideal Goddess'; a very corpulent John Bull is more articulate: 'Why we are fat and free! and live under a Glorious Constitution, its old and I venerate it—to be sure Time may have made a few flaws and cracks in it—but Dam it, it can never be mended with Plaister of Paris—so you can keep your Freedom and Your Fricassee to yourself!' Gillray, using the title of his Necker–Pitt plate of 1789, expressed a similar idea with characteristic irony on 21 December; in *French Liberty v. British Slavery* [Pl. 93] a ragged and famished sansculotte in a poverty-stricken room is contrasted with an obese and gouty 'cit', surrounded with luxury, carving a great joint of beef, and with a decanter of hock on the table. The Frenchman ravenously devours raw onions and has *assignats* for a few sous in his pocket: '. . . vat blessing be de Liberté. . .', he exclaims, '—no more Tax! no more slavery!—all free citizen . . . ve svim in de Milk & Honey'. The Briton: 'Ah! this cursed Ministry! they'll ruin us with their damn'd Taxes! why! Zounds!—they're making Slaves of us all, & Starving us to Death!' A statuette of Britannia has a big sack of 'Sterling' in place of a shield.

The burning question in 1792 was how far was the country in danger from Jacobins at home. There was a bad season, with dearth and bread riots; alarm was caused by the organization of a 'National Convention' in Scotland, by the astonishing circulation of cheap editions of Paine's (Republican) *Rights of Man Part II* (translated into Gaelic, Erse, and Welsh), and by the fraternal messages of the London Corresponding Society to the French Republic. An address delivered by a deputation on 28 November by John Frost and Joel Barlow[2] gave the impression that the

---

[1] The Prussian defeat was a great encouragement to malcontents: at a celebration of Dumouriez' victory (Jemappes, 6 Nov.) near Lewes an ox was roasted whole and a procession was formed, reputedly 10,000 strong, headed by the French tricolour and a picture of Dundas stabbing Liberty and Burke trampling on 'the swinish multitude'. J. H. Rose, *Pitt and the Great War*, 1911, p. 70. Cf. *E.P.C. 1793–1832*, p. 9 and n..

[2] An American; associate in England of Horne Tooke, Price, Priestley, Paine, and others;

country was honeycombed by seditious clubs. It assured the Convention that innumerable clubs and societies were springing up in England: 'After the example given by France Revolution will become easy . . . and it would not be extraordinary if in a much less space of time than can be imagined, the French should send addresses of congratulation to a National Convention in England.' A deputation from English and Irish residents in Paris assured the Convention that a majority of the British wished to copy the French example and that the old Government would soon exist only in memory.[1] If the Ministry at home were unduly alarmed, the French were completely deceived, and believed Britain on the verge of revolution; English caricatures of British Jacobins may well have contributed to their illusions.

The prints reflect a main trend of anti-Jacobinism, qualified by a few protests against scaremongering. In which category Gillray's *Patriots amusing themselves or Swedes firing at a Post* [8082] in April should be put is open to doubt—though scaremongering had scarcely shown itself. This is a burlesque suggested by the assassination of Gustavus III; the patriots are Fox, sinister and conspiratorial, firing a blunderbuss, Sheridan loading a pistol, and Priestley providing him with wadding: 'here's plenty of Wadding for to ram down the charge with, to give it force, & to make a loud Report.' He holds out two books 'on the Glory of Revolution' and 'on the Folly of Religion & Order'. Their target is a post roughly carved into a grotesque semblance of George III in a hunting cap, the bull's eye being on the object's posterior.

Priestley and Paine were the main objects of attack. Isaac Cruikshank's *The Friends of the People* [8131], though the title is that of the Reform society of the advanced Whigs, is a violent diatribe against these two *bêtes noires* as murderous and conspiratorial revolutionaries in which the guillotine makes a first appearance. With an altered title, *Sedition, Levelling and Murdering; or, the Pretended Friends of the People in Council*, it was used as an illustration to 'God save the King' with six interpolated verses attacking Paine, Priestley, and the Unitarians:

> Tom Paine and Priestley are
> More base and desp'rate far,
> Than vile Jack Cade

author of *Song of the Guillotine*, a parody of *God save the King* exulting at the death of Louis XVI and looking forward to that of George III: 'And when great George's Poll / Shall in the basket roll . . .': P. A. Scholes, *God save the Queen!*, 1954, p. 164.
  [1] J. H. Rose, *Pitt and the Great War*, 1911, pp. 70–71.

He for reform did cry;
They for equality
Wou'd stain true liberty
With British blood.

Two comprehensive attacks on Paine by Gillray followed, on 26 November and 10 December [8132, 8137], the second an elaboration of the first, both called *Tom Paine's Nightly Pest*. Paine lies asleep in a wretched room (in France). He dreams of his treasons and libels and of punishments: a prison wall, a gibbet, a pillory. The 'Guardian Angels' at the head of his bed are Fox and Priestley; a torn American flag covers the straw which makes his pillow. Both prints anticipate his trial for *Rights of Man, Part II*, as a 'scandalous libel on the Constitution Laws and Government of England', for which he had sent the Attorney General a defiant letter with a sneer at 'Mr Guelph and his profligate sons'. Cruikshank's *Wha Wants Me* [8146], on 26 December, is a vicious attack on Paine, who stands, pen in one hand, dagger in the other, with a bundle of weapons on his back: his 'Letter to the Convention' (on 25 September, three days after the proclamation of the Republic) is quoted, in which he offered his services, 'Convinced that the cause of France is the cause of all mankind . . . having borne a share in the commencement and complete establishment of one Revolution. . . .' The title is from the street cry of an Edinburgh character and was first applied to Dundas [8103]. Paine was burnt in effigy by the troops in various places in December.

On 11 December came the split in the Whig Party owing to the attitude of the left wing to France, when a majority decided to support the Government. Dent produced *Jacobine Wigs, or, Good Night to the Party* [8140] on 18 December, a meeting of the Whig Club, with a remnant of three members, Fox, Sheridan, and Grey, sound asleep, with French caps drawn over their eyes. On the same day Dent published an amusing caricature of Fox as a partisan of the French Republic, *French Ambassador* [Pl. 94], oddly suggesting the famous scene in the Tuileries in 1802. Isaac Cruikshank used the split personality device for an indictment of Fox, *A Right Honorarle* [sic] *alias a Sans Culotte* [8142].

In the meantime the Association for preserving Liberty and Property against Republicans and Levellers—Anti-levelling Society—had been founded on 20 November to discourage seditious publications and produce counter-propaganda. It was known as the Crown and Anchor Society, its headquarters being in the famous tavern. Among its tracts and leaflets it published at the turn of the year a few subsidized satirical prints. Gillray derided it—in terms that suggest that he had worked for it or had been asked to do so.

The first of his two explicitly anti-scaremongering prints of 1792 is *John Bull Bother'd:—or—The Geese alarming the Capitol* [Pl. 95] on 19 December, with a gibe at the new Association: 'Price 3 shill<sup>s</sup>—the engraving not having been Paid for, by the Association for vending two'penny Scurrilities.' The subject is the proclamation on 1 December for calling out the militia—partly to repress riots—on alarming news from Scotland and Ireland. Pitt and John Bull (again a yokel but in a militiaman's coat in place of a smock) stand together on a fortified tower; Pitt looks through a telescope at a flock of geese, his hair rising, his knees bending in terror. John, bewildered and almost equally frightened, holds an old musket with a broken bayonet; there are two favours in his hat: 'Vive la Liberté' and 'God save the King'; in one pocket is 'The Rights of Man', in the other 'One Pennyworth of Truth' (an anti-Jacobin tract 'from Thomas Bull to Brother John' denounced in the Commons by Grey as a libel). He is 'bothered', or 'botheared', that is, bemused by being 'talked to at both ears by different persons'.[1] The point of the satire is elaborated in the very Gillrayesque speeches engraved on the plate. Pitt begins by warning John to get his arms ready: '. . . they're Rising & coming upon us from all parts . . . theres Ten Thousand sans-Culottes . . . there's Five Hundred Disputing Clubs with Bloody Mouths; & twenty Thousand Bill-stickers with *Ça Ira* pasted on the front of their Red-Caps! . . .' John sees only a few wild geese, but adds, 'I dont know what reason for I to see at all, for that matter;—why Measter does all that for I,—my business is only to Fire when & where Measter orders, & to pay for the Gunpowder. . . .' Here, one supposes, is an echo of Fox's irony: 'An Insurrection! Where is it? . . . Good God! an insurrection in Great Britain, no wonder that the militia were called out. . . .'[2]

The other Gillray protest against scares, dated 30 December, is *The Dagger Scene;—or—the Plot discovered* [8147], a caricature of the famous scene in the Commons on 28 December. Burke has just thrown down the dagger and looks with a contemptuous frown at Pitt and Dundas on the Treasury Bench, though a bag-wig and a new corpulence suggest that he now draws funds from the Treasury. He makes a speech which parodies his own: 'There! . . . Three Thousand such Daggers are now manufacturing for this Country!—for where French principles are introduced, you must

[1] Grose, *Dictionary of the Vulgar Tongue*, 1796.
[2] *Parl. Hist.* xxx. 14 (13 Dec.).

prepare your hearts for French Daggers!—Nineteen Assassins are already here. . . .' Fox and Sheridan clutch each other in terror. Fox: 'Confusion! —one of Our daggers, by all that's bloody! . . . —' (&c., &c.) Cruikshank effectively satirized the same scene in *Reflections on the French Revolution* [Pl. 96], dated 1 January.

Gillray's ironic double-edged satires reflect the problems of the day. How great was the danger from revolutionaries at home? Did the Foxite attitude not only mislead France and so encourage the Republic to declare war, but lead to provocative and regrettable precautions? By the end of the year it was evident that war could hardly be averted, though negotiations went on. For the next eight years the prints directly or indirectly relate to war with the French Republic. The old contest between Pitt and Fox, with all its accumulated rancours, became the contest between Ministers and a small but vocal and socially powerful Opposition, refusing to recognize the aggressive character of the Republic, and bitterly opposed to the war; between anti-Jacobins and Jacobins, between those who thought the war 'just and necessary' and those who derided Pitt's phrase to pillory its whole policy and conduct, to whom Foxite protests were the defence of British liberties.

# INDEX OF ARTISTS

Allard, Carel (1648–1709). Engraver and print-seller of Amsterdam. 4.

Arcimboldo, Giuseppe (1527–93). Milanese. Court painter to Ferdinand I, Maximilian II, Rudolf II. Specialized in fantastic heads composed of flowers, fruit, animals, &c. See B. Geiger, *I dipinti ghiribizzosi di Giuseppe Arcimboldi*, Firenze, 1954. 6 & n.

Austin, William (1721–1820). Etcher, drawing-master, and print-seller. Occasional caricaturist. 148; Pl. 46. *See* Pl. 32.

Belloguet, A. French lithographer and caricaturist. 19th century. 7.

Bickham, George, the younger (d. 1753). Engraver and print-seller, son of G. B. (d. 1769), writing-master, engraver, and print-seller. 87, 91, 172, 175.

Boitard, Louis Peter (worked *c.* 1750–61). Engraver in London, born in France. 101.

Boyne, John (d. 1810). Watercolourist, engraver, and drawing master. Occasional caricaturist. 169, 170, 172; Pl. 64.

Braddyll, Lt.-Col. Thomas Richard Gale (1776–1862). Amateur caricaturist. 174.

Bunbury, Henry William (1750–1811). Draughtsman and caricaturist. His work engraved for publication by leading practitioners. Equerry to the Duke of York. 147, 163, 173, 205; Pl. 59.

Callot, Jacques (1592–1635). French engraver and painter. 76.

Caracci, Annibale (1560–1609). Italian painter. 11, 112.

Colledge or College, Stephen (1635?–1681). The 'Protestant Joiner'. Made the panelling for the Hall of the Stationers' Company. Tried and executed in Oxford. 12, 53 & n. 2, 55, 56–59, 60; Pls. 15, 16.

Colley, Thomas (worked 1780–3). Caricaturist. Published many of his own plates from a variety of addresses. 167, 174 & n. 2.

Collings, Samuel (worked 1784–91). Painter and caricaturist (pseudonym Annibal Scratch). Exhibited R.A. Designed *Picturesque Beauties of Boswell*, twenty plates etched by Rowlandson, 1786. 179, 186.

Cranach, Lucas (1472–1553). Painter and engraver, friend of Luther and protégé of Electors of Saxony. His sons: Lucas (1515–

86), Hans (d. 1537), John Lucas (d. 1536). 3, 5, 8.

Cruikshank, George (1792–1878). Etcher, caricaturist, and illustrator. 173.

Cruikshank, Isaac (1756?–1811?). Caricaturist and watercolourist. Exhibited R.A. 1790 and 1792. Occasional illustrator. 172, 174, 183, 205, 206, 210–11, 217, 218, 220, 221, 223; Pl. 96.

Darly, Mary (worked *c.* 1756–77). Printseller, etcher, and teacher of etching. *The Female Conoiseur* [4692] in 1772 is seemingly a self-portrait. 115–17, 127, 147.

Darly, Matthew (worked *c.* 1750–78). Etcher, drawing-master, and print-seller; occasional designer of caricatures. Designer of *chinoiserie* decorations. Styled himself (in 1771) 'Painter of Ornaments to the Academy of Great Britain': P.O.A.G.B. [4632]. 101–2, 103, 104, 115–17, 122, 123, 129, 147–8, 154, 155, 156, 175, 176; probably etched Pls. 28 *a* and *b*, 29 *a* and *b*, 33, 43. *See* Pl. 32.

Dent, William (worked 1783–93). Amateur caricaturist. Published most of his own plates, selling them through print-sellers. 125 n., 170, 173, 174, 179, 184, 187–8, 190, 193, 199, 200, 202, 210, 218, 219, 221; Pls. 76, 94.

Dixon, John (1740?–1780?). Mezzotint engraver. 151.

Dürer, Albrecht (1471–1528). Painter and engraver of Nuremberg. 5.

Faithorne, William (1616?–91). Engraver, portrait-painter, and print-seller. With Robert Peake (engraver) and Hollar defended Basing House, 1645. 12, 41 n., 44 n.

Fuseli, Henry, R.A. (Johann Heinrich Fuessli, b. Zurich 1741, d. 1825). Painter, author, and Keeper of the R.A. 186, 216–17. Pls. 74, 88.

Gaywood, Richard (worked 1653–64). Etcher, closely associated with Hollar. 12.

Ghezzi, Pier Leoni (1674–1755). Painter, engraver, musician, and man of letters in Rome. Noted for his caricatures of personalities (pen drawings). 11, 111–12.

Gillray, James (1757–1815, insane from 1811). Caricaturist. A caricature of 1769 is attributed to him; other attributions from 1775. His principal plates reissued by McLean as *The Genuine Works of Mr James Gillray*, 2 vols., 1830, with a key, *Illustrative Description.* . . . In 1851 the plates, worn and retouched, were again reissued by Bohn, with a key, *Historical and Descriptive Account . . .*, by T. Wright and R. H. Evans. *The Works of James Gillray . . . with the History of his Life and Times*, ed. T. Wright, 1873 but by J. Grego, is useful. 2, 21, 116, 147, 158, 163, 164, 165, 166, 167, 168, 171–2, 174 & n., 175, 177, 179, 185, 186, 188, 189, 190, 192, 193, 194, 195, 196, 198, 199, 202, 203, 206, 211, 212, 213, 214–15, 216, 217 & n., 218, 219, 220, 221, 222–3; Pls. 54, 60(?), 61, 62, 63, 78, 79, 81, 83, 87, 89, 91, 93, 95.

Gould, Sir Francis Carruthers (1841–1 Jan. 1925). Stockbroker, caricaturist, and journalist. Political cartoonist of strong Liberal sympathies, notably in the *Westminster Gazette* (to 1901). An amateur draughtsman but a professional cartoonist. 171.

Gravelot, Hubert-François (1699–1773, in England from 1732). Engraver. 90.

Grimm, Samuel Hieronymus (1734–94). Born in Switzerland. Watercolour painter and occasional caricaturist. Exhibited R.A. See R. M. Clay, *Samuel Hieronymus Grimm of Burgdorf, Switzerland*, 1941. 146; Pl. 44.

Guttenberg, Carl (b. 1743 Nuremberg, d. 1790 Paris). Engraver and illustrator. Worked in Paris. 151 & n.

HB = John Doyle (1797–1868). Lithographer, portraitist, and caricaturist. 177.

Heath, William (1795?–1840). Watercolourist, military painter, etcher, and caricaturist. 173.

Hogarth, William (1697–1764). Painter, engraver, and publisher of his own prints. His engravings catalogued by Austin Dobson, *Hogarth*, 1907; his paintings by R. B. Beckett, *Hogarth*, 1949. See A. P. Oppé, *The Drawings of William Hogarth*, 1948; P. Quennell, *Hogarth's Progress*, 1955. 7, 11, 73, 75–77, 80, 83, 85, 105 n., 107–8, 111–15, 117, 118, 121, 122 & n., 125, 128–31, 171, 172, 175, 177, 186, 193, 205; Pls. 20 (a), 21, 31, 35, 36, 90. *See* Pl. 32.

Holland, William (d. 1816). London printseller and occasional caricaturist. 175, 205 & n., 207, 209–10; Pl. 86(?).

Hollar, Wenceslaus (1607–77). Bohemian etcher and engraver. Worked in England 1637–44 (a Royalist) and 1652–77. Catalogue, by Parthey, *Wenzel Hollar*, Berlin,

1853–8. 7, 12, 21, 22, 25, 28, 44; Frontispiece, Pls. 4, 5.

Hooghe, Romeyn de (1648–1708). Painter, engraver, sculptor, medallist, and goldsmith. Ennobled by the King of Poland 1675. Worked for William III from 1689. Dutch political cartoonist in the grand manner, many anonymous and pseudonymous plates. 62.

Hook, James (1771–1828). Chaplain to the Prince of Wales. Dean of Worcester 1825–8. While at Westminster edited the *Trifler* and did caricatures. Published novels (pseudonymous), pamphlets, and sermons. 173, 194, 208.

Kingsbury, Henry. Portrait and landscape painter and engraver in London, *c.* 1775–98. Exhibited R.A. 1787–91. Occasional caricaturist. 172, 188.

Laroon, Marcellus, the younger (1679–1772). Painter and engraver. 12 n.

Loggan, David (1635–93). Born Danzig of Scottish extraction. Engraver. 'Public Sculptor to the University of Oxford' from 1669; afterwards also to Cambridge. 57 n.

Marshall, William (worked 1630–50). Engraver. The most prolific of contemporary illustrators, chiefly from his own designs. 7, 12, 19, 34–35 & n., 37; Pl. 12.

Metsys, Quentin (1466–1530). Painter, Flemish school. 215–16; cf. Pl. 92.

Mortimer, John Hamilton (1741–79). Historical painter. Designed caricatures, some of which were etched after his death. 171.

Newton, Richard (1777–98). Caricaturist and miniaturist. 173, 175, 215; Pl. 85.

Nixon, John (d. 1818). Merchant and officer of the Bank of England. Watercolourist, exhibited R.A. 1784–1815. Occasional caricaturist. Secretary to the Beefsteak Club. 173.

Ogborne, John (1755–1837). Engraver. Pl. 91.

Picart, Bernard (b. Paris 1673, d. Amsterdam 1733). Engraver and miniaturist. A leading engraver in Holland. Pl. 20b signed 'Picart'.

Pine, John (1690–1756). Engraver. The friar in Hogarth's *Calais Gate*. 74.

Pond, Arthur (1705?–58). Painter, etcher, and art-dealer. From 1736 to 1747 produced 25 plates in imitation of chalk and

# GENERAL INDEX

# PLATES

PLATE 1

The Image of Antichrist exalting himfelfe in the Temple of God.

771.

918. Ex lib. Examinû nationis Germanicæ.

About fiftie byshoppriches in Germany.

did it not for any duty to him, but onely for peace fake, what should I speake here of my dayly reuenues, of my first fruits, annates, palles, indulgences, bulles, confessionals, indultes and refcriptes, testaments, dispéfation, priuileges, elections, prebends, religious houfes, and fuch like, which come to no fmall maffe of money? In somuch that for one palle to the Archb. of Mentz, which was wont to be geuen for x. thousand. 218. florence, now it is growen to xxvij. thousand flo, rence, whiche I receiued of Iacobus the Archbyshop not long before Basill Councell: Besides the fruites of other Byshoprickes in Germany, cômyng to the number of fifty, wherby what vantage commeth to my coffers, it may part-

ly be coniectured. But what should I speake of Germany, 219. when the whole world is my Dioceffe, as my Cano= nistes do fay, and all men are bounde to beleue. 220. except they will imagine (as the Maniches do) two begyn= nynges, whiche is false and hereticall. For Moses fayth: In the begynnyng God made heauen and earth, and not in the begynnynges. 221. wherefore as I begon, fo I conclude, commaundyng, declaryng and pro= nouncyng, to stand vpon neceffitie of faluation, for euery humane creature to be fubiect to me.

Æneas Syluius.
219. Sext Decret.
De penis. cap. Felicis in Clofis.
Ité. De priuilegiis c. Autoritaté in Glofa.
220. Pope Bonifacius. 8. Ext. De Maio. & obed. c. Vnam fanctam.
221. Ibid.

¶ The end of the first Volume of the Booke of Martyrs.

¶ A liuely picture defcribyng the weight and fubftaunce of Gods moft blessed word, agaynft the doctrines and vanities of mans traditions.

¶ AT LONDON
Printed by Iohn Daye, dwellyng ouer
Alderfgate beneath Saint Martins.

Anno. 1576.

✠ Cum gratia & Priuilegio Regiæ Maieftatis.

PLATE 2

*a*. Copy of *Gorgoneum Caput*          *p.* 6

*b*. Copy of Reformation token     *p.* 6

PLATE 3

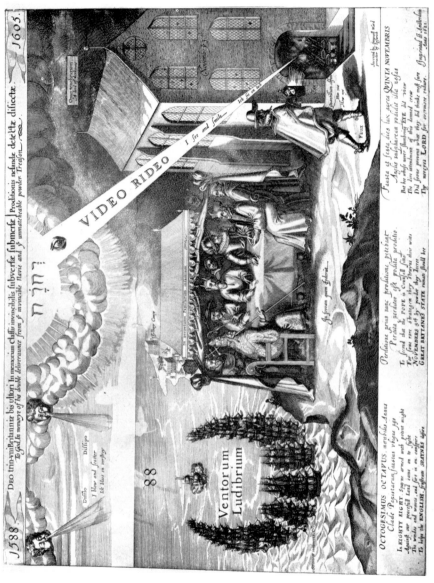

*The Double Deliveraunce*

pp. 15–16, 63–64, 88. Cf. Pl. 29 *a*

PLATE 4

Who am I, who am I like, what nobody,
Sure I'me the Picture of a Patenty

Ragges. P:

Wine P:

Pinnes. Pat:

Sope

Salte

Butter

Coles P.

Loe' here is he, whose Hogs:head now doth vent
Naught but Peccavies, since the Parliament,
Wolfe like, devourer of the Common wealth
That robs by Patent, worse then any stealth
Alls Fish, comes to his hooke,Tobaco wine & ragges
Make full his Cofers, with his numbred baggs

Coales, Salt, & Butter, pipes, Cards, Pynns, and Soape
Are free to buy, and sell, leaue him the Roape !
Hee feares no damning, this doth make him start,
That Patents damned are, this breakes his hart;
Strong scrues support him that hath scru'd vs all.
And now we liue, to see this strong man fall.

B.M. 264                    The Patenty. Hollar                    pp. 7, 21

PLATE 5

This Burden backe to *Rome*, I'le beare againe;
From thence it came, there let it still remaine.

When Times Great Maker (the most high Eternall)   He to his daughter Truth gaue straight Command   This trunke of trash, & Romish Trumperies
In mercy looked from his Throne supernall:   That shee those dang'rous Errors should withstand   Deluding showes infernall forgeries
And saw the Euils which began to grow   Then vp I tooke vpon my aged backe,   And therefore am I hence in post thus riding
In his deare Vine here Militant below,   This load of vaniti, this Pedlers packe   To Rome againe, for here is no abiding

PLATE 6

MADFASHIONS, 3o
OD FASHIONS,
All out of Fashions,
OR,
The Emblems of these Distracted times.

By *John Taylor*.

*LONDON,*
Printed by *Iohn Hammond*, for *Thomas Banks*, 1642.

A Purge for Pluralities, shewing the unlawfull-
nesse of men to have two Livings.

OR

*The Downe-fall of Double Benefices.*

Being in the Clymactericall and fatall yeare of the proud Prelates.
But the yeare of *Iubilee* to all poore hunger-pinch'd Schollers.

*LONDON,*
Printed for *F. Cowles, T. Bates*, and *T. Banks*. 1642.

PLATE 7

Much meate doth gluttony produce. Hee needes no napkin for his handes
And makes a man a swine——— His fingers for to wipe
But hee's a temperate man indeed Hee hath his kitchin in a box
That with a leafe can dine——— His Roast meate in a pipe

PLATE 8

PLATE 9

*The Kingdomes Monster Unclouked from Heaven*

PLATE 10

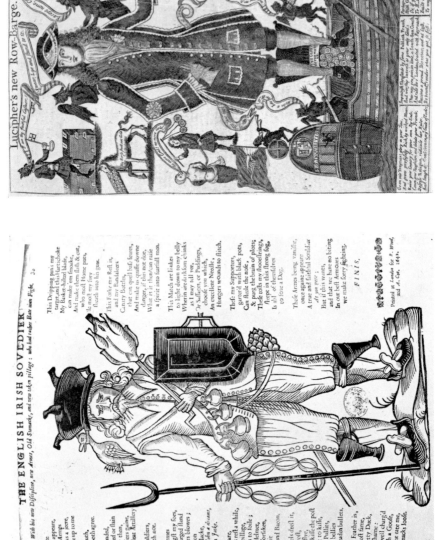

PLATE 11

*Englands Wolfe with Eagles Clawes*

*pp.* 12, 30

PLATE 12

PLATE 13

pp. 49-50

Copy of a Dutch print

B.M. 1044

PLATE 14

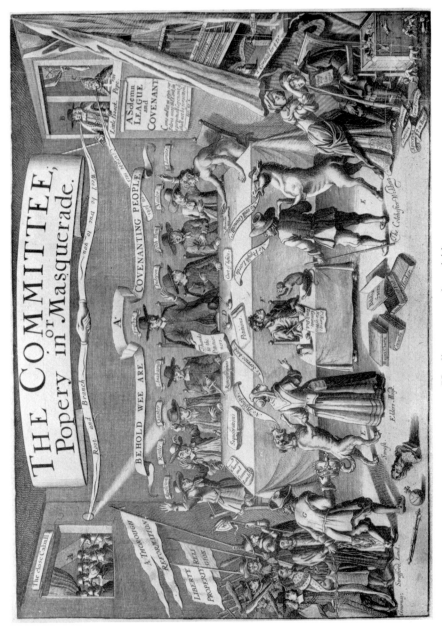

B.M. 1080

Heading to verse broadside

*pp.* 54–55

PLATE 15

# STRANGE'S CASE, STRANGEY ALTERED.

Or, a HUE and CRY after a *Strange* old *Torkiſh Tike* full of Black and Blue, Red and Yellow Spots, of a Motley, Dun, Brindled, ill-livered Colour; neither *Maſtiff* nor *Mungrel, Tumbler* or *Lurcher, Lap-Dog* nor *Setter, Bull-Dog* or *Bear-Dog, Wolf-Dog* or *Sheep-Biter*, but all of them : of a *Strange* Amphibious Nature, lives on Land or on Water, in *Court* or in *kennel*, run away from his Maſter, about the 25th Inſtant, leen on *Saturday* laſt behind a Coach, between *Sam's* Coffee-Houſe, and *Madam Cellier's,* whoever hath (or that) take him up, have a ſpecial care of him (unleſs you know his ill qualities) for he has a thouſand *Dog-Tricks,* (*ſiz.*) to Fetch for the *Papiſts,* Carry for the *Prateſtants, Whine* to the *King,* Dance to *Nill's Fiddle, Fawn* on the *Courtier, Leap* at their *Croſſis,* wag his Tail at all *Bitches,* hunt Counter to the *Plat, Tonge-Pad* the *Evidence,* and Cringe to the *Crucifix* ; but above all this, he has one damn'd old trick of ſlipping the *Halter.* If there be any that can give notice of this dangerous *Carr,* to the men in *Authority* (who have been ſeveral days in *Grand Queſt* after him) or bring him (if he be not there already) to the Sign of the *Popes Demi-Caſtorin,* next Door to the *Maſquera'le Committee,* in the Street of *St. Lud.* or to the *Tantivit Abhorrers,* at the *Levitical-Club-Houſe* in *Ave-Mary-Alley,* ſo that he may be tyed up from his Meat, for the Good of the Publick; he will do his Country good Service, the *Prateſtants* Right, the *King* Juſtice, the *Law* Juſtice, the *King* a Kindneſs, un-deceive the *Church,* and himſelf a mighty Favour in obtaining the *Marks-Royal,* of a Loyal true *Engliſhman,* a Right good *Proteſtant,* and a hearty Lover of his *King* and Country ; all which is ---- ---- ----

*The Figures above may be thus Explained.*

PLATE 16

A RA-REE SHOW.

*To the Tune of* I am a Sencelefs Thing.

Heading to a verse broadside

Bodleian

*pp.* 56–57

PLATE 17

The happy INSTRUMENTS of ENGLANDS Preservation.

Come and behold ẏ salvation of ẏ Lord

HEAVEN SHALL TURN THY WEAPONS AGAINST

By our discoverys you may know what damn'd Intreagues are hatche'd here

THE INFERNALL CONCLAVE

Behold th'Infernall Conclave, mett in state. Contriving Englands, and its Monarchs Fate. Assassinate the King, Subvert his Laws, They cry'd, and on their Ruin, build our Cause.

Pardons were streight prepar'd, and men made free Of Heaven, to perpetrate their Villany. And thus secure, their Plotts went briskly on, Against our fixed Laws and settl'd Throne.

But he that sitts enthron'd, in mercy chose, Those instruments, that did the whole disclose. And thus to Oates and all the rest wee owe The Kingdoms Peace, if wee can keep it so.

London Printed for Ben: Combe at the ball and Anchor in Lombard street. 27. Aprill 1681.

PLATE 18

Since Moderation is so much in vogue.
And few can tell a Trimmer from a R——;
I am perswaded such a Print 'as this,
Thus modell'd and contriv'd can't be amiss.
At such a juncture, such a time as this,
When to be loyal is esteem'd a fault,
Obedience hist at, Scripture sett at nought,
And ÿ reverse for pure sound doctrine taught:
I mean by them this picture doth resemble,
Who preach not half so fine as they dissemble.
Of Heterogeneous parts as opposite
Compos'd, as darkness to Meridian light.
Made up of halves that can no more agree,
Than Regal pow'r and Independency.
A British Janus with a double face,
A Monster of a strange Gigantick Race:
His head half Mitre, and half hat doth bear;
His looks are sainted; and refin'd his air.
Not more preposterous in his black & white,

Than the true semblance of an Hypocrite.
Always Conformist to the strongest Party;
Always deceitful, Ever more unhearty.
The Moderate Man ne'er yet a Martyr dy'd;
But tack'd about, & chose the strongest side
Always recanted in the time of trial:
Is ever best extempore at denial.
Scorns to be moderate then in any thing.
But where to be immoderate is a sin.
In eating, drinking, and such things as these
Be moderate as moderate as you please.
But in Religion there's no Medium. No
Who is not truly zealous, is not so.
Glory to be esteem'd an High-c —h Man:
Let them prove Low-c —h true c-h if they can
Zeal for the c —h's Cause a Crown will gain;
And Martyrdom for He'ven's an easy pain.
Dare to be true, tho' in a suffring time:
A Bare Denial then's a Double Crime.

PLATE 19

PLATE 20

B.M. 1722      The South Sea Bubble. Hogarth      *pp.* 73, 75–76

B.M. 1710      The Skreen. Picart      *pp.* 78, 92

PLATE 21

Some of the Principal Inhabitants of y͡e MOON, as they Were Perfectly Discover'd by a Telescope brought to y͡e Greatest Perfection since y͡e last Eclipse; Exactly Engraved from the Objects, whereby y͡e Curious may Guess at their Religion, Manners, &c.

Price Six Pence

PLATE 22

EXCISE IN TRIUMPH

PLATE 23

THE PLURALIST.

B.M. 2618

pp. 24, 84

PLATE 24

Monument to Gin. Vandermijn

PLATE 25

The Stature of a
Great Man        or the English        Colossus.

Why Man, he doth bestride ÿ narrow World | Men at some times are Masters of their fates:
like a Colossus, and we petty Men          | The fault, dear P— —y is not in our Stars,
Walk under his huge Legs, & peep about     | But in our selves, that we are Underlings—
To find our selves, dishonourable Graves.  |                              Shakespear.

Description.

The Colossus at Rhodes, a Stature of ÿ Sun 70 Cubits high, placed at ÿ Mouth of ÿ Harbour; one Man could not grasp its
Thumb with both his Arms. Its thighs were stretch'd out to such a Distance, that a large Ship Sailing might easily pass
into ÿ Port betwixt them. It was Twelve Years a making, & cost 300 Talents (a Rhodian Talent is worth 322 Pounds 18
Shillings & 4 Pence in English Money.) It stood 50 Years, & at last was thrown down in an Earth-quake. And from this
Colosfs ÿ People of Rhodes were named Colossenses, & every Stature since of an unusal Magnitude is called Colosfus.

PLATE 26

pp. 89-90

*The Motion*

PLATE 27

The Butcher,

Taken from ŷ Sign of a Butcher in ŷ Butcher Row.

Old Æsop who in Morals did surpass,
Wrapt in a Lions Skin produc'd an Afs,
And sure as fit a Cloathing we provide,
Who dress a Butcher in an Oxes Hide
The Candle serves his Foe-men to disclose,

The Tray's a Breast-Plate to withstand their Blows,
His Axe Knives, Cleaver is prepar'd for fight,
And Death & Slaughter are his sole delight,
Thus arm'd he Terror all around does spread
He's rot bereaved if from a Calf his Head.

Decem: 19: 1746

PLATE 28

B.M. 3371        Newcastle and Fox        *pp.* 102, 116

B.M.        Fox and Newcastle        *pp.* 6, 102

PLATE 29

Henry Fox          *p.* 105

Bubb Dodington, Fox and his sons          *p.* 105

PLATE 30

BRITANNIA in DISTRESS
under a Tott'ring Fabrick with a Cumberous Load.

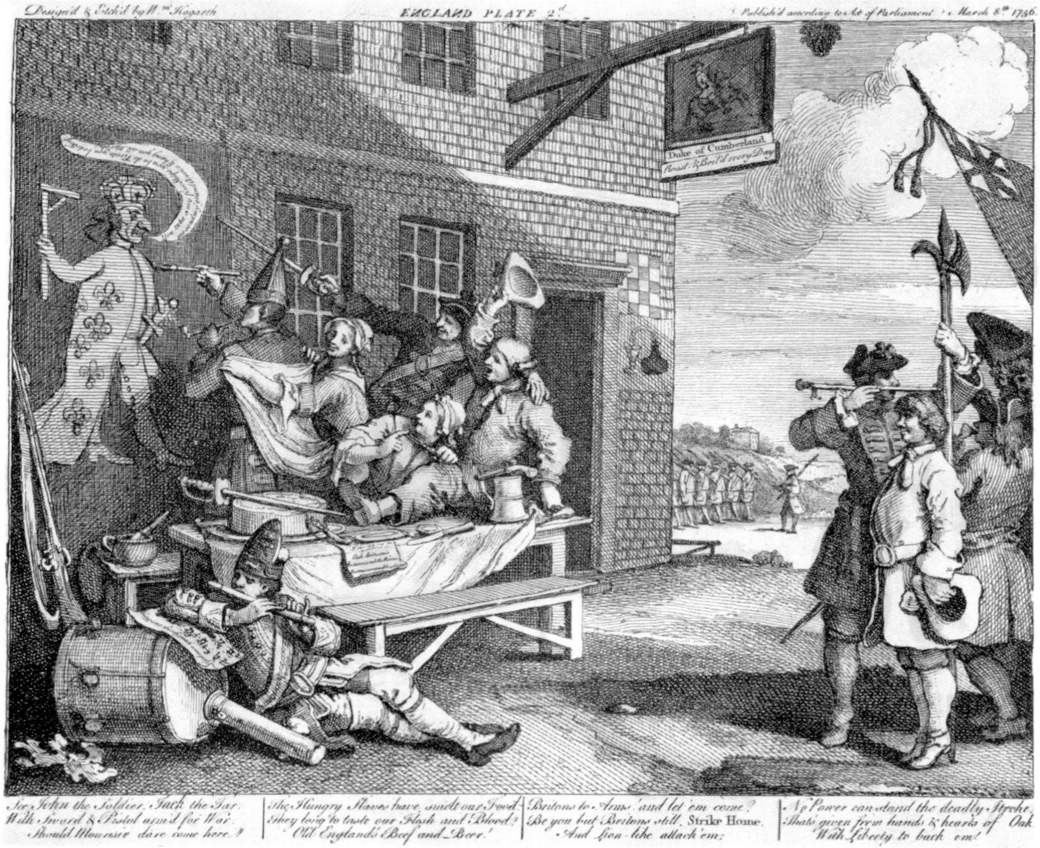

PLATE 31

The Invasion. England Plate 2ᵈ. Hogarth

pp. 114–15

PLATE 32

B.M. 3844

The Hungry Mob of Scriblers and Etchers

p. 122 and n.

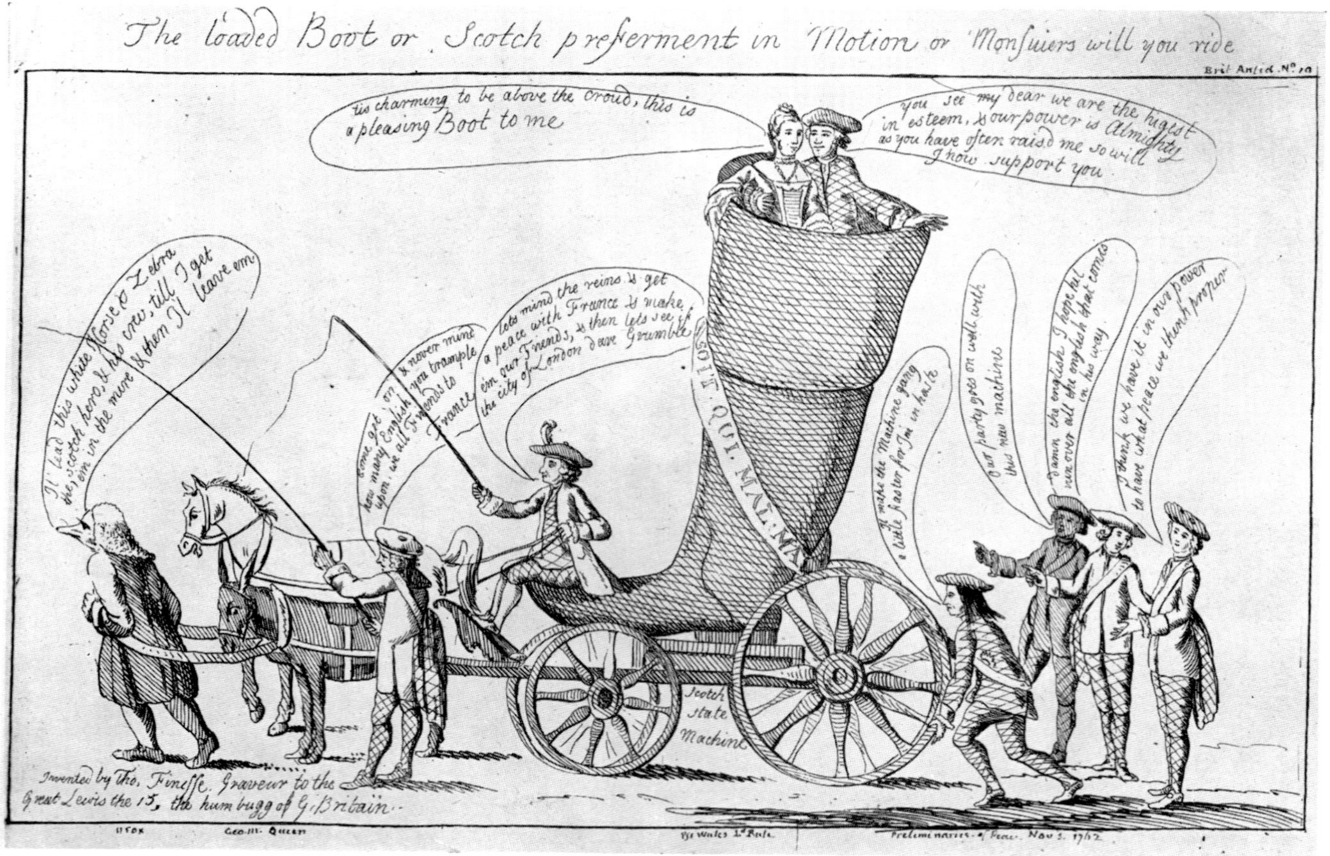

The Loaded Boot

PLATE 33

PLATE 34

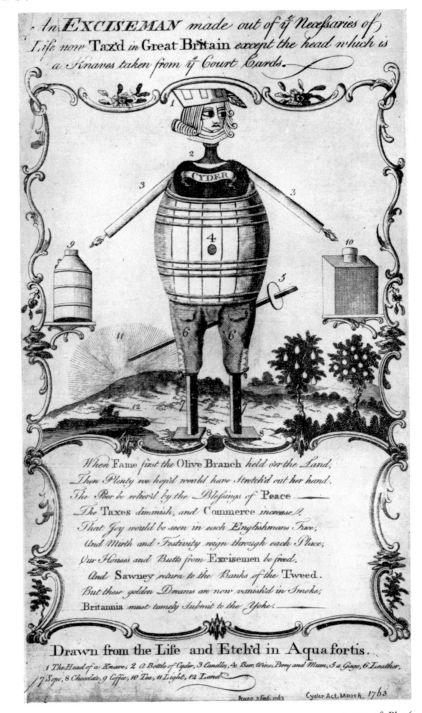

PLATE 35

The Times
Plate I

Designed & Engraved by W. Hogarth

Published as the Act Directs Sepr 7 1762

Hogarth

B.M. 3970

pp. 128–30

PLATE 36

*John Wilkes Esqr.*
*Drawn from the Life and Etch'd in Aquafortis by Willm. Hogarth.*
Price 1 Shilling.        *Publish'd according to Act of Parliament May 4.16.1763.*

PLATE 37

The Great Financier

pp. 133-4

PLATE 38

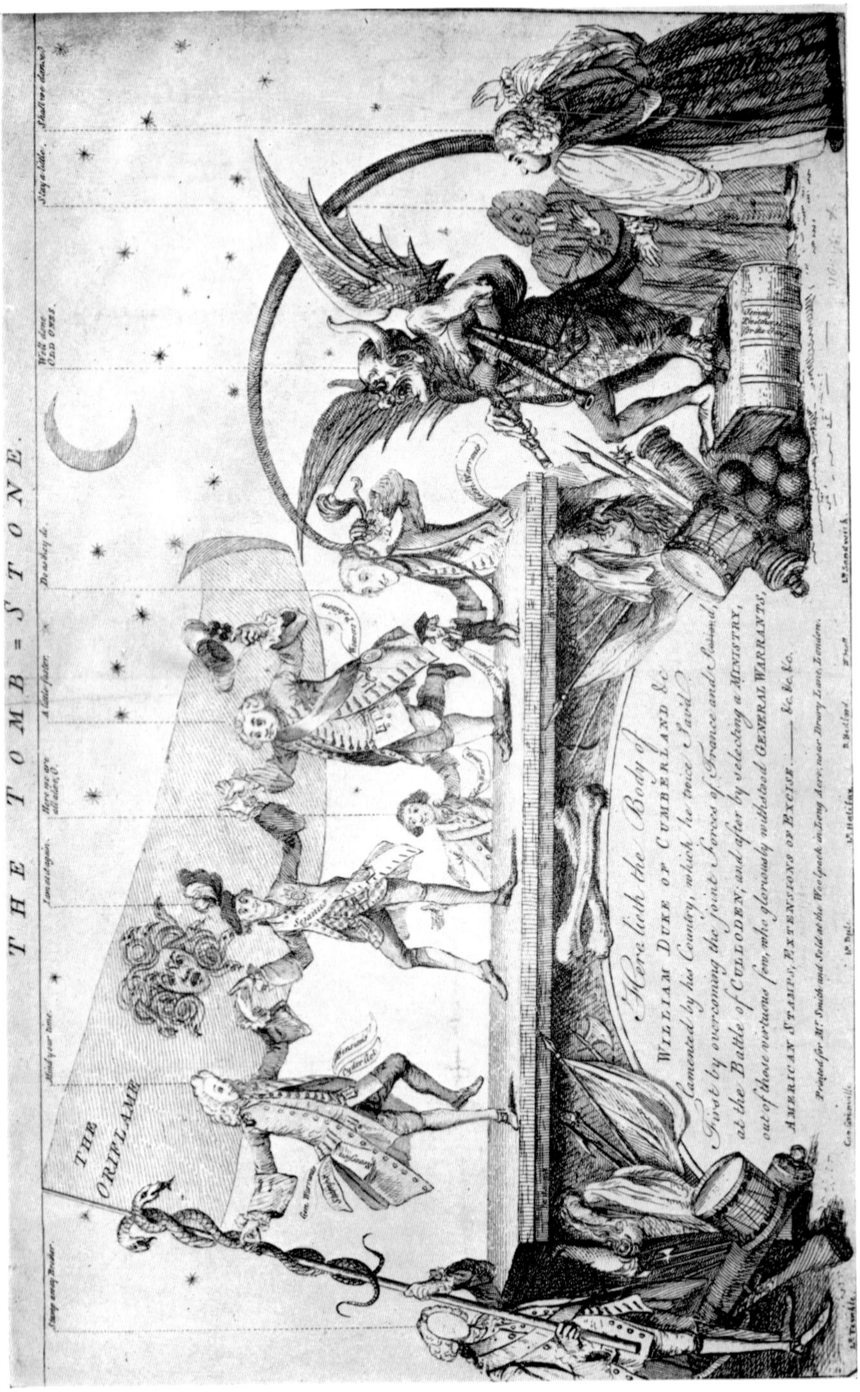


B.M. 4124

B. Wilson

pp. 134–5

PLATE 39

pp. 135-6

B. Wilson

B.M. 4140

PLATE 40

PLATE 41

PLATE 42

THE SCOTCH VICTORY

pp. 143-4

PLATE 43

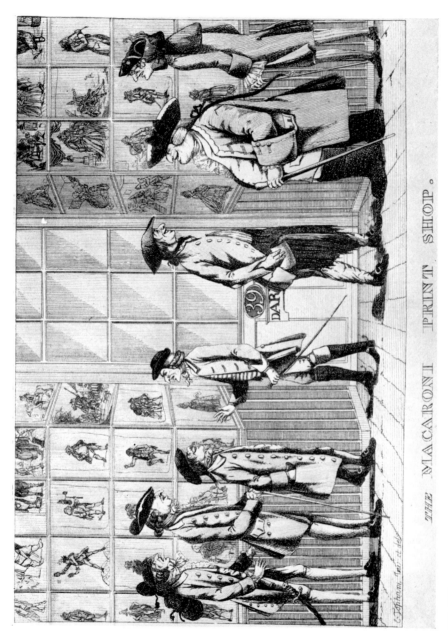

THE MACARONI PRINT SHOP.

p. 147

PLATE 44

The POLITICIAN.

*Done from the ORIGINAL DRAWING by S.H. GRIMM.*

Printed for S. Sledge Printseller, in Henrietta Street Covent Garden. Publish'd as the Act directs 4 May 1771.

B.M. 4857

*p.* 146

PLATE 45

C.J.Fox.

THE YOUNG POLITICIAN

Publish'd accor.ᵈ to Act by H. B rger London.

PLATE 46

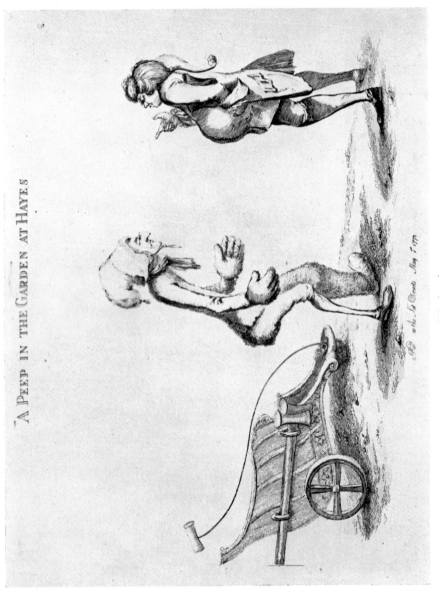

A Peep in the Garden at Hayes

W. Austin

*p.* 148

B.M. 5113

PLATE 47

*The able Doctor, or America Swallowing the Bitter Draught.*

B.M. 5226

*p.* 150

*The Parricide.*
*A Sketch of Modern Patriotism.*

B.M. 5334

*pp.* 152-3

PLATE 48

A Picturesque View of the State of the Nation for February 1778.

PLATE 49

America to her mistaken Mother

PLATE 50

THE CURIOUS ZEBRA.

alive from America! walk in Gemmen and Ladies, walk in.

London, Printed for G. Johnson as the Act directs 3 Sep. 1778 and Sold at all the Printshops in London & Westminster.

PLATE 51

PLATE 52

Pub.<sup>d</sup> as the Act directs Aug.<sup>t</sup> 1<sup>st</sup> 1779 by W<sup>m</sup> White. Amp<sup>l</sup> touch Westminster.

THE HORSE AMERICA, throwing his Master.

1 Aug. 1779.

PLATE 53

THE ALLIES. — *Par nobile Fratrum!*

The Party of Savages went out with Orders not to spare Man, Woman, or Child. To this cruel Mandate even some of the Savages made an Objection; respecting the butchering the Women & Children but they were told the Children would make Soldiers, & the Women would keep up the Stock.

*Remembrancer Vol.8.p.77*

Scalping Knives.
Crucifixes.
Tomahawks.

D—n my, dear Eyes, but we are hellish good Christians.

That thy Ways may be known upon Earth, thy saving Health among all Nations.

G E O R G E by the Grace of the King Defender of the Faith &c.

Pub.<sup>d</sup> as the Act Directs Feb.<sup>ry</sup> 3. 1780 by J. Almon Piccadilly.

*Qui facit per alium, facit per se.*

B.M. 5631

*Indignatio facit*  3. Feb 1780

*p.* 158

PLATE 54

THE STATE TINKERS.

The National Kettle, which once was a good one,      The Master he thinks, they are wonderful Clever,
For boiling of Mutton, of Beef, & of Pudding,      And cries out in raptures, tis done! now or never!
By the fault of the Cook, was quite out of repair,      Yet sneering the Tinkers their old Trade pursue,
When the Tinkers were sent for, ____Behold them & Stare.      In stopping of one Hole____they're sure to make Two.

Publish'd Feb.º 10.th 1780. by W.Humphrey.Nº 227 Strand.

PLATE 55

p. 158

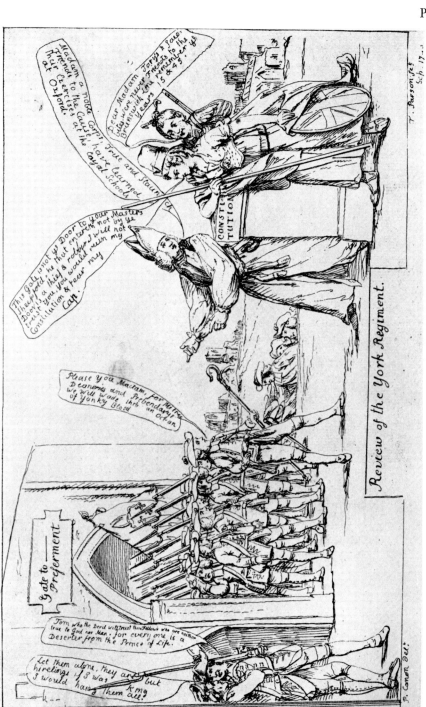

PLATE 56

pp. 150–60

PLATE 57

OPPOSITION DEFEATED

27. Feb. 1780

*pp.* 160–1

PLATE 58

*Who's in fault?* (NOBODY) *a view off* Ushant

The Anatomists will have it that it can have no Heart having no Body—but the
Naturalists think if it has a Heart; it must lay on its Breeches

Pub.d Dec.r ye 1 1779 by W.m Humphrey N.o 227 Strand

PLATE 59

After Bunbury

PLATE 60

? Gillray

p. 165

B.M. 5979

PLATE 61

Gillray

PLATE 62

St GEORGE & the Dragon.

Gillray

PLATE 63

To thee I call,
But with no friendly voice & add thy name.
Shelburne: to tell thee how I hate thy beams
That bring to my remembrance from what state
I fell: &c &c &c

GLORIA MUNDI,

or ___ The Devil addressing the Sun. Par.Lost.Book IV.

Pub. July 22. by W.Humphrey
1782.

C.J.Fox                                    Lᴰ Shelburn.

Gillray

PLATE 64

London Publish'd as the Act Directs May 16 1783. by I. Boyne No. 2 Shoe Lane Fleet S.

PRI. *There is a Gentlewoman in this Town her name is* —— FALSTAFF & HIS PRINCE FAL. *Master George I will first make bold with Your Money next give me Your hand & last as I am a Gent.ᵐᵃⁿ You shall if you will Enjoy* —— *Wife*

PLATE 65

A Transfer of East India Stock.

Sayers

PLATE 66

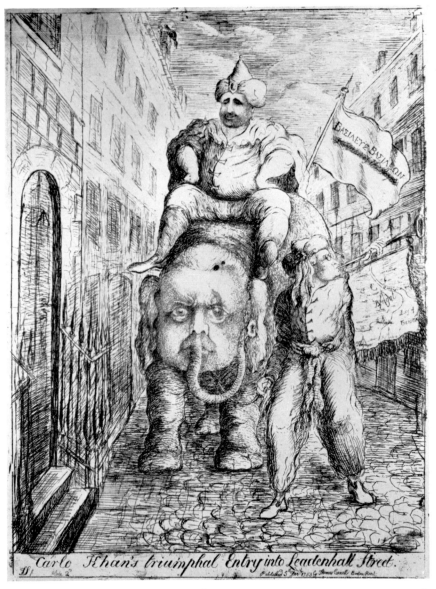

B.M. 6276

Sayers

*p.* 169

PLATE 67

The Mirror of Patriotism.

C. J. FOX

PLATE 68

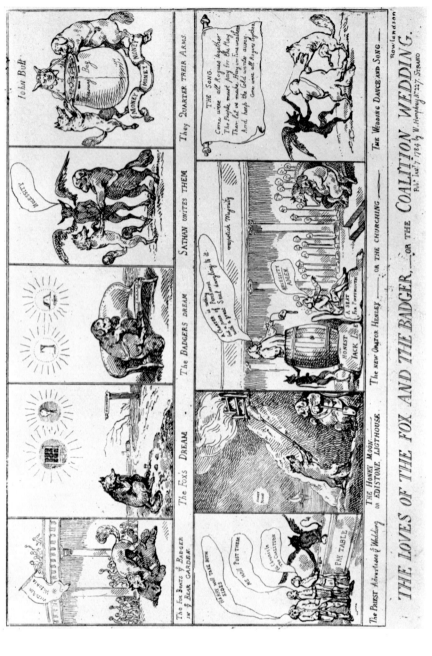

Rowlandson

PLATE 69

BRITTANNIA ROUSED,
OR THE COALITION MONSTERS DESTROYED

Rowlandson

PLATE 70

THE HANOVERIAN HORSE AND BRITISH LION.

A Scene in a New Play lately acted in Westminster with distinguished applause. Act 2.ᵈ Scene last.

Pub.ᵈ March 31 1784 by W.ᵐ Humphrey 227 Strand.

Rowlandson

PLATE 71

The POLL.

Rowlandson

B.M. 6526

PLATE 72

B.M. 6234          Sayers          *pp.* 168, 186

PLATE 73

Cheek by Joul or the MASK

D/s Devonshire    C.J. Fox.

Two faces here in one you see defign'd, | One rough & virulent, th' other fair & free,
Each ftrongly mark'd declares the inward mind, | with looks that promife fenfibility.
One feems ambitious of a daring foul, | When fuch as thefe in harmony unite,
The other foft the pafsions to controul. | The contraft furely muft amize the fight.

Publifh'd by C. Hedges Nº 92 Cornhill May 8ᵗ 1784

PLATE 74

The Nightmare.  After Fuseli

*p.* 186

PLATE 75

THE COVENT GARDEN NIGHT MARE.

Rowlandson

p. 186

B.M. 6543

PLATE 76

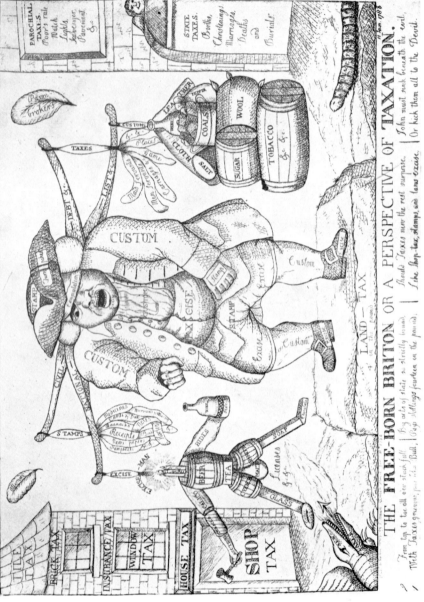

THE **FREE-BORN BRITON** OR A PERSPECTIVE OF TAXATION.

Dent

B.M. 6914

pp. 187–8

PLATE 77

A SCENE in the SCHOOL for SCANDAL.

PLATE 78

The POLITICAL-BANDITTI assailing the SAVIOUR of INDIA.

PLATE 79

Gillray

p. 193

PLATE 80

PLATE 81

PLATE 82

Rowlandson

PLATE 83

_p._ 199

The _VULTURE of the_ CONSTITUTION.

Gillray

B.M. 7478

PLATE 84

The Comet. Sayers

PLATE 85

p. 205 n.

Watercolour by R. Newton

PLATE 86

THE KNIGHT OF THE WOFUL COUNTENANCE
GOING TO EXTIRPATE THE NATIONAL ASSEMBLY.

PLATE 87

B.M. 8072

Gillray

pp. 214–15

PLATE 88

p. 216

The Three Witches. After Fuseli

PLATE 89

To H. Fuzelli Esq. this attempt in the Caricatura-Sublime, is respectfully dedicated.

WEIRD-SISTERS; MINISTERS of DARKNESS; MINIONS of the MOON."
"They should be Women!_ and yet their beards forbid us to interpret_ that they are so."

Gillray

PLATE 90

p. 217

Satan, Sin, and Death. After Hogarth

PLATE 91

SIN, DEATH, and the DEVIL. - Vide Milton.

Gillray

p. 217

PLATE 92

*From the Originals at Windsor.*

L——C——tonn's Dream.

London Pub.d by Jacb Dowse, near Turnstile, Holborn, March 20. 1791.

*pp. 215–16*

PLATE 93

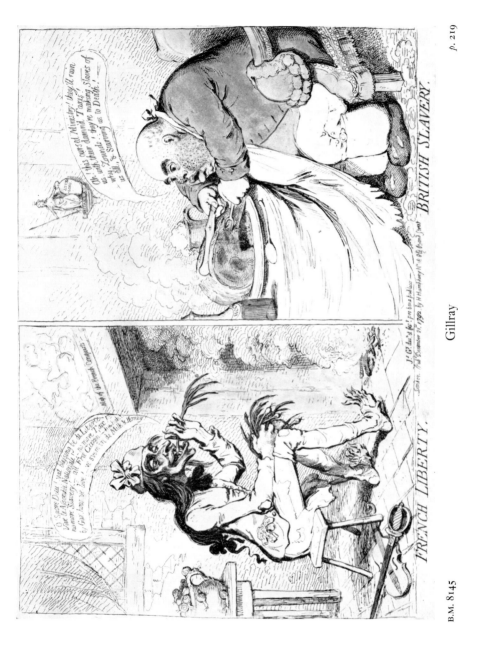

Gillray

PLATE 94

FRENCH AMBASSADOR.

Executed by Citizen

PLATE 95

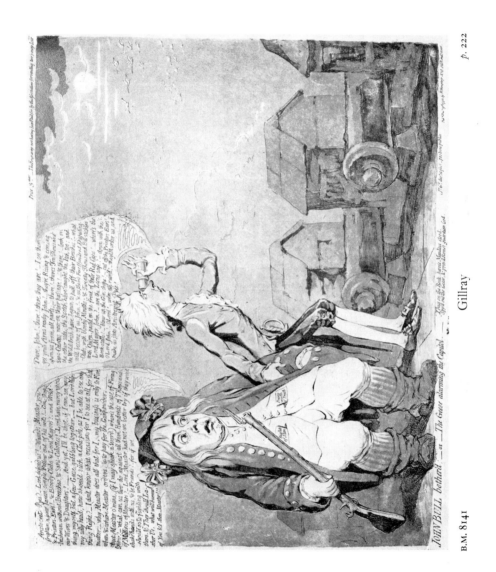

Gillray

PLATE 96

Reflections on the French Revolution.

B.M. 8285 I. Cruikshank pp. 222-3